LONDON
TRANSPORT
from the 1930s to the 1950s

1897.
BLACKWALL TUNNEL.

Michael H. C. Baker

Ian Allan PUBLISHING

Contents

First published 2009
ISBN 978 0 7110 3391 7
Published by Ian Allan Publishing
an imprint of Ian Allan Publishing Ltd, Hersham, Surrey, KT12 4RG
Printed in England by Ian Allan Printing Ltd, Hersham, Surrey,
KT12 4RG
Code: 0907/B
Visit the Ian Allan Publishing website at www.ianallanpublishing.com

Front cover: RT549 of 1947 circumnavigates Eros in Piccadilly Circus, c1950. *Ian Allan Library*

Back cover (top): Acton Town Piccadilly Line station, designed by Charles Holden. *London Transport Museum*

Back cover (bottom): A Matilda tank on its way to 'somewhere in England', accompanied by two STLs in Marble Arch, 19 May 1940. *London Transport*

Title page: One of the NSs specially adapted for working through the Blackwall Tunnel and seen there c1931. *London Transport*

Introduction

No 40, a former South Metropolitan Electric Tramways car built by Brush in 1906, stands at the West Croydon terminus of the Crystal Palace route in February 1936. This archaic vehicle would be replaced a few days later by an almost-silent, smooth-running, state-of-the-art trolleybus.
E. G. P. Masterman

DID the motor bus ever make such strides in comfort, technical specification and performance as in the years between 1930 and 1940? As this is a rhetorical question I shall, dear reader, provide an instant answer, which is 'No'. And nowhere was this more obvious than in London. When the decade opened some bus journeys would have been in vehicles with solid tyres, many double-deckers had no upper-deck roofs, and practically all would have brackets, pillars and various protruding fitments seemingly designed to catch unwary passengers in various painful parts of their anatomy as they lurched and bumped over what, in places, were far-from-smooth road surfaces. Most passengers would still have been pretty content with all this, having in their younger days been accustomed to horse-drawn modes of transport.

The tramcar was still the standard conveyance for many Londoners. No fewer than 423 trams passed along the Embankment within sight of the Houses of Parliament every hour during peak periods. Most cars, but not all, did have upper-deck roofs, although the seats were probably not upholstered, and the driver would be exposed to everything the weather and the often dirty streets — for there were still tens of thousands of horses at work — could throw at him. But many of the trams, particularly those belonging to certain boroughs, were old-fashioned and worn-out, and even the standard LCC car dated back the best part of 30 years to before World War 1. Revolutionary designs were just over the horizon, but the tram was essentially seen as out of date, an archaic means of transport holding up the march of the internal combustion engine.

Probably the most comfortable form of public transport was the Underground train, particularly on the District and Metropolitan lines, although the fact that it was possible to rattle below London's streets with the doors wide open was somewhat disconcerting. Deeper down, in the 'Tube', the ride was distinctly lively, and not all of each carriage was available to passengers, technology not yet having reached the point where everything electrical and mechanical could be stowed away beneath the floor.

Out in the furthest suburbs, in 'Metro-land' and the rural Home Counties, the scene was highly varied, with a host of operators, large and small, providing services with a huge mixture of vehicles, some of them very small with fewer than 20 seats, designed to penetrate the rural vastness down often-unmade country lanes. Car ownership was still very much for the more affluent, male-dominated middle and upper classes, and nearly everyone was dependent upon public transport for both getting to work and pleasure trips.

The Green Line network as such did not officially come into being until 1930, but a number of express services from the outer suburbs and beyond were already in existence. These were, in the main, worked by much the most comfortable of public-service vehicles, almost luxurious, fitted with handsome interiors, well-upholstered seats and mounted on the latest AEC Regal and Leyland Tiger chassis. At weekends vast numbers of Londoners travelled out into the country, to Epping Forest, the Surrey and Chiltern hills, historic towns such as Tunbridge Wells, Westerham, Windsor, St Albans, Guildford, and many routes from Central London and the inner suburbs were extended on Saturdays and Sundays to cater for this traffic. On Saturdays the exodus would not begin until early afternoon, most people working Saturday mornings.

The London General Omnibus Co, the London County Council and the Underground Electric Railway Co, collectively known as the Combine, were

Above left: A Fox cameraman films the burning of withdrawn K-type buses in the grounds of Alexandra Palace in 1930. *London's Transport Museum*

Below left: Hyde Park Corner in 1937. A policeman holds up a collection of taxis, saloon cars, a van and a lorry to allow two standard STLs and various other vehicles to make their way westwards. *London Transport*

Above: ST409 and NS2236 stand on Crystal Palace Parade in 1931. Despite its covered top the NS retained solid tyres, emphasising the advance in design represented by the ST. This location is still much used as a bus terminus, although Paxton's magnificent Crystal Palace, relic of the Great Exhibition of 1851, was to burn down on the night of 30/31 November 1936. *The Omnibus Society*

ST.ALBANS
ROUTE **84** FROM GOLDERS
GENERAL✦ GREEN

Left: An Edward McKnight Kauffer poster of 1929 for the LGOC, featuring one of the Central London routes which penetrated deep into the Home Counties countryside. *London's Transport Museum*

Right: Streamlining reaches its apotheosis. One of the remarkable-looking, streamlined 'Tube' trains of 1935. *London's Transport Museum*

Below right: London Transport took the welfare of its staff and their families seriously. An egg-and-spoon race approaches a nail-biting finish at a Chiswick sports day in 1938. *London's Transport Museum*

far and away the biggest providers of public transport in and around London. There were also no fewer than 54 bus companies that were totally independent of any of the Combine, but although they operated a fascinating collection of vehicles and have attracted much historical interest they were actually of little significance, providing a mere 6% of services within the Metropolitan area.

Rather bigger players, taken together, were the tram networks of the municipalities. Some 20 or more years earlier, at the dawn of the new century, it had been virtually a matter of pride for a town which considered itself of any importance to emphasise its forward-looking attitude by providing electric trams for its citizens. They did not come cheap, track-laying being not only disruptive of other traffic but also expensive, as was all the necessary ancillary equipment, but many authorities considered it worthwhile. However, once the system was up and

running it was usually highly efficient and popular and made a profit that could be ploughed back to subsidise the rates.

Having been born in 1937 I cannot claim an intimate first-hand experience of the decade, although I do have a distinct memory of a coach trip to Broadstairs in the summer of 1939, as well as a vivid recollection of being on Richmond station on 3 September of that year when air-raid sirens began to wail (a false alarm, as it turned out) and feeling that something very unpleasant was happening. Whatever the horrors of the war, the fact was that London Transport had by September 1939 become such a finely tuned, highly organised concern that it was able to cope in an admirable manner with the totally unprecedented demands placed upon it.

Michael H. C. Baker
Wareham
March 2007

• 1 •

Four Great Men

JUST as there had been a considerable body of opinion in the first decades of the century which argued that the main-line railway companies should come under public control, so there were those who felt the same about public transport in the capital. The trauma of World War 1, if it had not brought about rail nationalisation, had resulted in the 'halfway house' of amalgamation into the Big Four in 1923, and when Labour won the general election of 1929 few doubted that changes were coming to London too. Our story is dominated by four men, who, ably assisted by many others, ranging from those in positions of considerable power — managers, engineers, designers, administrators — right through to the drivers, conductors, motormen, ticket collectors, porters etc who were in everyday contact with the travelling public, were instrumental in creating what, it is generally agreed, was by 1939 the most forward-looking and best-organised transport undertaking of any capital city. The four were Herbert Morrison, Charles Holden, Lord Ashfield and Frank Pick.

Herbert Morrison was a Londoner through and through. Born in Lambeth in 1888, he left school at 14. His parents were working people, sufficiently well off to afford an annual week's holiday in Ramsgate. As he wrote in his autobiography, 'Secondary education was hardly thought of by parents of my class and time', and he took up work as an errand-boy in a shop. Always interested in politics, he sought ways of bettering both himself and working people generally. The loss of sight in his right eye meant he did not serve in World War 1, to which he was anyhow opposed, arguing that the working men of Britain and Germany had much in common. A founder member of the London Labour Party, by 1920 he had become Mayor of Hackney; two years later he was elected to the London County Council, and in 1923 he entered Parliament as MP for South Hackney. Defeated in the 1924 election, he returned to Parliament in the Labour victory of 1929 and was appointed Minister of Transport by Prime Minister Ramsay MacDonald.

Morrison, with his trade-union background, was somewhat wary of handing over the assets of the LCC to 'Lord Ashfield and his wicked Combine', as he once wrote, but he was also a realist, warning against favouring any one form of transport against another and stating that he would be 'guided by the facts'. In December 1929 he announced that it was the Government's view that public ownership of transport in London must be established, and, despite his earlier comments about Ashfield, it is generally agreed that the two were instrumental in the foundation of the London Passenger Transport Board (LPTB).

Above: The Prince of Wales (later Edward VIII) and Lord Ashfield on an Underground train during a Royal visit in 1935. *London's Transport Museum*

Left: A wartime David Low cartoon of Herbert Morrison, second from right in the front row, alongside Ernest Bevin, Clement Attlee and Winston Churchill. The title was 'All Behind You'.

Morrison refused to serve in MacDonald's National Government of 1931, which relied upon Conservative support, and instead devoted his formidable energies to the London County Council, becoming its leader in 1934, by which time London Transport was a *fait accompli*. He returned to Parliament in 1935, and by 1940 he was Deputy Leader of the Labour Party and Home Secretary under Winston Churchill in the wartime coalition, being still very much concerned with the fate of Londoners, especially during the Blitz, when the East End suffered grievously.

Serving between 1945 and 1951 as Deputy Prime Minister, Leader of the House of Commons and Foreign Secretary, Morrison could be hard and ruthless and had enemies in his own party as well as amongst his opponents. Eileen Wilkinson, the first woman to serve in a Labour government (and, according to Hugh Dalton, Chancellor of the Exchequer, 'a devoted worshipper of Herbert Morrison'), described

him as 'an able administrator' but 'a bit of a brute — the rudest man I know', conceding that 'he is giving to London almost exclusively gifts needed by the nation'. It was once remarked of Morrison that he was his own worst enemy. 'Not while I'm around', was the riposte of arch enemy Ernest Bevin, Foreign Secretary in the 1945-51 Labour Government but who as leader of the Transport & General Workers' Union in the 1920s and '30s had had many dealings with the London Transport management. With his John Lennon-type glasses and Tintin-like quiff, Morrison was a gift to cartoonists. One of the towering political figures of the first half of the 20th century (and the grandfather of Peter Mandelson), he remained active in politics, latterly as a life peer, until his death in 1965.

Lord Ashfield was Chairman of the LPTB from 1933 until 1947, and Frank Pick was his Chief Executive from 1933 until 1940. To quote Sir John Elliot, Chairman from 1953 to 1959, 'It was the combination of Pick and Ashfield, rather than the work of either, that brought about the remarkable development of public transport in the 30 years prior to the outbreak of war in 1939. The two men were essentially complimentary; Ashfield was best in dealing with politicians, shareholders and the public. Pick, on the other hand, was a very shy man, but he had great qualities as an administrator.'

Albert Stanley, 1st Baron Ashfield, came from a humble enough background, his father being a Derbyshire coachbuilder who had emigrated to

was appointed its publicity officer. Although a solicitor by profession, he soon revealed a remarkable sense of design, such that, in a tribute after his death in 1941, he was described by Nikolaus Pevsner as 'the greatest patron of the arts whom this century has so far produced in England and indeed the ideal patron of our age'. Like Charles Holden, Frank Pick spurned honours, refusing both a knighthood and a peerage. He worked extremely long hours, often ending his day in the early hours with a 'spot inspection' of a station to check that the most detailed aspects — signs, litter bins etc — had been completed correctly.

Pick encouraged artists, many of them amongst the most progressive, to produce posters and good design in every aspect of public transport. He was founder member of the Design & Industries Association and founding chairman of the Council for Art & Industry, the forerunner of the Arts Council. His achievements gained international recognition, perhaps most extraordinarily in the form of an honorary Badge of Merit from the Soviet Union for his work on the Moscow Metro in 1932.

In many respects Ashfield and Pick *were* London Transport in the 1930s, and, reading of their achievements, from such seemingly minor examples as the introduction in 1935 of compulsory bus stops to their worldwide fame, and their characters, so different yet so perfectly complementary, one is simply lost in admiration. Frank Pick resigned in 1940 and was appointed by Winston Churchill as Director of Information. Sadly he died the following year, aged 62, no doubt worn out by his Herculean efforts. Lord Ashfield died in 1948, aged 74.

Charles Holden, the architect responsible for the London Transport building style of the 1930s, was a most interesting man. He had a strong social conscience, twice refusing a knighthood because he believed 'architecture should be a collaborative effort'. Born in Bolton in 1875, he did not have things easy as a child, his father going bankrupt and his mother dying when he was six. Studying in Manchester, he

Chicago. Young Albert showed exceptional managerial skills, becoming head of the Detroit Street Railways by the age of 28, and in 1907, at the age of 33, was appointed General Manager of the Underground Electric Railways Co of London. Rapidly turning around its precarious financial position, he was appointed Managing Director in 1910. Knighted in 1914, he was appointed President of the Board of Trade during World War 1. In 1919 he returned to head the Underground Group, was created Baron Ashfield in 1920 and with Pick as Commercial Manager established a unique partnership, the benefits of which are still felt by anyone who travels by bus, tram or train in London today. It was indeed, as it has often been described, a 'Golden Age'. In 1928 Lord Ashfield handed over the role of Managing Director to Pick, remaining Chairman and concentrating on the complex, long-drawn-out negotiations that led to the setting-up of the LPTB.

Frank Pick, four years younger than Stanley and born into a devout Congregationalist family in Lincolnshire, had joined the Underground Group in 1906 — a year earlier than Stanley —and in 1908

was trained in the classical tradition, of which he was a master, and from this he developed a style based on a deep respect of materials and the function of a building. Thus he saw no need of 'cornices, pilasters, mouldings . . . when in doubt leave it out'.

Very much influenced by the post-1914 generation of Northern European masters — Arnos Grove station, for instance, is based on Gunnar Asplund's Stockholm City Library — Holden had a huge influence in Britain and, to a degree, abroad. A man of ascetic habits, he was practically hero-worshipped by his colleagues. 'Fitness for purpose' was his creed. Buildings should take account of their surroundings, be aware of their function. Their interiors and their fittings (lamps, escalators, ticket offices and shop façades) were as important as their exteriors — something which has been adhered to pretty faithfully in the decades since the Morden extension, the rebuilt Piccadilly station and all the rest that were erected. Few architects of the 20th century have had a greater impact on London than Holden, for he also designed what is now Zimbabwe House in the Strand (almost opposite Charing Cross station), 55 Broadway, completed in 1929 and which in 1933 would become the headquarters of London Transport, and, most spectacular of all, Senate House, the administrative headquarters of the University of London and described at the time as 'London's first skyscraper'.

• 2 •

The Workers

Possibly just about the toughest job on London Transport, a points operator at a tramway junction. In later years this tended to be the responsibility of uniformed inspectors who were given a canvas shelter to keep out of the worst of the weather.
London's Transport Museum

MORRISON and the LCC as a whole were much concerned with unemployment, which was a persistent problem throughout the 1920s and '30s. Received wisdom is that it grew much greater after the Wall Street Crash of 1929, but it had existed ever since soldiers returning from World War 1 found that 'a land fit for heroes' could not necessarily provide them with a job. London and the South East was not as hard hit as the industrial North, the Midlands or South Wales; in 1932 some 5% of males were unemployed in London, whilst in parts of the North the figure could be as high as 33%. But the fear of unemployment was ever present, and there was relatively little industrial agitation; which is not to say that it was entirely absent. In *A Lifetime of Bus Work* (Transport Publishing Co, 1979), Bob Scanlan, who worked in the machine shop at Chiswick in 1932, recalls hearing 'through the grapevine' that redundancies were on the way; one of his colleagues, 'a skilled man and an ex-apprentice of the company', found himself sweeping station platforms for £2 a week.

With the full effects of the downturn in business hitting London's bus, tram and Underground services it was announced that there would be a cut in wages. The Transport & General Workers' Union, led by Ernest Bevin, reluctantly accepted this, but a number of his members did not, and early in 1933 a militant group called a strike in which between 20 and 30 bus garages took part. Negotiations continued and the strike was called off. The Communist party newspaper, *The Daily Worker,* backed the strike action and accused Bevin and the Union leaders of being 'agents of the management' and 'fighting for the company against the men, Bevin sued for libel — and won.

A number of the leaders of the militants were Communists — or sympathetic to Communist ideals — at a time when fascism was taking root in Germany, Italy and Spain, with adherents all over Europe. In Britain the charismatic Sir Oswald Mosley was active in the East End, provoking many who

A Central bus inspector stands sternly at the head of a queue whilst a business lady (possibly a stenographer) hurries by, newspaper under her arm. The inspector still wears an LGOC jacket, although the date is August 1934. *London's Transport Museum*

opposed his extreme-right-wing views to see Communism as the one force unequivocally prepared to stand up for the rights of workers everywhere, and throughout the 1930s there was a strong element within London's busmen which believed this and was prepared to act on it. The tram, trolleybus and railway workers seem to have been less militant.

An example of the differences manifested itself in May 1937, at the time of the Coronation of King George VI and Queen Elizabeth. Negotiations over a reduction in the working day had been dragging on for months. In late April the LPTB issued a definite 'No' but asked the Union to resume negotiations after the Coronation. The grievances were shared with busmen in many parts of the country, and there were strikes by employees at Maidstone & District, Eastern National and Luton Corporation, among others. The London tram men were sympathetic but not to the extent of striking. Bevin managed to persuade the provincial busmen to return to work whilst he negotiated their case, but the militant Londoners struck, no buses ran during the Coronation, and the Government set up a Court of Inquiry. Bevin spoke on behalf of the men, asserting that London Transport railwaymen had, in effect, the 7½-hour working day that the busmen wanted.

One of the strongest planks of Bevin's argument was that the harsh conditions of driving and conducting buses in London's streets was detrimental to the men's health and called doctors as witnesses of their nervous disorders. Frank Pick, in response, doubted the relevance of these assertions and said that the Board simply could not afford the £½ million that the reduction in working hours would cost. The findings of the Court were that the whole matter of conditions of work and the health of the employees should be properly investigated. The Executive Council of the Union declared this to be a '75-80% victory'. The strike ended on 28 May, and at a subsequent conference a number of the militants were expelled. One of them commented: 'I have never seen fascism operated so clearly!' Ironically, to quote H. A. Clegg in his book *Labour Relations in London Transport*, 'It was said that, owing to the crowds of Coronation Week, the buses were best off

Right: A Country Area inspector parks his BSA motor-cycle and checks an ST double-decker working the 417 somewhere in the Windsor area in January 1938. The motor-cyclist hardly seems to be appropriately attired for riding in the depths of winter. *London's Transport Museum*

Below: Driver and conductor of a Merton STL take refreshment from a Catering Department pedal-tricycle, Epsom, 1936. *London's Transport Museum*

the streets'. But the men had always claimed that it was mere coincidence that the strike occurred at this time, asserting that the Board could have settled the dispute much earlier.

Working in public transport was perceived as a job with considerable status; it was usually secure, and the uniform suggested the wearer exercised a certain authority. But it was no sinecure. In *Bare Empty Sheds* (Tramway & Light Railway Society, 1986) G. Harry Guilmartin recalls working with tram drivers from the inter-war years whose memories were of 'working long hours . . . in all weathers, often drenched, often frozen'. They had sometimes to suffer 'petty tyrants' who made their lives a misery, and a public complaint, 'probably unjustified or possibly untrue', might result in suspension and loss of wages.

The Unions were generally in favour of the creation of London Transport. Their leaders agreed with the directors of the Combine that 'wasteful competition' should be ended, that a unified authority meant greater prosperity for all, and that union representation was much weaker in the smaller concerns. There were worries about how members of the LPTB should be appointed, but these were generally allayed when John Cliff, Assistant General Secretary of the T&GWU was invited to join, even though he had to give up his union office to do so. The militant members, who called themselves the 'Rank and File Movement', were less impressed.

By and large most employees were not only content to work for London Transport but were even proud of doing so. Compared to many other employers London Transport treated its staff well. It provided various forms of welfare, and there were numerous sports clubs, drama groups and all manner of recreational activities in which wives and children were encouraged to take part. If 'Bonnie Baby' contests would nowadays be considered politically very incorrect, they are just one example of dozens if not hundreds of activities, some frivolous, some serious, that attracted contestants and spectators and were aimed at involving as many as possible, so that they would feel part of the London Transport family, however large this might be.

Six members plus the chairman made up the London Passenger Transport Board, appointed by, amongst others, the chairman of the London County Council, the chairman of the Committee of London Clearing Banks, the president of the Law Society and the president of the Institute of Chartered Accountants in England and Wales. It was clearly not an organisation to be taken lightly.

The welfare of staff (or, as the establishing Act describes them, 'officers and company servants') was a priority. No one 'shall, without his consent, be by reason of such transfer [to London Transport] in any

A guard gives the 'right away' to a Metropolitan Line train. *Author's collection*

worse position in respect of the conditions of his service formerly obtaining'. Pensions were protected. The possible closure of the tramway system would have worried many LCC and borough employees. There was reassurance here. 'If . . . their services . . . are dispensed with by the Board upon the abandonment . . . of a tramway... that officer or servant shall, unless the contrary is proved, be deemed . . . to have suffered a direct pecuniary loss' and would be compensated.

Wages and salaries were not high, although they were sufficient to retain staff, particularly those doing shift work, who might have been tempted to look elsewhere. Anthony Bull, who rose to become Vice-Chairman of London Transport and received the CBE, recalled that he started with the Underground Group in 1929 as a Grade 5 Clerk on a salary of £120, rising to £130 a year later. A 16-year-old joining

Above: The typing pool, 55 Broadway, mid-1930s. *London's Transport Museum*

Below: The tracing section, Chief Engineer's drawing office, 55 Broadway, 23 August 1938. *London's Transport Museum*

Above: The proud LPTB mothers seem rather jollier, despite the inclement weather, than their bonny babies, *c*1936. Presumably these are the winners for the two on the left are clearly wearing rosettes. Note big brother attempting to get into the picture whilst being skilfully elbowed into the background. *London's Transport Museum*

Left: An interesting variation, perhaps unique to London Transport, on the egg-and-spoon race, photographed around the same time. *London's Transport Museum*

Left: An elegant forehand shot performed, one suspects, especially for the camera, during a tennis tournament final at Keston sports ground with a pair of LT six-wheelers parked on the adjoining road, 10 September 1933. *London's Transport Museum*

the Underground as a clerk in 1939 would have started at £55 per annum, this rising to £90 at the age of 18. At the other end of the scale a Class 1 clerk could reach £345 per annum after two years in that grade. For some reason women's salaries were quoted in weekly terms rather than yearly. A 16-year-old received 21s 6d (£1.07½) per week, virtually the same as her male counterpart. A Class 1 lady clerk, after two years in this grade, received 71s 6d (£3.57½) per week, which works out at £371 per annum — considerably more than her male counterpart, which is most surprising. An Underground ticket collector (Class 1) was paid 62s 6d (£3.12½) per week, a porter a maximum 56s 6d (£2.82½) per week.

A Central Area bus driver's wage after 18 months' service was 90s (£4.50) per week, a conductor's 84s 0d (£4.20). Their average working time was 6hr 27min a day. A tram or trolleybus crew worked rather longer, 7hr 10min a day, drivers and conductors both being paid 84s per week. The maximum wage for a Country Area bus driver was 75s (£3.75), for his conductor 66s 6d (£3.32½); they worked 6hr 59min a day.

Many LPTB employees took more than a passing interest in their vehicles and trains, and, although in the 1930s there was nothing like the enthusiast movement of today, there were certainly those who studied, noted, photographed and wrote about the bus, tram, trolleybus and train fleets, despite information being much harder to come by than it would be once the Ian Allan 'ABCs' began to appear in the next decade.

Above: Two Central Area bus conductors pose in winter uniform, 1935. *London's Transport Museum*

Most, whether observers or employees, understood the realities and did not wear rose-tinted spectacles. They appreciated that what might bring joy to the enthusiast would be seen in a different light by the ordinary passenger. G. Harry Guilmartin describes being regularly sick as a child on the Underground: 'I think it was the unpleasant smell the trains had in those days.' He was similarly afflicted on buses, by 'petrol fumes, dusty upholstery and Lord knows what else'. One sometimes hears elderly folk complaining that public transport is not as comfortable as it was. It is easy to forget what an unhygienic, pungent world it was in the 1930s when homes with hot running water were the exception, when few people bathed more than once a week, when we were generally poorer, changed our clothes far less often, and when cigarette fumes impregnated upholstery and clothing.

Right: A conductor with a white-topped (summer uniform) hat helps a lady passenger aboard his Central Area LT *c*1935. *Author's collection*

Below left: Looks a lot worse than it is. A volunteer demonstrates how to be run over by STL1143 whilst watched by a truly horrified (honest!) group of onlookers, none of whom have been dragged away from their otherwise gainful employment in various parts of Chiswick Works *c*1937.
London's Transport Museum

Below: Whatever the first glance at this apparently rural idyll might indicate it is actually a scene at a suburban Underground station during an inspection (by Neville Chamberlain?) for best garden competition *c*1938.
London's Transport Museum

• 3 •

The Double-deck Bus Fleet in 1933 — before the Regent

THE most numerous double-deck bus type in the fleet on 1 July 1933 was the NS. In all 2,385 NSs had been built between 1922 and 1928, the LGOC's standard double-decker of the period. Although the majority came from the London General Omnibus Co (LGOC) a limited number was acquired from three other sources — London General Country Services, Thomas Tilling and the British Automobile Traction Co (BAT).

At the beginning of 1930 1,781 of the NSs still had solid tyres and 61 were open-toppers. Withdrawal began in 1932, and by July 1933 183 had been taken out of service. Such was the pace of progress in bus design at the end of the 1920s and the early '30s that they already looked archaic, despite the majority having been modernised with pneumatic tyres and covered tops. Those which were missing one or other of these features looked even more out of date. Of 56

working in the Country Area no fewer than 35 were without upper-deck roofs. The Tilling and BAT NSs did have tops but retained their solid tyres.

The chief feature of the NS which distinguished it from its predecessor, the S of 1920, was that it possessed a cranked (and therefore lower) chassis. This meant that passengers could step much more easily onto the rear platform and from there make just one more step into the lower saloon. It was also low enough to enable a roof to be fitted although that bastion of conservatism, the Metropolitan Police, refused to countenance this until March 1926. Although the NS was lower than the S there was still a significant gap between the bottom of the panelling and the road surface.

A total of 776 S types were at work on 1 January 1930 with London General, but all the red LGOC versions had been withdrawn before London Transport was created. There were six S types proper still in service with London General Country Services which lasted for just over a year with London Transport. Eleven examples of the PS, an East Surrey version of the S, were still in stock in July 1933, being needed for the 410, which ran from Bromley to Redhill beneath the famous (or perhaps infamous) low bridge at Oxted, although their successors were on order. Apart from their higher

Above: George Street, Croydon, c1931. A solid-tyre S is on the left, working on route 12 and bound for Oxford Circus with conductor perched atop the staircase, whilst the bus on the right, on local route 178, is an NS with roof and pneumatic tyres. *Author's collection*

Left: The first six-wheel double-deck motor bus to enter service in London was this 45-80hp Guy of the Public company, dating from 1927. It seated 60 passengers, and was finished in a predominantly blue livery. *Ian Allan Library*

floor level they did not look any more old-fashioned than the NS in its original form.

Predecessor to the S was the K, which came out immediately after World War 1, in 1919. These were London's first forward-control buses with the driver seated alongside the engine rather than behind it. In all 798 Ks were still at work in London on 1 January 1930, and rather remarkably 15 entered London Transport ownership, although all were delicensed and would be scrapped by the spring of 1934. These 15 had been retained to work on route 90 which passed over a bridge with severe weight restrictions, until June 1932.

The NS type, like its predecessors, was originally without windscreens — another police restriction —

One of the extraordinary-looking mammoth LS six-wheelers of the LGOC poses for the camera at Chiswick when brand-new. By 1930 all 11 LSs were working the 29, moving on to Cricklewood garage and the 16. Several were converted to lorries and survived World War 2. *Ian Allan Library*

and did not begin to acquire them until the late spring of 1931. Some were still without in 1933. When fitted with covered tops the upper deck window frames did not match up with those downstairs. Other features which dated them were their top-lights, a radiator which was as wide as it was high (and it certainly was high), whilst the front wings were pretty minimal. Only the Country Area NSs had headlamps, and although the downstairs seat cushions were quite deep there was little else in the way of comfort, with plenty of protrusions likely to catch the unwary passenger as he or she either made for his or her seat or rose to leave it.

Similar to the NS but several steps ahead of it was the LS, introduced in 1927. The LSs were actually ADCs rather than AECs, although all had (either from new or shortly afterwards) AEC engines. The

LGOC's first six-wheelers, they were built new with an enclosed upper deck, an enclosed staircase and pneumatic tyres. There were seats for 60 passengers, later reduced to 56. The 11 LS double-deckers and one single-decker are said to have been less than entirely successful, but for all that they worked the 16 group of routes from Cricklewood garage for 10 years, finally being withdrawn at the same time as the very last NSs. Four were then converted as breakdown tenders and in this form lasted well into the postwar era, not being withdrawn until April 1951.

ADC was the result of a brief amalgamation of AEC and Daimler. AEC had always supplied the vast majority of London's buses and would do so right up until the late 1960s, but although Daimlers would make a comeback during World War 2 (and again in the late 1960s) a mere five double-deck Daimlers entered the LPTB fleet in 1933, and all were gone two years later — well, sort of. Three rather sophisticated CH6s with epicyclic gearboxes and fluid-flywheel transmission were bought as an experiment by the LGOC in 1931 and fitted with standard ST bodies. They influenced the later versions of the AEC ST and LT types, but they

Above: WR20, a Sunbeam 70/142hp six-wheeler of the Westminster company working route 73, August 1933. Impressive and up-to-date the bus may be in most respects, but it is rather let down by the Metropolitan Police's insistence that the driver be exposed to the elements.
Ian Allan Library

Left: An NS in original condition with solid tyres affords the upper-deck passengers an unrestricted view of the glorious Surrey countryside on its way to Hook in the summer of 1930. *Pamlin Prints*

Left: Covered-top, pneumatic-tyred NS1445 of Chalk Farm garage stands beside the Crystal Palace *c*1933. *Author's collection*

Below: An archaic-looking Thomas Tilling normal-control petrol-electric near New Cross ahead of a General NS, with solid tyres but upper-deck roof, both on their way to Chislehurst *c*1930. *W. Noel Jackson*

Left: A bowler-hatted gentleman, carrying an intriguingly shaped parcel, boards a covered-top NS on route 24 near Trafalgar Square *c*1932. *Ian Allan Library*

Below: Contrast in design. By the mid-1930s the outside-staircase NS looked archaic and far removed from this light, airy, functional bus shelter in Epsom. *London's Transport Museum*

themselves soon departed, the chassis being sold and the bodies being transferred to new AEC chassis. These were placed in the STL class, which was highly confusing to bus spotters, as they looked like STs and were the same length as STs. Two further Daimlers were acquired from independents, and were soon sold.

World War 2 Daimlers were placed, logically, in the D class, but this could not be done in 1933 as this letter was reserved for the more numerous Dennis double-deckers. These were four-ton normal-control buses owned by various independents, 69 of which were at work in 1930. Not surprisingly the LPTB got shot of the 26 it acquired, all being withdrawn by the end of July 1935. There were also some rather more

Left: The very last run by an NS in passenger service (there were just four left, working peak-hour route 166 from West Green garage), captured by the LT official photographer on the evening of 30 November 1937. *London's Transport Museum*

Below: A scene full of interest, recorded at Mile End in 1931. Of the many pedestrians, only one seems to be without headgear. Partly obscured by the tram-stop lamp-post is what looks like a Guy FCX six-wheeler of City. *London's Transport Museum*

Right: TD130, a Leyland Titan TD2, originally of the Prince Omnibus Co (and later sold to Red & White), working the 18c from Hanwell garage shortly before withdrawal in 1939. *Author's collection*

modern H-type forward-control Dennises, which London Transport classified DH. The LGOC had itself bought three in 1929 but found them inferior to the AEC LTs and STs. The rest of the type, 18 in total, came from independents, and all were gone by the end of May 1936.

Finally, in the Dennis stable, was the Lance. This model was introduced in 1931 and did well enough nationwide against the otherwise all-conquering AEC Regent and Leyland Titan to remain in production into the 1950s. The LGOC bought 25 of the earliest examples, fitted them with ST-type bodies, classified them D and sent them to its subsidiary, Overground, at Potters Bar. Eight more came from independents; they too worked from Potters Bar, the whole class being now DLs. Transferred to Sutton at the end of 1936, these modern and efficient vehicles might have lasted until 1939 had not the busmen's strike of 1937 led to service cuts and their withdrawal at the end of November that year.

Below: Interesting use for a redundant double-deck bus. NS2052 was converted to a mobile betting shop at the Brooklands motor-racing track. *London's Transport Museum*

• 4 •

The All-conquering Regent

THE AEC Regent would be the standard London double-decker for the best part of 50 years. So we'll start with the Renown, which was simply a Regent with two extra wheels. (Even this needs qualifying, for in one sense a Regent also had six wheels, the back pair being actually doubles mounted one inside the other, but the Renown had one behind the other at the back; everyone could see it was a six-wheeler, and this is the accepted definition.) Had regulations not intervened there would have been no need for the Renown, for it was only restrictions on the length of a four-wheel chassis that brought about the 1ft-longer Renown.

LT1 seated 54 passengers, the next 149 of the type would seat 60 passengers, and most of the rest 56,

Open-staircase LT42 in original condition without a windscreen follows a Metropolitan NS in Trafalgar Square in 1930. *Author's collection*

except for the final, 'Bluebird' version, which, with the upper deck extended over the driver's cab, accommodated 60. In 1931 the police allowed the length of four-wheel chassis to be extended to 26ft, rendering the Renown redundant, and no more LTs entered service after 1932. Although basically a huge step forward from the NS in terms of its far superior interior, almost luxurious upholstery and permanent roof, the LT body had features that looked backwards, the most obvious being the outside staircase of the early examples and a frontal design with the upper deck set well back from the lower. The lucky drivers of LT1 were protected by a windscreen, but this caused a sharp intake of breath from the Metropolitan Police, which would not allow this civilised feature to become standard until March 1931. The majority of London's tram drivers had to put up with exposure to the elements for getting on for another 10 years.

The LT was modernised progressively throughout its three-year production run, enclosed staircases becoming standard from LT151 onwards, and a much more comprehensive route-number and destination display arriving in the latter half of 1931. LT345 had an inward curve to the upper-deck sides which became standard, whilst most dramatic was the appearance of LT741. This had the upper deck extended right over the cab (slightly ahead of it actually), and in essence the standard layout of the London half-cab double-decker had been arrived at. Mechanically, equally startling experiments and developments were afoot — Lockheed hydraulic brakes, the Wilson preselective gearbox and fluid transmission and the oil (diesel) engine being the most notable. Some 1,227 double-deck LTs were built, all of which passed into London Transport ownership. There was also a single-deck version, which we will consider elsewhere.

The prototype Regent entered service with East Surrey in July 1929 before moving on to Autocar; the first LGOC example, classified ST, was licensed in October of that year. What was so special about the Regent that London would fall in love with it and sustain the love affair for half a century? Simply that it was the best. It was designed by George Rackham, who had already produced the Titan and Tiger designs for Leyland, and between them the Regent and the Titan established a virtual monopoly of the British (and much of the overseas) double-deck market. The ST was in production between 1929 and 1932, the type totalling 1,137, being superseded by

Above: Two LTs, that on the left being of the final, 'Bluebird' variety, pass in Bow. In the distance can be seen are at least two more LTs, while just entering the picture(right) is an 'E1' tram. *London's Transport Museum*

Below: ST91 heads along the South East London tram tracks towards London Bridge on the 218 *c*1932. *Author's collection*

Above: An LT, ST437, a traffic policeman, and a choice selection of vehicles, including one horse-drawn (just about visible in front of the LT), in the Strand, 1932. *Arthur Ingram collection*

Below: A wonderful assortment of cloche hats, bowlers and bobbed hairstyles, plus an ST, c1931. *London's Transport Museum*

the longer but otherwise initially identical STL. The vast majority of the ST fleet looked exactly like a shorter version of the earliest standard type of enclosed-staircase LT, although there were, inevitably, a great many variations. Some, absorbed by London Transport from East Surrey and National, had square cabs, some round, with slightly smaller destination indicators. (Twenty years later a curious decision saw one of these smaller-indicator, round-cab versions selected to be the official preserved example, and when it went on display, painted red, at Clapham a number of faces turned the same colour, some with embarrassment, some with apoplexy.)

Unlike the Renowns, short-wheelbase Regents were acquired by London Transport from sources other than the LGOC. Some 191 came from Thomas Tilling. They looked completely different and distinctly old-fashioned, not least because they had open staircases. (Having said that, in December 2005 I travelled up from Cobham and toured the final Routemaster route, the 159, in the preserved example, ST922, and found its ride perfectly acceptable, even if

Right: The smiling Romford-based crew of ST154 (note the raised letters and numbers) pose in their summer uniform c1933. The *Sunday Pictorial* advert is a reminder that Hitler is about to assume power in Germany and that Lloyd George, Prime Minister during the latter days of World War 1, was, like Churchill, one of the few prominent politicians of the 1930s who early on saw the terrible dangers this presaged. *Alan B. Cross*

Above left: The lower deck of an ST. The protrusion of the long, straight staircase is particularly noticeable; also the gearbox casing upon which small boys with long legs sitting in the front seats used to love to place their feet in order to feel the vibrations; and *(right)* the beautifully designed, almost luxurious upper deck of an ST, with its generously padded seats. *London Transport*

Top: An AEC Regent of Chariot. An official LT picture taken shortly after passing into LPTB ownership in 1933. *Ian Allan Library*

Above: A Regent of the Lewis company ostensibly *en route* to Rickmansworth, 3 July 1930. *Pamlin Prints*

An idyllic glimpse of the Surrey countryside at Mickleham, with an ST toiling past a group of cottages which, despite it being summertime, are all smoking away like a small Cunard liner, probably to provide hot water which very few homes had 'on tap' in the 1930s. *London's Transport Museum*

rather more fresh air was circulating than one normally expects in a 21st century bus.) There were also a handful of other open-staircase STs from independents, eight lowbridge examples which spent all their long lives (they would be the last STs to remain in service with London Transport) in the Amersham and Watford areas and, most handsome of all, 23 that were effectively ST (*i.e.* two-axle) versions of the LT 'Bluebird' and entered service with London General Country Services in 1932.

The successor to the ST was the 26ft-long STL. This was to be London's standard double-decker throughout the 1930s, although it would change greatly in appearance, evolving from something of an ugly duckling to one of the all-time classics. The first examples, following on directly from the last LTs, arrived in late 1932. Like the final LT design, the 'Bluebird' (so called because of the colour of its upholstery), the STL seated 60 passengers. It lacked the well-proportioned panache of the 'Bluebird' but served London well, the considerable increase in capacity over the 48-seat ST being much appreciated by operators if not passengers, for it was not as spacious, and the seats were less comfortable than those of the ST or the majority of LTs. An initial batch of 50 for the LGOC was followed by a further 100 buses, most of which entered service after the creation of London Transport. The other principal constituent of the STL class upon the formation of London Transport was a batch of 80 built for Thomas Tilling. These bore some resemblance to the Tilling STs but were more modern, with completely enclosed, rather rounded bodies. However, to get the show on the road the driver still had to give the starting handle a hefty swing, making sure he didn't break his wrist in the process, and the engine was less powerful than that in the LGOC version; both shortcomings were soon addressed by London Transport. There were also six STLs inherited from independents.

The original LGOC STL1 design was succeeded in August 1933 by the very much better-looking and more comfortable 56-seat 3STL2. This had a sloping front and rounded back, a petrol engine and Daimler preselective gearbox and, although designed by the LGOC, was the first variation of the theme to be introduced by the newly formed London Passenger Transport Board. The seating capacity would remain standard for double-deckers right through the production run both of the STL and its successor, the RT.

Tilling STL93, lettered 'General', heads north at Victoria in 1934, passing 'E1' tram No 1528 which is about to return southeastwards, having got as far into the West End as trams were allowed. *Photomatic*

STL609, which entered service in November 1934, was the first example of the perfectly proportioned standard London double-decker of the later 1930s. To quote Ken Blacker, in his book entitled simply *The STLs* (Capital Transport, 1984), 'the gently curved frontal profile . . . was quickly copied by almost every other coachbuilder in the country'. The standard was set for the rest of the decade, although there would be many variations in chassis, engine and body. Diesel engines (or oil engines, as they were then known) were now standard. Whilst preparing this chapter I had the great good fortune to be introduced to Jack Lemmer, a remarkable centenarian who started work with the General in 1924 and was much involved with the STL. One of his projects was STL760, which was fitted with an automatic gearbox and sent to Merton garage. 'At the end of its first week in service I went down to see how it was performing,' recalled Jack. ' "I've got a complaint," said one of the drivers. "I don't know what to do with my left leg!".'

Hendon garage in 1935. On the far left is an NS, which, despite the STLs now allocated to the garage, was still employed on one of Central London's most famous routes, the 13. In the centre of the picture is one of the 253-608 series of STLs dating from 1933/4, whilst on the right is one of the earliest examples built by the LGOC in 1932/3. *London's Transport Museum*

Specially modified STL1866 with domed roof and reinforced tyres emerges from the north portal of the Blackwall Tunnel shortly after replacing NSs on this service in 1937. *Ian Allan Library*

One variation of the standard STL was a forward-entrance version for the Country Area that followed on from some forward-entrance lowbridge examples (with provincial Weymann bodies) which worked the 410 from Godstone garage. Another comprised a batch with heavily domed roofs and strengthened tyres for working through the Blackwall Tunnel. Then there was an oddity, in the shape — that being the operative word — of STL857, which, in keeping with the times, was given a streamlined full-front and was renumbered STF1. It was neither pretty nor practical.

Best remembered of all was the roofbox variety, which appeared in the spring of 1937. Meccano Dinky Toys, whose products were deeply desired by every boy with sufficient pocket money (or an indulgent uncle), brought out a model of this; although never identified as such and not painted in London colours, a roofbox STL was clearly what it was, thus ensuring that the design achieved near-immortality. Similar in appearance to the standard

STLs were the 100 Leyland Titan TD4s of the STD class, their Leyland bodywork being skilfully disguised to look very like the standard Chiswick product.

The entry into service of the very last standard STL, STL2647, coincided with the outbreak of World War 2. This did not, however, immediately bring double-deck bus production to an end, for already the STL's successor, the RT, had appeared. Much has been written about this superb vehicle, without doubt the finest half-cab, rear-entrance 56-seat double-decker ever built. Suffice to say here that, although RT1 entered service in August 1939, the vast majority of the 4,825 eventually built for London service appeared between 1947 and 1954.

Above: Streamlined, full-fronted STL857 before renumbering as STF1, January 1936. *London Transport*

Right: Q2. It bears some (although not a particularly striking) likeness to the full-fronted STL. *Ian Allan Library*

Above: A lady hails STL901 at one of the newly installed standard LT request stops in the Strand in the summer of 1937. *London's Transport Museum*

Below: Cricklewood garage in the winter of 1938 with a line of STLs, STDs and STs, all wrapped up and prepared for whatever the weather might inflict. Nearest the camera is roofbox STL2037, delivered in March 1937, next is STL856 of August 1935. *London's Transport Museum*

Above: Although more and more middle-class families now owned a car, causing huge traffic jams at weekends on the largely inadequate main roads leading into and out of London, the vast majority of the population still relied on public transport. Crowds queue patiently beside 1938-built STL2403 on the edge of Epping Forest, 29 May 1939. *London's Transport Museum*

Right: Changing styles as the end of the decade approaches. The bobbed haircuts and cloche hats of the early 1930s had quite vanished by the time this picture was taken of office workers heading across London Bridge in 1939. A Tilling ST, a standard STL and two STs go about their business. *London's Transport Museum*

Right: The Lawn Tennis Championships at Wimbledon have always generated vast crowds of train and bus travellers. Hats are more prominent in this June 1939 view. *London's Transport Museum*

Above: Another view of the crowds waiting for a bus home, which looks like being an STL, from the Royal Forest Hotel, Chingford, after spending Whit Monday (29 May) 1939 in Epping Forest. Interestingly very few are wearing hats. *London's Transport Museum*

Left: The shape of things to come. The white-coated driver of RT1 sits upright and vigilant in charge of the prototype of what many consider to be the finest bus design ever to run in London — a service provided for 40 years, from 1939 to 1979. *London's Transport Museum*

· 5 ·

The Single-deckers

TO some extent the London single-deck fleet had its double-deck equivalents; but there were plenty of exceptions, not least because right through the 1930s experiments were being conducted, in close co-operation with AEC and Leyland, on where to place the engine, these being confined, with one exception, to single deck chassis. The single-deck version of AEC's Regent was the Regal. This remained in production right through the decade, and although there were many variations all were placed in the T class. The first entered service in 1929, and 370 came into LPTB stock. These were

Central and Country Area buses and a very large number of Green Line coaches.

The beginning of the Green Line adventure is very much the story of the early versions of the T class, for although a number of different makes operated under the Green Line umbrella in its early days it was the T class that was dominant. The first was T38, quickly followed by another 250 in 1931. Their bodies were built by a number of manufacturers, and whilst they were not all identical they were all built to a very similar, Chiswick-inspired style. Green Line was set up by the LGOC in 1930 as it became aware that it was losing traffic to a number of independents that had tapped into the demand for travel from the Country Area into Central London. The creation of London Transport simplified the situation, and by the beginning of 1936 a complex network of regular

T116 and forward-entrance STL980 inside Chelsham garage c1936. Green Line livery and lettering was subject to constant variation at this time.
Author's collection

Left: T217. This 1/7T7/1 variant with standard Chiswick-designed bodywork, dating from 1930, was an absolute classic. Although soon rendered obsolete by the magnificent 10T10s and lasting on Green Line work for less than 10 years, these coaches never lost their looks, and (as may be judged from the restored T219) in their livery of two-tone of green and black, with chromium embellishments, they looked superb.
London's Transport Museum

Below: Green Line T232. Although dating from 1931, in this picture it sports its unique all-metal 35-seat Metro-Cammell body, fitted in 1933 after an accident. *The Omnibus Society*

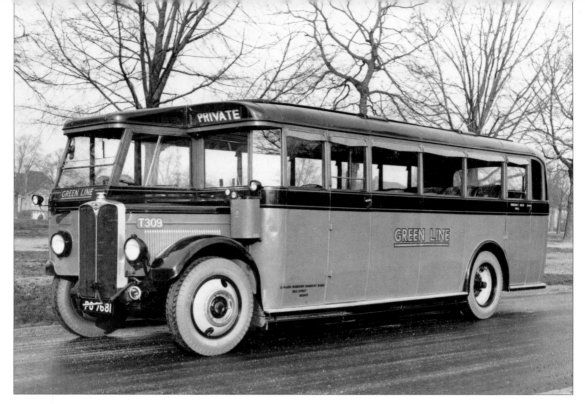

Above: T309, a Hall Lewis-bodied AEC Regal of 1930, delivered to East Surrey. *London's Transport Museum*

Below: London General S439 in Cheam High Street. Dating from 1921, the vehicle had the driver exposed to the elements. This outer-suburban 113 route bore absolutely no relation to the double-deck 113, which terminated at Oxford Circus. S439 managed to survive until July 1935, by which time it looked extraordinarily antiquated compared with the modern Chiswick-designed single-deckers then entering service. *Pamlin Prints*

10T10 T505 poses in the early spring of 1938 before entering service on route C1. There could be no more fitting destination than Tunbridge Wells for a vehicle of such classic proportions. *London's Transport Museum*

services, identified by letters, extended around the compass from Tilbury, Brentwood, Ongar and Bishop's Stortford in the east by way of Baldock, Hitchin, Luton, Dunstable, Aylesbury, High Wycombe, Windsor, Ascot, Guildford, Horsham, East Grinstead, Tunbridge Wells and back to the Thames Estuary at Gravesend. Various stopping places were established in the West End, notably, in the early days, Poland Street coach station, near Oxford Circus, but it was Eccleston Bridge, above Victoria railway station and a few yards from London Coastal Coaches' Victoria terminus, with which Green Line was most commonly associated.

Although two experimental Green Line double-deckers — an LT and a Q — were tried out, single-deckers were the norm, with successive variations on the T-type theme dominant.

Among its predecessors was the S class, which consisted of 64 solid-tyred 30-seat buses dating from 1922-4 plus a further 14, with pneumatic tyres, built for National in 1928. Of the 58 acquired by London Transport all had gone by January 1937 (although a remarkable sight on the HCVC London–Brighton run of 2005 which took practically everyone by complete surprise was that of newly restored S433, most enthusiasts not even being aware of its existence).

In the late 1920s AEC and Daimler products were marketed as ADCs. Exactly 100 coaches and buses of this make passed to the LPTB in 1933, most of which had gone by the end of 1936. Among the ADCs were the earliest examples of AEC's Reliance

model, introduced in 1927. Althogether 49 Reliances came into London Transport stock, the last being taken out of service by the end of January 1939.

Single-deck Renown buses received the same classification (LT) as their double-deck counterparts. Some 202 were acquired by London Transport, and all were still at work as 1940 opened. Although production of the LT class ended in 1932 and sales of the Renown went into deep decline nationwide with the easing of restrictions on the length of a four-wheel chassis, a little surprisingly another 34 Renown single-deckers were placed in service in 1937/8. Classified LTC, they were 30-seat private-hire coaches with Weymann bodywork and looked very like the 10T10 Green Line coaches. The six-wheel chassis, with less wheel-arch intrusion into the body, was chosen with comfort in mind; they were also given petrol engines to keep noise levels to a minimum.

The LPTB's most numerous single-decker was the 10T10, a slightly modified version of the 9T9 of 1936. Weymann-bodied Green Line coaches, the 50 9T9s were nice-looking vehicles apart from a rather clumsy-looking built-up front end; in the event they did very little Green Line work, being demoted to Country Area buses within three years. The 10T10 has always been regarded as a classic design. There were 266 of them, fitted with 30- or

43

Right: Q43. Placed in service in August 1935, this side-engined, 37-seat BRCW-bodied bus of revolutionary design was destined to serve in the Country Area for the best part of 20 years. *R. J. Snook*

Below: Rather less beautiful — but then revolutions seldom are. The prototype underfloor-engined Leyland Tiger TF1. It also carries Tunbridge Wells side route boards but these were probably fixed for photographic purposes as it is also sporting trade plates. *London Transport*

34-seat composite bodywork (a tidied-up version of the 9T9), and they replaced all Green Line vehicles pre-dating the 9T9s.

The Q was an AEC innovation, a breakaway from the traditional engine-at the front layout, and London Transport owned far more than all other operators put together. The prototype, Q1, had an LGOC body, but the first production vehicles were 102 buses with slightly odd-looking 35 seat bodies, higher at the front than at the back, and went into service in 1935/6. Although intended for bus use in the Country Area, some worked for a short while as Green Line coaches. Next came 80 vehicles designed for Central Area service, although some initially worked in the Country Area. They were in one important respect the direct link with the postwar RFs, for they had the entrance ahead of the front wheels, beside the driver. Fifty Green Line coaches followed in 1936/7, bringing the grand total of single-deck Qs to 233.

The Q was followed by two more designs with unconventional engine positions, both of which appeared in 1937. The TF was a modified Leyland Tiger, with the engine mounted beneath the floor. The first had the oddest-looking cab imaginable; like something out of 1930s science fiction, it was practically all-glass and was seemingly designed by

Production TF16 — a far tidier design, owing much more to that of the 10T10s. Rather curiously it is still of half-cab layout, no advantage being taken of the extra floor space. *London Transport*

someone who had not the slightest interest in what the rest of the vehicle looked like. Next came 12 private-hire coaches; with deep windows, glass roof panels and well-proportioned cab these were truly beautiful vehicles, but sadly all but one were destined to be destroyed during the Blitz. Finally came 75 Green Line coaches. All TFs bar the prototype dated from 1939.

The other innovation of 1937 was the rear-engined Leyland Cub, 49 of which formed the CR class. All had bus bodywork very much in the Chiswick tradition of the late 1930s. Neither the TF nor the CR took advantage of their respective engine positions, both types retaining the conventional half-cab layout. There were two earlier Cub varieties. First came 96 front-engined, normal-control buses, one-man 20 seaters, for both Central and Country work; C1 appeared in 1934, the rest in 1935. Eight quite different buses went into service in 1936. These were forward-control one-and-a-half-deckers, painted in an attractive blue and cream livery and used on the 'Inter Station' service between the main-line termini.

Above: The career of the CR class of rear-engined Leyland Cubs would span 15 years. In the twilight of their lives several were transferred to the Country Area and repainted green; allocated to Epping, CR10 is seen in Hoddesdon in the late 1940s. *Ian Allan Library*

Left and below left: The neat interior of one of the CR class. *London Transport*

Right: Leyland Cub C26 poses at Chiswick on a wet day in May 1935 before being sent off up north to work the 303. According to the contemporary caption on the back of this photograph the C class was delivered at the rate of six a week from May 1935.
Ian Allan Library

Above: C106 posed at Chiswick in all its blue-and-cream glory on delivery in 1936.
Ian Allan Library

Left: Looking towards the rear of Inter Station forward-control Cub C106. The interior fittings show how closely related was the RT to the single-deck fleet of the later 1930s. *Ian Allan Library*

newer vehicles, all being out of service by December 1939. London Transport also acquired 45 larger Dennis single-deckers, which it quickly disposed of. Also disposed of were the 42 Leyland Tigers and 21 Titans fitted with single-deck bus or coach bodywork which the LPTB had inherited from various sources.

Gilfords had been very popular in the 1920s and very early '30s, and London Transport acquired no fewer than 220. However, Gilford could not compete with the Tiger and the Regal and folded in 1935. The LPTB had little use for these non-standard vehicles, with a variety of bus and coach bodies, and had disposed of all of them by the end of January 1938. Most found new owners, and some returned to London Transport service for a short while during the vehicle shortage of the late 1940s.

Twenty-seven Bedfords, most of them 20-seaters, came into the LPTB fold, and, perhaps surprisingly, a few lasted right through to 1939. Amongst a bewildering array of other single-deck types, some long forgotten and all quickly removed from the LPTB fleet, were Albions, Bristols, Beans, Chevrolets, Commers, Daimlers, Fords, Dodges, Guys, Lancias, W&Gs, Thornycrofts, Tilling-Stevens, Karriers, Lafflys, Manchesters, AJSs, GMCs, Morrises, Reos, Saurers, Stars, one BAT, one Brockway, one International, one Minerva, one Overland, and one British Associated Transport Cruiser (!).

Predecessors of the Cubs were the LGOC Dennis Darts of 1930-3 (42 of them, with Chiswick-designed 20-seat bodies) plus three inherited by London Transport in 1934 from Romford & District. They were replaced towards the end of the decade by

Below: A delightful study of a Rayner's Horsham Bus Services normal-control Vulcan at Horsham Carfax in 1930. It is clearly in no hurry to depart, for there is no sign of a driver and the lady with the bicycle seems to be engaged in conversation with one of the passengers through the window which, on what is clearly a very warm summer's day, has been dropped right down. By the end of 1933 practically all the many routes serving Horsham were divided between the LPTB, Southdown and Aldershot & District, although the independents always kept a toehold. *Pamlin Prints*

Above: A little Dennis Ace with 20-seat Waveney body, BPF 318, ordered by Gravesend & District but delivered to London Transport in March 1934, climbs through the Chilterns. It was sold by the LPTB after a mere four years' service. *London's Transport Museum*

Below: Hertford garage in October 1935: as varied a selection of single-deckers as one could wish for, plus a 'Bluebird' ST and two NSs. *London Transport*

· 6 ·

The Underground, Metropolitan and District Lines

The trains that the London Transport Passenger Board found itself operating on that July day in 1933 were a very mixed bunch. They ranged from metal, riveted 'Tube' stock, which looked as if it had been built from left-over bits of 'Dreadnought' battleships, through wooden-bodied surface carriages that had somehow got diverted from their intended destination of Coney Island and were now more familiar with Sloane Square, to several of the archaic original Beyer Peacock 4-4-0Ts, put out to grass in the rural fastness of the Brill branch, and smooth-looking 'Tube' and surface stock with automatic sliding doors — and, most incongruously, two Pullmans, called *Mayflower* and *Galatea*.

Without its complex network of electric railways, running at various depths beneath the streets of the City, the West End and the inner suburbs, London would, by 1933, have pretty well come to a halt. In 1932 this network carried 498 million passengers, a figure more or less evenly divided between the 'Tube' and the surface lines. It might be as well to make sure that when we refer to surface stock we mean the trains which worked the Metropolitan, Inner Circle (as the Circle Line was then called) and District lines (which of course, spent much of their time below the surface but not as far down as the 'Tube' lines) and which in their dimensions were more or less comparable to main-line vehicles. 'Tube' trains were considerably smaller. Which, incidentally, meant that the electrical traction equipment had to be above floor level, thereby restricting the amount of space for passengers. One of the many innovations London Transport would introduce in the 1930s would be a solution to this problem.

The Metropolitan was the very first underground railway in the world, its original section, from Bishops Road, Paddington, to Farringdon, in the City, opening on 10 January 1863. By 1864 the first

Left: Difficult to believe that this rural idyll has any connection with the London Underground system, but this is the Metropolitan's 4.4pm from Quainton Road passing Wood Siding in high summer, 22 June 1935, hauled by one of the original 4-4-0Ts. *H. C. Casserley*

Right: A year earlier Mrs Casserley smiles for Henry's camera at Chesham with an 0-4-4T heading the branch train. *H. C. Casserley*

of the famous Beyer Peacock 4-4-0Ts was in service. Although long displaced from the capital by electrification, five managed to survive into the 1930s, mainly for the Brill branch. As John Glover records in *London's Underground* (Ian Allan Publishing, 1999), 'The train was sometimes quite empty, in which case the crew would often stop and go rabbiting in the woods'. Can one imagine a greater contrast than with the hustle and bustle 30-odd miles away around the Inner Circle? (One can get something of the flavour of this today if one stands on the platform at Quainton Road, where the Brill branch connected with the rest of the system and where preservationists have done a most sensitive job in re-creating a rural junction deep in the Buckinghamshire countryside.) Not surprisingly 55 Broadway soon put an end to this idyll: the branch closed on 2 December 1935, and the rabbits were left in peace — or perhaps the crews could now concentrate on harassing them. All but one of the 4-4-0Ts were scrapped, the lone survivor, No 23 (which in 1937 became L45) being found light duties in the service department until 1948. It had been somewhat modified over the years, the most noticeable alteration being the fitting of a cab. London Transport, pursuing its estimable preservation policy, then restored No 23, as it once again became, to a close approximation of its 19th-century days working underground.

The Metropolitan was the most distinctive of London Transport's railways, being in some respects more like a main line, with its goods yards, steam locomotives (some of them big, modern, Maunsell-designed 2-6-4Ts), electric locomotives and compartment-type carriages, as well as more conventional open-layout, sliding-door stock. It connected Central London with Uxbridge, Harrow and the Buckinghamshire towns of Rickmansworth, Amersham, Chesham and Aylesbury and on to Verney Junction.

For its territory beyond Swiss Cottage the Metropolitan Railway coined the term 'Metro-land', in doing so creating one of the most effective advertising ploys of all time. Colourful posters featuring neat, carefully set-out leafy estates of semi-detached 'Tudorbethan' villas complete with bow windows and add-on beams proved irresistible to city bank clerks, insurance salesmen, West End department-store managers and the like, and they moved in with their families throughout the 1920s and '30s, travelling to and from their places of work by, of course, the Metropolitan Line. It was a seemingly cosy, easily mocked world, but one must remember that many of the husbands would be survivors of the carnage of World War 1, and it was a way of life which the next generation would be prepared to fight and die for. It would later be celebrated with great affection by the Poet Laureate, Sir John Betjeman, who made a television programme (which still sells well as a DVD) of its delights, among them a man who had installed in his lounge — all 'Metro-land' houses had lounges — an electronic organ from a West End cinema, an ornithologist who proudly listed an astonishingly varied selection of birds found in a park in Neasden, and a Conservative ladies' luncheon (these ladies having been the young wives of 30 years earlier) featuring the finest collection of hats to be seen since the French Revolution.

As a child growing up in the 1940s I was fascinated by a picture in one of my big, colourful train books of a Metropolitan electric locomotive (I was familiar with electric multiple-units which were ten a penny in Thornton Heath, but an electric locomotive was something again) passing a bank of enormous poplar trees near bucolic-sounding Rickmansworth, although I was equally intrigued by Pinner (such an odd name), where Great Aunt May lived and whence she would visit us, travelling not by the Metropolitan Line but by trolleybus — which seemed to me an enormously long journey by this mode of transport. By the end of the 1930s London possessed the greatest trolleybus system in the world, and it was quite possible to make lengthy journeys all around suburbia. One of Betjeman's most evocative poems compares the hissing of the trolleys below Harrow-on-the-Hill with waves breaking on the shore in North Cornwall. The great illustrator W. Heath Robinson also lived for a time at Pinner and used to meet with his two

Above:
The photographer wrote on the back of this print: 'Old Metropolitan 0-6-2T No 93 makes quite a nice picture on a ballast train near Rickmansworth'. How right he was.
F. R. Hebron

Left: No 111, one of the handsome Maunsell-designed 2-6-4Ts, heads an up goods near Preston Road, Metropolitan Railway, in 1934.
Ian Allan Library

Above: A Metropolitan Railway 'H'-class 4-4-4T heads a five-coach train through the Chilterns north of Rickmansworth. *E. R. Wethersett*

Right: A Metropolitan Line Bo-Bo electric locomotive about to come off its train at Rickmansworth and hand over to steam for the rest of the journey to Aylesbury. *O. J. Morris*

illustrator brothers and friends in the Queen's Head, 'with its old oak panels and timbered ceilings' — a reminder that this was a village outside London until 'Metro-land' arrived. I never got to visit Pinner until Great Aunt May was long gone, together with daughter Wyn, who was married to Alf, known by the rest of the family as 'Know-all Alf' (although obviously not in front of Aunt May and Wyn). I, of course, was dying to meet him, for we were not a generally vindictive family, and for him to have received such an epithet, I reasoned, his boasting must have been something to behold. Alas 'Know-all Alf' never accompanied Aunt May and Cousin Wyn on their epic trolleybus rides around the western suburbs, and I later began to wonder if perhaps there had been a parting of the ways. Divorce was not something our family, or indeed any family we knew, indulged in, and Mum never quite got over her beloved Prince of Wales' deserting the throne in 1936 to marry the divorced Wallis Simpson.

Above: A Hammersmith & City Line train of 'L' stock of 1931, photographed in July 1936. *Ian Allan Library*

Right: 'Day trip from Ravenscourt Park' is the title of this postcard depicting a school party of young ladies climbing aboard a District Line train. *London's Transport Museum*

Far right: A GWR '97xx' condensing pannier tank specially designed for working through the Underground tunnels heads past Paddington goods depot towards Smithfield with a train of 'Mica B' insulated meat vans c1938. *Author's collection*

The Hammersmith & City Railway dated back to 1864, when it had opened between Hammersmith and Green Lane Junction, Westbourne Park. For three years it was worked by the GWR, being taken over by the Metropolitan in 1867. In 1884 it was extended through Brunel's Thames Tunnel to New Cross, adjoining the SECR station, whilst the District shared most of the route, diverging south of the tunnel to the LBSCR New Cross station (which the Southern Railway would rename New Cross Gate). From 1905/6 the section between Shoreditch and the two New Cross stations was independently worked, by the East London Railway, still using steam-hauled trains. Electrification came in 1913, and through trains once again ran between Hammersmith and the two New Cross stations.

The District Line — the Metropolitan District, to give it its proper title — was similar in several ways to the Metropolitan, originating in 1868. It provided what would become the southern part of the Circle Line and gradually extended eastwards and westwards. It favoured the Beyer Peacock 4-4-0Ts which the Metropolitan Railway had introduced in 1864 and eventually owned 54 of them. Six survived electrification in 1905 and one, No 34, was still at work in 1930, its principal duty being to clear ice from the conductor rails. It was withdrawn in 1932, replaced by a Hunslet 0-6-0T.

By the 1930s the District Line extended eastwards to Barking and then paralleled the LMS's London, Tilbury & Southend line as far as Upminster, which it reached in 1932. Built on the flat Essex marshes, this extension served a huge area covered mainly by council estates — an area, it must be said, rather lacking in character compared to 'Metro-land'. There, I've probably upset hundreds of nice Essex people now. Westwards it shared the Metropolitan route between Rayners Lane and Uxbridge — one of a number of branches from its main route out to Hounslow West. Other branches northwards were those to South Acton and Ealing Broadway. Southwards the Wimbledon line branched off at Earl's Court, whilst that to Richmond left the Hounslow line beyond Turnham Green. A feature of the District Line was that its several termini were situated alongside main-line stations. These were at Wimbledon, Richmond (which station would be rebuilt in the 1930s in distinctive art-deco style), Ealing Broadway, Kensington Olympia and Upminster. It was, of course, not unique in this respect, but the District seemed to have a particular affinity with above-surface routes.

· 7 ·

The 'Tube' Lines

THE City & South London (later Northern) Line incorporated London's first 'Tube' railway, which had opened in 1890 between the Elephant & Castle and the Bank. This was somewhat unusual; even now much the greater part of the 'Tube' system is north of the river. Powered, rather impractically, by locomotives, the carriages possessed tiny windows, not much bigger than the arrow slits in Norman castles, whilst the accommodation was scarcely more comfortable. The assumption was that, as there was nothing to see except unlit tunnels, who would want to look? This, like Bulleid with his notorious 'Tavern Cars' 50 years later, showed a profound ignorance of the basic desire of all train passengers to see where they are going, and especially which station they have arrived at; even in thick fog at midnight. Not that you get a lot of fog on the 'Tube', but you know what I mean. By 1930 the City & South London Line extended northwards to Highgate and Edgware and southwards to Morden. This made the Morden to Golders Green the longest tunnel in the world, as any right thinking schoolboy could have told you.

The Central London Railway, later the Central Line, opened in 1900, connecting the Bank, and soon, Liverpool Street, with Shepherd's Bush. This too was originally worked by locomotives, but these were soon ruled out of order, conversion to multiple-unit operation being effected in 1903. An extension was opened to Ealing Broadway in 1920, and others eastwards and westwards would be effected under London Transport control.

Above: One of the little Model T Ford vans used by the Underground Group to provide garages and stations with tickets and stores in the late 1920s and early '30s.
London Transport

Left: Coming up. *London's Transport Museum*

Above right: Service vehicle V48 of the Underground's Commercial Advertising Department outside Lambeth North station.
London Transport

Right: One wonders how the hats fared as these travellers, having posed for the flash camera, pushed their way into this clerestory roof, American-built 'Tube' train.
London Transport

The Bakerloo Line began business on 10 March 1906, setting out from beneath the Metropolitan Railway station at Baker Street southwards by way of Waterloo to the Elephant & Castle and northwards to Edgware Road. In 1915 it expanded northwards to Queen's Park and two years later, using tracks built by the London & North Western Railway, to Watford. This was at that time far and away the furthest point north reached by 'Tube' trains.

The Piccadilly Line had also opened in 1906, running between Finsbury Park and Hammersmith. There had been no further extensions, but these were planned and would come about in the 1930s.

The Great Northern & City Railway ran from Finsbury Park to Moorgate. Opened on 14 February 1904, it was built to main-line dimensions, the intention being that Great Northern Railway trains should use it, but 70 years would elapse before this finally happened.

• 8 •

Curtains for the Trams — and What Might Have Been

THIS chapter is not about providing a more homely *ambience* for the tram fleet but about its impending doom. Throughout the 1920s there had been proposals to extend the LCC tram network. Elsewhere in Britain the future was far less rosy, and the motor bus was seen as a much more up-to-date, flexible, less costly alternative to the tram. The advent in 1927 of the first really successful double-deck chassis, the Leyland Titan, relatively low-floored by the standards of the time and with pneumatic tyres, hastened this process enormously. In 1931 the Royal Commission on Transport recommended that no more tramways should be built and

that gradually motor buses and trolleybuses, running on wider, smoothly surfaced roads, many of them dual-carriageways and featuring roundabouts, would best provide public transport in the years to come. Meanwhile the LCC was building a fleet of new trams, which, whilst sturdy, well engineered and built to last, were nevertheless not much of an advance in the eyes of the general public on the traditional cars, the 'E1s', which dated back 30 years.

Yet there appeared in 1932 a completely different animal, a tram which not only looked different externally but which internally was light-years ahead of its immediate predecessors and rode like a dream.

Above: The classic view of the Westminster skyline at the beginning of the 1930s. Amongst the traffic crossing Westminster Bridge are four LCC 'E1' trams and at least five LGOC NSs, plus what looks like a normal-control 'pirate' open-top double-decker. *Author's collection*

This was No 1, and although I rode on it only once I saw it often and was immensely impressed. No 1 didn't just materialise on the streets of London one fine day in 1932: it must have been well into the planning stage when the 'HR2s' and the 'E3s' of 1930/1 were entering service, and I find it extra-ordinary that the LCC could not have held back for a year or so and then introduced a large fleet of 'No 1s', which together with the revolutionary 'Felthams' of the LUT and MET would have really given the anti-tram lobby something to think about.

In April 1929 *Tramway and Railway World* wrote: 'The greatest improvements yet effected in the double-deck tramway car have been credited to the three tramway companies operating in the Metropolitan area . . . The new car thus evolved may be said to constitute a model for the world.' Thus was the 'Feltham' introduced to a world grown cynical to the notion of steel rails in city streets. The magazine's claim was a huge one, but anyone who has sampled the delightful interior and riding qualities of prototype 'Feltham' No 331 at the National Tramway Museum at Crich — let alone those of my generation who every day rode the 'Felthams' through the streets of Croydon — will surely not disagree. The 'Feltham' had much in common with

the PCC car, introduced in the USA in the 1930s and taken up with enthusiasm in Europe. So successful was this design that it survived in its thousands long enough for the love affair with the tram or streetcar to revive worldwide from the 1980s onwards. Would the same have happened in London if, say, there had been 500 'Felthams' and 500 LCC 'No 1s' running by 1935? We cannot say, and in the event the beginning of the end for London trams came in 1931, when London United trolleybuses replaced trams operating in the Kingston, Twickenham and Hampton Court areas.

The first generation of London United trams was wearing out, as was the track. The Kingston area was not the most heavily used part of the network, so, whilst the company considered it worthwhile to invest in 'Feltham' trams for the profitable Uxbridge Road services, in 1929 experiments were conducted with trolleybuses; in 1931 authorisation was received to introduce them, and they took up work in May. Mounted on AEC chassis was bodywork built by the Union Construction Company at Feltham, a wholly owned Metropolitan Group subsidiary, and, despite having parts in common with the elegant 'Feltham' trams, the trolleybuses — 'Diddlers' as they came to be nicknamed, although no-one now seems to know

Left: An animated scene in the Seven Sisters Road, Finsbury Park, on 29 April 1930, with a variety of LCC and MET trams and a couple of normal-control open-top buses amongst the equally varied private cars. *London's Transport Museum*

Right: The magnificent LCC No 1 in its original 'streamlined' blue livery. *Author's collection*

Left: Passengers board experimental MET 'Feltham' No 320 (the only one of the prototypes to survive with London Transport postwar) at Golders Green. *London's Transport Museum*

Right: Boarding a standard MET 'Feltham' on route 21. *London's Transport Museum*

Above: 'Diddler' No 43, in original LUT livery,
is overtaken by a single-deck LGOC LT1059
outside Wimbledon Town Hall, 3 May 1933.
London's Transport Museum

Below: In sylvan Thames-side South West London a
'Diddler' does little to disturb the peace as it heads
almost silently on its way c1932.
London's Transport Museum

why — were rather ugly, brutish-looking contrivances, although, to be fair, vastly more comfortable than the trams they replaced; which was what mattered.

The 60 'Diddlers' were merely the prelude to what would eventually become the largest trolleybus fleet in the world. The true forerunner of this fleet was No 62. Completed early in 1934, it was, like just about every aspect of 1930s London Transport design, a classic. There were similarities with the standard STL, but the markedly different livery and route indicators disguised these; in any case the former tram people based at Charlton Works retained a good deal of independence within the London Transport set-up, so the standard London trolleybus — a design which would hardly alter between 1934 and 1950 — was distinctive, elegant and original. It certainly put the advocates of retaining the tram on their back foot and finally ended any lingering hopes they might have had. No 62 seated 70 passengers in its all-metal body, which was built by Metro-Cammell. The use of established bodybuilding firms, other than London Transport itself, was a feature of the trolleybus fleet, although LPTB ensured that strict guidelines were followed, so that differences between one manufacturer and another were largely superficial.

There were in addition two further prototypes which were rather different from No 62 and did not lead to production versions, although both remained in service throughout the 1930s. No 61 was a centre-entrance six-wheeler, introduced by London United in 1932. An AEC/English Electric, it had a body built by the LGOC at Chiswick and looked extremely modern. In one sense it set the pattern for the future, for it bore little resemblance to any Chiswick bus body, being much smoother and more streamlined than contemporary STLs. The ex-tram men of the Trolleybus Department retained a good deal of independence within the LPTB set-up and always maintained an individual approach to registrations, livery, indicators, and upholstery, ignoring what the motor-bus boys were up to. No 61 was probably nearer to what a Q-type trolleybus would have looked like — one was planned but never built. No 63 was a four-wheeler with a modified standard provincial English Electric body, the only four-wheeler in the fleet.

Right: 'X3' No 63, London's one and only four-wheel trolleybus. *London Transport*

Below: 'X2' No 62, prototype for the largest and most up-to-date fleet of trolleybuses in the world, at the AEC works in Southall. In the background is a Q coach for an independent operator. *Ian Allan Library*

· 9 ·

Trolleybuses for Trams — the Services

I F the introduction of the Kingston-area trolleybuses in 1931 was the prelude to the end of London's trams, the actual programme was signalled on 23 November 1933, when a parliamentary Bill to replace 80 miles of route was published by London Transport. The Act received Royal Assent nine months later, and on 27 October

1935 the work began. Two more ex-London United routes, linking Hounslow with Shepherd's Bush and Hampton Court with Hammersmith, were replaced by trolleybuses; then in November the worn-out Dartford-area trams succumbed. Early 1936 saw trolleybuses taking over the routes between Sutton and Crystal Palace via Croydon, these being combined into one through one, the 654. The replacement of the Hammersmith–Acton route in April saw only two ex-LUT services (7 and 55) still operated by trams, and even these lasted just a few

The almost-completed Bexleyheath depot in November 1935. *Ian Allan Library*

Acton depot, now home to trolleybuses but with the network of tram tracks still intact, in 1936. *London Transport*

months longer. This was doubly ironic, for the 7 was the long and heavily used Uxbridge Road route and was home to the scarcely five-year-old 'Felthams' — trams designed with this route partly in mind. And now, in the first decade of the new millennium, there are serious proposals to reinstate trams here. But as far as the 1930s were concerned, go the trams must. West London's loss was South London's gain, for the 'Felthams' were transferred to Telford Avenue, Streatham, where the entire class would take up residence before the decade was out.

July saw the Hammersmith–Acton tram route replaced, this being followed by two ex-MET routes linking Acton and Canons Park. In some ways the MET was the most progressive of all the tram concerns taken over by London Transport, for as far back as 1925 its Manager, C. J. Spencer, who had visited Canada and the USA in 1919, was asked by Lord Ashfield to design a completely new, advanced type of tramcar. The result, after various experiments, was the 'Feltham'. Some years ahead of the LCC the

MET had put in hand a modernisation programme for its older cars, and although all of these were withdrawn for scrap by the end of 1938, there was more than a hint of the ex-LCC people at Charlton favouring their own, for the ex-LCC 'E1' was noticeably slower than its modernised ex-MET counterpart.

The MET trams between Edgware and North Finchley and between Paddington Green and Sudbury and Edgware were replaced by trolleybuses in August 1936, whilst early autumn saw inroads into the former LCC East London network serving the Docks and the edge of Epping Forest. This continued in 1937 with the replacement of the ex-Walthamstow Corporation route 85, the updated Walthamstow

Above: Surely the conductor of this 'E1', bound for London's oddest (and most approximate) destination on what is clearly a warm summer's day, is not trying to catch the passing breeze?
J. Bonnell, courtesy LCC Tramways Trust

'E1'-type trams (faster than the standard ex-LCC cars) being moved south to Telford Avenue to work alongside the 'Felthams'. That summer saw a wholesale wiping-out of East London tram routes serving the Docks and Stratford and the introduction, *inter alia*, of London Transport's highest-numbered trolleybus route, the 699 (actually the highest LPTB route number of any sort), which ran between Chingford Mount and the Victoria & Albert Docks.

In the West tram route 32, which terminated just north of Chelsea Bridge, was replaced by a revised 137 motor-bus route, whilst much further south London's longest regular trolleybus route (630) came into existence, connecting West Croydon with the quaintly named (and a constant delight to collectors of curios) 'Near Willesden Junction'. One wonders just what mayhem *I'm Sorry I Haven't A Clue . . . ?* would have made of it, if only this programme — and *Mornington Crescent* — had been around at the time. There were a number of cutbacks, rather than outright withdrawals, in the Wandsworth/Battersea area, which meant that Wandsworth depot would until 1950 be home to both trolleys and trams.

Over in the mysterious East the march of the trolleybus continued with the disappearance of one of the two No 1 tram routes, together with 1A, the result being that trolleybuses far outnumbered trams on Stratford Broadway; the Wanstead Flats–Canning Town and Wanstead Flats–Upton Park routes also succumbed to the trolleybus. In February 1938 the Barking local routes were converted; then, before the month was out, the unique Alexandra Palace route was replaced by motor buses. What made it unique was that it was worked by single-deck cars — bogie vehicles built by the MET, the only examples in London. With their clerestory roofs and absence of windscreens they made a curious contrast when lined up in Wood Green depot alongside 'Feltham' cars. Up North, Waltham Cross said goodbye to trams, Edmonton becoming a trolleybus depot, although its address remained Tramway Avenue.

The year 1939 inaugurated a huge drive to remove trams from North and East London, no fewer than

Above: Two stylish gents, clearly in no hurry, cast a critical eye over an 'E1' on route 9 as it changes from conduit to overhead power. Trolleybus wires for replacement route 609 are already in position in this March 1938 view. *Author's collection*

23 routes being replaced by one motor-bus and 20 trolleybus routes. February saw trolleys taking over the Holborn Circus–Wood Green, London Docks–Stamford Hill and Moorgate–Stamford Hill services from seven different tram routes, whilst a month later the big, looping, much-used 53 from Tottenham Court Road to Aldgate via Stamford Hill became the 'K1'/'K2'-operated 653; 'K1s' and 'K2s' would always be associated with Stamford Hill. Summer saw trams depart from the green fastness of Epping Forest, routes 55, 55ex, 57, 57ex, 81 and 81ex being replaced.

Although World War 2 would prolong the lives of most south-of-the-Thames routes, initially its outbreak had no effect, and early in September route 77 between West India Docks and Smithfield gave way to trolleybuses, whilst in November routes 61 and 63,

linking Aldgate with Leyton and Ilford respectively, were replaced. Peace, of a sort, still reigned in the East End, this being the period of the 'Phoney War', although its inhabitants were only too aware of hostilities, for ships sailing out of the Docks — the busiest in the world — were regularly being sunk by German submarines and surface raiders such as the *Admiral Graf Spee*. The last tram-replacement scheme of 1939 saw 'J3' and 'L1' trolleybuses fitted with a special braking system plying up and down the steep hill to/from Highgate Village on route 611. The final trolleybus-for-tram replacements would occur in 1940.

What did the travelling public think of the change from trams to trolleybuses? All the evidence suggests it was delighted. They were softened up by LPTB's highly sophisticated publicity department with, under a heading 'The Street of Tomorrow', phrases such as 'the silence of smooth-running and silent new trolleybuses, successors of 30-year-old trams', and 'the new vehicle falls into line with road custom and plays its part in the evolution of the street of the future'. Traffic receipts almost always went up wherever trolleybuses replaced trams, even if they sometimes dropped back a little once the novelty of the new mode of transport had worn off.

• 10 •

Trolleybuses for Trams — the Vehicles

LONDON Transport inherited 1,662 trams from the LCC, 150 from the LUT, 316 from the MET, 52 from the South Met, 40 from Ilford Corporation, 56 from East Ham Corporation, 134 from West Ham Corporation, 50 from Leyton Corporation, 54 from Croydon Corporation, 62 from Walthamstow Corporation, 33 from Bexley and 19 from Erith — a grand total of 2,628. Not all saw service with the LPTB, for some were so decrepit that they were withdrawn immediately. Many belonged to the very first generation of tramcars, the oldest dating

One of the hazards of tram travel — and one which played a significant part in its decline — is illustrated in this 1933 view of intending passengers stepping far into the road at Finsbury Park to board MET 'G'-class No 233, fitted with an LGOC-built top cover.
London's Transport Museum

back to the year of Queen Victoria's death. Which was one very good reason why the tram was doomed; imagine what a hoo-ha there would have been if passengers had been asked to ride around London in 1933 in a motor bus dating from 1901.

The standard tramcar was the 'E1'. This was scarcely more modern, the design dating from 1907, although examples continued to be built until 1930 — and not just by the LCC. Over the years there had been improvements, 'Pullmanisation' being the term applied, possibly by a joker within the LCC, to the fitting of upholstered 2+1 seating downstairs and upholstered cushions (but not to the backrests) upstairs. Very few of any of the cars inherited by London Transport had windscreens or vestibule screens, which was the term generally used. In other words the poor motorman had to stand, exposed to everything the weather could throw at him. Even many of

Above: An open-top SMET four-wheeler dating from the first decade of the 20th century stands at the top of Anerley Hill, with the magnificent (if by now somewhat careworn — and soon-to-be-burned-down) Crystal Palace dominating the scene, c1933. *Author's collection*

Below: The Embankment, along which more than 400 trams passed every hour. Heading towards Blackfriars Bridge is 'E1' No 952, whilst ahead of the windscreen-fitted 'E3' is 'E1' No 1101 working the 18A to Norbury station, the boundary between the territories of the LCC and Croydon Corporation. The photograph dates from July 1933. *Author's collection*

Above: Mile End Road in November 1933, with
trams, including 'E1' No 912 on route 63, buses,
a costermonger with barrow, pony and cart, etc.
London's Transport Museum

Below: An 'E3' emerges from Kingsway Subway
on its way to Highgate as a policeman bars the way
to an LT on route 177, September 1933.
London Transport / Pamlin Prints

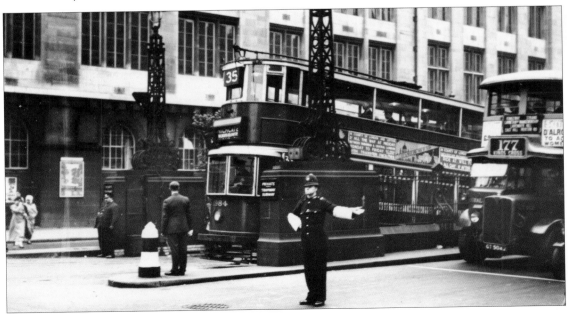

the 'E3s' and 'HR2s' of 1930 were built in this condition. Perhaps the most extraordinary attempt to hold back progress was the purchase by Ilford Corporation in 1932 of eight brand-new open-fronted, four-wheel cars from Brush — this at a time when the MET and LUT were already operating 'Felthams'. Four-wheelers never rode as well as bogie cars, and as for specifying no windscreens in 1932, one wonders whether the genius in the corporation that made this decision didn't also ask that shafts be provided in case electric traction proved to be a passing fad and a reversion to horses proved necessary.

Above: An 'E1', still sporting the three colour lights (albeit now painted over) used to indicate its route in the days before World War 1, stands at a loading island, complete with shelter. *Charles F. Klapper / The Omnibus Society*

Below: Car No 795 and a Thomas Tilling STL pass the Catford 'Bon Marché' in 1933. A standard 'E1', No 795 was rebuilt in 1932, fitted with a metal-framed windscreen and painted aluminium and grey. By 1933 it was painted in standard livery of red and off-white livery. Despite the modifications, No 795 would be broken up by 1940. *A. D. Packer*

Above: Ex-MET 'G'-class No 2264 heads past the high cinema wall by the 'Tally Ho', North Finchley, on its way to Holborn, shortly before being replaced by trolleybuses in late 1938. *Photomatic*

Right: A postman empties a box outside an Underground station — which he might do half a dozen times a day — as three MET 'G'-class cars (the first, No 2279 with a windscreen, the other two without) pass by. *London's Transport Museum*

The LPTB decided that this really was not on, and although it very quickly took the decision to fit screens to the entire fleet, the actual fitting took very much longer and was not quite complete by the end of the decade. In the mid-1940s one of the highlights of a journey to Purley was to peer over the gates of Purley depot from the upper deck of a 'Feltham' and view what was stored out of service therein. This consisted of open-fronted 'E1s', a condition I assumed had been caused by bomb damage, but I later realised that these cars, made redundant by the final conversions of 1939/40, had never received screens and had been placed in store in case they were needed to replace cars destroyed by enemy action.

East Ham, West Ham, Walthamstow and Croydon all had variations on the 'E1' theme, whilst Leyton went one better with 50 'E3s'. All continued to operate throughout the 1930s, eventually transferring to South London depots, some lasting until the final day of trams in 1952. As the programme of replace-

ment by trolleybus rolled on through the second half of the 1930s so the tram fleet diminished.

Practically all of it was reduced to scrap, at various sites around the network, but some examples escaped and migrated north. The Ilford four-wheelers of 1932 were sold to Sunderland and, ironically, outlived the London network, lasting until 1954. They made an extraordinary contrast with another London exile, the centre-entrance 'Feltham', No 2136. This could not be equipped with plough pick-up like the rest of the 'Feltham' fleet when it was transferred to Telford Avenue, so the lucky citizens of Stockton became the beneficiaries when in 1937 it became No 100 in the Teesside fleet. Today, back in MET livery as No 331, it is the sole surviving 'Feltham' upon which one can regularly travel, at the National Tramway Museum at Crich — an experience greatly to be savoured.

Another survivor is a West Ham four-wheeler, UEC car No 102 of 1910; set aside for preservation in 1938, initially in London Transport livery, it now forms part of the LT Museum collection at Covent Garden and has been restored to West Ham livery, complete with period passengers. Three 'HR2' cars of 1930 were sold to Leeds in 1939 — a decision which the LPTB probably regretted, for the class suffered badly during the war, 16 being destroyed. Luckiest by far was No 1858. This was bought for preservation in 1952, put on static display at Chessington Zoo, where it was lucky to escape vandalism (and I don't mean by the inmates), and eventually made its way to that home for semiretired London trams and

trolleybuses, the East Anglia Transport Museum at Carlton Colville, where it has been lovingly restored to working order.

Two 'E1s' are still with us. Although withdrawal began in 1938, and more than half had been scrapped by the end of 1940, the survivors formed the most numerous type of tram in the fleet throughout the 1940s. No 1025 was saved for posterity and, preserved in the condition in which it ran in its final years, now forms part of the LT collection. A few others were sold for holiday homes on Hayling Island, and one of these, most remarkably, is once again at work at Crich. This is No 1622. What remained of it was rescued, and it was decided that, as a representative of the standard 'E1' already existed in preservation, No 1622 should be restored as one of the rehabilitated examples, of which more anon, and this is the form it now takes as it plies up and down the Pennines — a rather different setting from where it began.

A substantial section of MET No 94, a bogie car of 1904, originally double-deck but now a single-decker with a handsome clerestory roof, operates on the Seaton Tramway in Devon. Then there is LUT 109, which, like No 1622, is being put back together, some seven decades after it last ran, by those indefatigable people at the National Tramway Museum.

The LCC's pride and joy, No 1, saw little service, most drivers being wary, so the story goes, of its air brakes. It was repainted red in 1938, sent south to Telford Avenue, whence it appeared at rush hours on

short workings — I never saw it come south of Thornton Heath Pond — migrated to Yorkshire along with the 'Felthams' in 1951 and eventually moved a little way southwest from Leeds to Derbyshire, where it can be seen, restored to London Transport red, as a static exhibit at Crich. It would be nice to see it running again.

London Transport took over a number of four-wheel cars and quickly got rid of all but the ex-LCC 'M' class, which looked just like shortened 'E1s'. Their riding was best described as 'lively', and despite various attempts to sober it up remained so until the class became extinct, in 1939. Three were rebuilt extensively as bogie cars. One, No 1446, did not actually re-enter service in its new form until after the London Transport takeover, whilst No 1444 (soon renumbered 1370) was rebuilt again in 1935. Both looked much more modern than anything else in the fleet, other than the 'Felthams' and Nos 1 and 2, to which they bore more than a passing resemblance, with their roller-blind indicators and domed roofs. No 2 is sometimes referred to as the only tram to be built by London Transport. It was actually an extensive rebuild of damaged 'E1' No 1370 and re-emerged modernised with fully upholstered seating and a much more up-to-date external appearance, being clearly related to No 1.

The final attempt at providing London with a modern fleet went off very much at half-cock. Knowing that it would be at least 10 years before all the trams were replaced (Herr Hitler's delaying tactics

Above: One of the ex-LCC 'M'-class four-wheelers drafted in by the LPTB to take over from the worn-out Corporation cars at Dartford. *London's Transport Museum*

Right: Wheel-carrier No 012, converted from an LCC 'L'-class car of 1909. *Author's collection*

Far right: Class B2 short-wheelbase trolleybus No 105 at the Woolwich terminus of route 698 on a damp day in 1936. *London's Transport Museum*

having not yet entered into the calculations), the LPTB announced in 1933 that it would 'rehabilitate' 1,000 'E1s'. This number was subsequently whittled down to 250 and then 154, and the rehabilitation proved to be very disappointing. Some, initially, did not even have windscreens, and the flat roof was retained, despite the vast improvement a domed one was seen to effect on Nos 2 and 1370. Certainly internally and externally there were improvements, and the preserved No 1622 displays these to perfection, but the 'rehabs' could hardly be described as state-of-the-art.

The trolleybus, by contrast, had achieved total modernity, No 62 setting the standard for the entire fleet, and the various 'K', 'L', 'M', 'N' and 'P' classes of 1939/40 were little different from No 62 or the 'C' types of 1935/6. The 'B1s', 'B2s'and 'B3s' of 1935/6 were a window-length shorter and had 60 seats against 70 for the rest of the fleet, being designed for the routes that scaled the heights of Highgate and Crystal Palace. It is most curious that despite

numerous variations the AEC double-deck motor bus throughout the 1930s remained classified STL, whilst the slightest change from the trolleybus norm meant a new designation, such that 'P1' had been reached by 1940.

Chassis for the trolleybus fleet were supplied by AEC and Leyland, in roughly equal quantities, but six firms built the bodies, all to the London standard but with subtle variations; these were BRCW, Brush, Weymann, Metro-Cammell, Park Royal and Leyland. Most of the earlier trolleys had spats over the rear wheels and a longitudinal seat beside the driver; this latter was soon seen to be not a good idea, and the driver was soon provided with a proper full-width, glazed bulkhead.

In 1938 there came a small but surprisingly significant change in the appearance of the standard trolleybus when 'J3' No 1054 arrived from BRCW with valances along the tops and sides of the front upper-deck windows elegantly curved into the frames, producing a distinctly streamlined effect — if not quite

as dramatic as that achieved by the contemporary streamlined LNER 'A4' and LMS 'Coronation' Pacifics and Malcolm Campbell's *Bluebird* land-speed-record-holder. By contrast the Leyland 'K1' and 'K2' classes of 1938/9 — and, indeed, the 'K3s' of 1940 — refused to succumb to even the modest nod towards streamlining around the upper-deck front windows that was now standard on all other body suppliers.

Although chassis suppliers were restricted to AEC and Leyland, the 'L1', 'L2' and 'L3' classes of 1938-40 were of 'chassisless' (integral) construction with AEC running units and Metro-Cammell bodywork. They proved to be just as sturdy as vehicles with chassis, remaining in service until the very end of the system. They were for long associated with the East End, spending most of their lives, along with the contemporary Leyland 'K' classes, in East and North East London.

Above left: 'C1' No 182 being demonstrated to a group of trainee trolleybus drivers — presumably ex-tram men — at Fulwell depot on 26 November 1935.
London's Transport Museum

Left: Unlike motor buses the trolleys nearly all had registrations that corresponded with the fleet number. 'J1' No 932 is saluted by Prince Albert as it rounds his statue at the Holborn Circus terminus of route 621 in 1938. *Ian Allan Library*

Above: A February 1939 picture of 'K2' No 1223 being driven onto the traverser at Stamford Hill depot. *Ian Allan Library*

Silver was the preferred colour for the roofs of London buses and trolleybuses, but in 1938 experiments began on the latter with red, which would become standard; almost certainly this was nothing to do with the Munich crisis, when war almost arrived only to be postponed for a year, following which every shiny silver roof, be it on a motor bus or a trolleybus, would be rapidly be overpainted to make vehicles less visible to Nazi bombers.

One oddity was No 1671 (the highest number reached by 1939), a Leyland demonstrator with twin steering and a single rear axle; in other respects it was more-or-less identical to the 'K1's, 'K2s' and 'K3s'. Another oddity was 'X5' No 1379, which was designed to operate through the Kingsway Subway and had both near- and offside entrance/exits. Tests were carried out on battery power, but clearances in places were extremely tight, and, with the three subway trams routes surviving the cull of all other North London trams by 1939/40, No 1379 took up duties as an ordinary vehicle with its offside doors permanently fastened, and the idea of running trolleybuses through the Kingsway Subway was quietly dropped.

· 11 ·

The Underground Expands

IN some respects congestion in Central London in the 1930s was as bad as it had ever been or ever would be, and although there would be no extensions to the railways beneath its streets there were many to the suburban lines bringing passengers into the heart of the City and the West End. Thus London Transport's railway system — like so much of the Board's activities during this period —saw unparalleled expansion. Much of this involved the construction of new lines, the remainder the takeover of existing lines from the LNER, LMS or GWR.

A year before the creation of London Transport the Metropolitan Railway had opened a branch from Wembley Park to Stanmore. In 1939 this would be handed over to the Bakerloo Line, which would reach it by way of new tunnels from Baker Street to Finchley Road and then running parallel to the Metropolitan tracks. The 'Tube' trains stopped at all stations between Baker Street and Wembley Park, the surface trains became 'expresses' stopping only at Finchley Road. Staying with the Metropolitan Line, not all was expansion, for the remote rural fastness beyond Aylesbury, to Quainton Road, Brill and Verney Junction, was abandoned, the line to Brill being given up entirely in November 1935, and that to Quainton Road and Verney Junction in July 1936. Quainton Road was still served by LNER trains (and decades later would become one of the most eclectic preservation centres, with the London Underground well represented), whilst LMS trains still served Verney Junction. On the last day of December 1933 passenger trains ceased to run between Rickmansworth and Watford, although the connection remains as I write.

In September 1932 the Metropolitan District extended services over LMS tracks from Barking to Upminster. In the west the Piccadilly Line greatly extended its empire by taking over some Metropolitan District services. From October 1933 the Piccadilly assumed the Hammersmith–Ealing/ Uxbridge services, extra tracks being constructed between Turnham Green and Northfields, on the

Hounslow branch. From March 1933 Piccadilly Line trains shared the route to Hounslow West with the Metropolitan District. Some splendid new Charles Holden-designed stations were erected, and the area, which at the beginning of the 1930s was still fairly rural and in character quite distinct from London, now underwent huge changes, thousands of houses, shops and all that went with suburbia appearing at a bewildering rate. This, of course, would continue after World War 2, Heathrow being chosen to replace Croydon as London's principal airport.

In October 1932, after a sustained campaign by a certain football club, the name of the Piccadilly Line station at Gillespie Road was changed to 'Arsenal (Highbury Hill)'; the result was a dramatic upsurge in attendances, this providing the ultimate vindication of the club's move some years earlier from the old Woolwich Arsenal south of the Thames (one of the advantages claimed for this having been that the new North London ground would be 'within 12 minutes' "Tube" ride of the centre of London'). Meanwhile work was proceeding apace on one of the most significant of all the Underground and 'Tube' extensions, that of the Piccadilly Line northeast from Finsbury Park.

Finsbury Park has always been an extremely busy traffic interchange, being the location of the first station on the East Coast main line out of King's Cross as well as a meeting point for trams, trolleys, Green Line coaches and motor buses, and by 1930 overcrowding on the 'Tube' was so bad that Parliament passed a Bill authorising a 7.7-mile extension of the Piccadilly Line to Cockfosters, then on the edge of the countryside. Known as the Southgate Extension, it was completed in the remarkably short time of three years, the first trains running the full length of the line on 31 July 1933. More than any other, it is an example of why London Transport was held in such high esteem throughout the world, for its eight new stations have come to represent all that was best about urban transport architecture. The consulting architects were Adams, Holden and Pearson.

Above: Acton Town Piccadilly Line station, typical of
Charles Holden's superb work for London Transport.
London's Transport Museum

Left: The distinctive cylindrical form of Charles Holden's
Southgate station, completed in 1933.
London's Transport Museum

Frank Pick and Charles Holden had toured
Northern Europe in 1930, studying the striking new
buildings there, much influenced by the Dresden
Bauhaus (which would be an early victim of Hitler)
and the work of W. M. Dudok in the Netherlands
and Gunnar Asplund in Sweden. 'Fitness for
Purpose' was the creed, and although Holden,
perhaps tongue in cheek, called his stations 'brick
boxes with concrete lids' they were superbly fitted for
their purpose, at both platform and street level
distinctive, without surplus ornamentation — a
reaction to late Victoriana and High Edwardiana —
but with a deep regard for appropriate materials.
Almost all now have listed status, and although
aspects have been modernised this has been done
with great care, and they remain essentially as
completed in the 1930s, still performing with great
efficiency, and in a sense have become timeless, a
tribute to the foresight of those remarkable men who
planned and built them.

Above: Art-deco interior of Cockfosters Underground station. *Author*

Right: Underground sign outside Southgate station. *Author*

Below: A recent portrait of Arnos Grove Underground station. This building, in common with many other Charles Holden designs, holds Grade II listed status. *Author*

Their fame was instantaneous. In the 1930s Nikita Khrushchev, later to become leader of the USSR and the denouncer of Josef Stalin, was in charge of the Moscow Underground (then being extended with little consideration of cost) and sent two young engineers to look at the Piccadilly Line stations. They were much impressed but on returning home were told by Khrushchev that if they were to have any chance of Stalin's approving a decadent capitalist design they needed at least to double its size — which was what they did, and the results are there today for all to see!

Amongst the many impressive statistics associated with the Southgate extension is that 12 million bricks were used (numbers of bricks used in large construction projects is always mind-blowing). Many millions more went into the estates of rather upmarket houses which sprang up along the line. That at Oakwood was described by its builders, Laing, as 'the most beautiful estate in North London'. Often they were bought by East Enders and others from inner-city areas who were moving up the social scale, in terms of both employment and general aspirations. The style of the houses was generally a good deal less adventurous than that of London Transport's stations. 'Tudorbethan', with its bay windows, stuck-on beams and leaded windows, was all the rage, although in some houses art-deco touches could be found, particularly in the metal-framed, curved windows. The developers often gave them daftly pretentious names: goodness knows what they were doing labelling their bottom-of-the-range, three-bedroom semis (costing £910) as 'Lockerbies'.

The Northern Line, as it became in August 1938 (the long-winded City & South London & Hampstead & Highgate 'Tube' had already been renamed once before, in 1934, as the Morden–Edgware Line), was much involved with taking over LNER suburban lines. The LNER had electrification plans but not the money to carry them out, and its articulated, high-capacity, low-comfort, teak-bodied suburban carriages were a byword for all that was bad about steam-hauled commuting; it is interesting to note that the carriages provided by the LNER for its most affluent commuters on the line out of Marylebone to the Chilterns were far superior. The London Transport New Works Programme of 1935-40 included the takeover by the Northern Line of the LNER branches from East Finchley to High Barnet, from Finsbury Park to Edgware (and construction of an extension thence to Bushey Heath) and from Highgate to Alexandra Palace. A good deal of construction work was carried out, and 'Tube' trains began running to East Finchley in July 1939 and to High Barnet a year later. However, a slowdown in house building, the looming war and then the war itself put paid to the other planned Northern Line extensions — just for the time being, it was supposed, but after 1945 the creation of the Green Belt, amongst other factors, meant that the curtailment became permanent. Others planned or under construction, notably the Central Line out to West Ruislip alongside the GWR main line to Birmingham to the west and to Loughton and the Roding Valley in the east, taking over from the LNER, were duly completed in the immediate postwar era.

Above: Alexandra Palace LNER station in 1932. The Alexandra Palace branch was intended to become part of the Underground system, but World War 2 intervened, and it never did, eventually closing in the 1950s. Class N1 0-6-2T No 4587 has charge of a train for King's Cross. *H. C. Casserley / Pamlin Prints*

Below: London Transport's takeover of the LNER branches north of East Finchley under the New Works Programme of 1935-40 involved considerable construction to link the new sections with existing Northern Line metals. *Ian Allan Library*

• 12 •

The Ultimate
in Commuter Trains

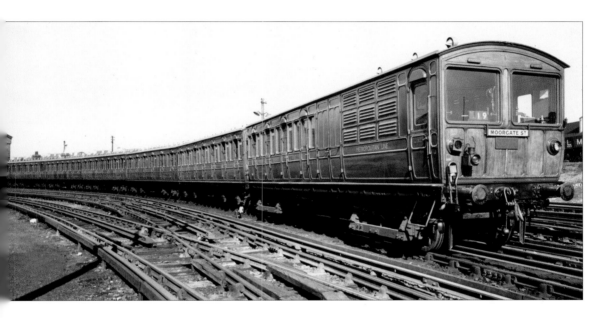

A train of arc-roof 'Ashbury' stock.
Ian Allan Library

LONDON Transport inherited a very mixed bag of 'Tube' and surface stock; to replace most of this it had by 1939 produced two designs, which, like so much of that to which the Board's inspired innovators turned their hands, became classics. First, though, we'll take a look at their predecessors.

On the Central Line cars dating back to Edwardian times, albeit considerably modernised, continued at work until the summer of 1939. Part of this modernisation involved replacing the original labour-intensive gates with automatic doors. The first 'Tube' trains so equipped from new entered service in 1920 on the Piccadilly Line, being transferred some 10 years later to the Bakerloo Line, where they stayed until 1939, then being withdrawn — but not broken up, in case wartime depredations required their reinstatement.

Next came what would be known as the 'Standard' stock. Six prototypes were revealed to the press at the beginning of 1923 as 'Underground Pullman Specials'

— a particularly silly title that merely debased the currency, for, although they were a commendable advance on what had gone before, no 'Tube' carriage ever has been or ever could be comparable to real Pullman comfort. Orders were then placed, initially for 191 cars. Production would continue until 1934, by which time 1,466 'Standard' carriages were in service.

There was much variation in surface stock. We'll begin on the Metropolitan. The most archaic were the 'Ashburys'. These were arc-roofed compartment vehicles dating from 1898-1900 and designed to be hauled by electric or steam locomotives. A number were converted to operate as multiple-units. Eight driving motor carriages, eight driving trailers and 41 trailers passed into London Transport ownership and

Above: A seven-car Metropolitan Line train of compartment stock in original lined livery. *London Transport*

Below: A similar train in London Transport days in plain brown livery. The third, fourth and fifth carriages are examples of the final, steel-sided variation of the MET's compartment stock. *London Transport*

Above: A Circle Line train of 1913 stock. *London Transport*

Right: The motorman's view ahead of a Circle Line train. *London Transport*

soldiered on until 1939. To complete the story, we must note that six were converted in 1940/1 to work as two steam-hauled push/pull units on the Chesham branch, thus ensuring the eventual preservation of several of them.

Next came the 'Dreadnoughts'. These were vastly more modern, elliptical-roof, compartment-type hauled carriages, of a design which would not have looked out of place at Glasgow Central, Carlisle, Crewe or Manchester Central, although the curved top to the doors was a distinctive feature. The first were placed in service in 1910, the last in 1923. Very similar in appearance were some compartment-type multiple-units. Twelve motor cars entered service in 1927, and 15 'Dreadnoughts' were converted to run with them; a further 55 motor cars and trailers arrived in 1930, and a final 65 in 1932.

We have noted the inappropriate use of the

Pullman term for trams and 'Tube' trains, but two proper Pullmans did work on the Underground. Named *Galatea* and *Mayflower*, they were bought by the Metropolitan Railway in 1910. Their chief purpose was to provide refreshment on certain Aylesbury-line trains, which they did until 1939.

The Metropolitan Railway's saloon stock entered service over a long period, between 1904 and 1926, and its history is very complicated — not surprising, considering that there were no fewer than 535 cars in all, of which all but 13 passed into LPTB ownership. Like most long-lived Underground vehicles they were much modified and modernised. Systematic withdrawal began in 1935, but there were still plenty working the Inner Circle, as it was generally known when, as a small child, I began to travel in them in the early 1940s. As they rattled through the tunnels there was something about their antiquated interiors that I

found spookily threatening in a Grimm's Fairy Tales sort of way, and, as a consequence, for several years I refused to let my parents take me underground.

The District Railway classified its carriages built between 1905 and 1914 as 'B', 'C', 'D' and 'E' stock. 'B' stock had wooden bodies, the rest steel. Some 287 'B'-stock cars passed to the LPTB, along with a total of 112 'Cs', 'Ds' and 'Es'. Withdrawal of the 'B' stock began in 1935, but virtually all the later types continued in service throughout the 1930s. Much more modern-looking, despite their rather small oval cab windows, were the 100 all-steel 'F'-stock cars ordered in 1919. On these the clerestory roof was abandoned, and they were capable of much faster acceleration and higher speeds than their predecessors. They lasted long into postwar days.

Fifty 'G'-stock cars came next, in 1924/5. These

had larger, rectangular cab windows but (rather surprisingly, perhaps) reverted to clerestory roofs. Similar, but with a smoother appearance, were the 101 'K'-stock cars of 1928/9. The final District cars to enter service before the London Transport takeover were the 37 'L'-stock cars of 1931/2. London Transport would bring this series of largely identical cars to a conclusion in 1936, when 28 'M'-stock and 26 'N'-stock vehicles took up work. Remarkably they perpetuated the tradition of clerestory roofs — a feature long considered outdated on the main line. This ensured that regular travel in a clerestory-roofed carriage could be sampled as late as the 1970s on the East London Line, where this stock ended its days — the very last clerestory-roofed carriages in ordinary service in the UK.

'Tube' trains by necessity have to be small, and not

Left: A Metropolitan Line train of seven compartment carriages, hauled by one of the Bo-Bo electric locomotives, and a Bakerloo Line 'Tube' train of 'Standard' stock. *London's Transport Museum*

Above: A four-car train of 1932 stock destined for the Piccadilly Line poses at Lillie Bridge depot against the impressive backdrop of Whiteley's. *Ian Allan Library*

Right: Servicing a Piccadilly Line train of 1932 stock. *London's Transport Museum*

being able to use the entire space above the floor for people had always been a source of frustration to designers. By the mid-1930s advances in technology meant this was no longer the situation, so yet another icon of transport design, the 1938 'Tube' stock, was born. First of all came some fascinating but not entirely practical highly streamlined prototypes. The last of these was given a flat front and — Bingo! — perfection was achieved. Just as Holden's stations were designed without unnecessary decoration, with respect for the materials of which they were constructed and with their purpose always in mind, so it was with the 1938-stock 'Tube' trains that passed beneath and through them. The production cars first entered service in 1938 and eventually reached the impressive total of 1,121, built by Metro-Cammell and BRCW. They served London faithfully for many decades, and even as I write in 2009 a handful are still in service, far away across the water on the Isle of Wight.

Above: A Bakerloo Line train composed largely of 1938 stock (although the third and seventh vehicles are earlier) leaving Bushey alongside the West Coast main line. *J. C. Flemons*

Below: A Bakerloo Line train of 1938 stock on its way to Stanmore pauses beside at a Holden-designed station. *London Transport*

Right: Interior of 1938 stock. *London Transport*

Left: A close-up of the elegant, flared sides of the 'Metadyne' stock. *London's Transport Museum*

Below: Interior of 'Metadyne' stock. *London Transport*

Equal in terms of purity of design but perhaps just that bit more revolutionary in appearance was the 1938 stock's big brother, the 'O' or 'Metadyne' stock for the District and Metropolitan lines. The two types had much in common, with flush-fitting windows, excellent use of internal space and fine detailing. But the one big variation was that the surface stock had flared-out sides. This was said to be to stop the dangerous practice of passengers' leaping onto footboards at the last minute and being carried off into the tunnel hanging onto the handrails. However, one wonders if this really was a serious consideration and suspects that, just like the flared-out fronts of the streamlined 'Tube' stock, this was more a matter of styling, very much in tune with the times. Initially there were 116 cars made up into two-car sets, but variations soon appeared, a trailer being added to each set. Then came the 'P' stock for the Metropolitan Line, which began work in July 1939. Thirdly came the 'Q' stock, which was designed to work with older stock. The grand total of all three variations was 573.

The future is now. The high-point of high-capacity, urban railway design. 'Metadyne' surface and 1938-stock 'Tube' trains north of Neasden.
London's Transport Museum

· 13 ·
War

London Transport had prepared itself well for the war that by 1938 just about everyone knew was inevitable. War was declared on 3 September 1939 and, in anticipation of immediate deadly bomber raids on London, an evacuation plan that had been finalised at a meeting held five months earlier at the Ministry of Transport was put into effect. Provision had been made for approximately 1,218,000 people to be moved to safer areas, 609,000 of these being schoolchildren and their teachers, the others 'children under school age with their mothers, escorts, blind persons and expectant mothers'.

The evacuation was carried out within four days — a quite remarkable achievement. The effect on many of the children, removed with sometimes not even the opportunity to say goodbye, was also remarkable — and highly distressing. Some 1,280 motor buses and 670 trams and trolleybuses were used to take the people to '129 entraining stations' away from the main-line termini (to avoid too much congestion) to Ealing Broadway, Acton, Burnham (Bucks), Sudbury Hill, Harrow, Edgware, Enfield West, Bounds Green, Richmond, Wimbledon and New Cross Gate, amongst others. Use was also made of Underground trains where these connected with main-line stations. The plan stipulated that the vehicles used were to be 'taken off their normal services at the times they are required to make the special journeys' and would 'return to their normal services as soon as they have completed the conveyance of the evacuation traffic'.

Various measures were immediately put into effect in early September, although a strange, halfway state existed with no raids on England — although elsewhere, particularly at sea, hostilities began at once. Services were cut, leading to the withdrawal of hundreds of buses, particularly those with limited capacity, such as all the remaining Dennis Darts, as well as double-deckers — practically all the Tilling STs, many of the General version and the forward-entrance Country Area STLs. These all eventually returned to service, the Tilling STs in particular being sent to help out all over Britain. The entire Green

Left: A policeman warns of an air raid as the drivers of ST212 and an unidentified STL hurry to take cover on the day World War 2 broke out, 3 September 1939. The primitive use of pedal-cycle and whistle was a relic of World War 1; vastly more sophisticated methods — chiefly sirens, which could be heard over a long distance — would be in place by the time the bombs began to rain down on London a year later. *London's Transport Museum*

Right: A smiling nurse emerges from a 10T10 Green Line coach converted to an ambulance and engaged in evacuating patients and staff from Westminster Hospital, 1 September 1939. *London's Transport Museum*

Line network disappeared, most of its coaches being converted into ambulances, although it was later, temporarily, partially reinstated, being worked by double-deck buses.

Probably the most noticeable change on the home front was the imposition of the Blackout, with reduced interior lighting on all trains, buses, trams and trolleys, and masked headlights. The result was many accidents, some fatal. Manufacturers of white paint prospered, for platform and mudguard edges, tram fenders and boarding platforms were all painted white in an attempt to make them more visible.

The Dunkirk evacuation and the fall of France in June 1940 was succeeded by the intense bombing campaign on London so long anticipated. It was because so much had been achieved by London Transport in the previous decade that its buses, trams, trolleybuses and Underground trains — and, above all, the men and women who controlled and operated them — were able to keep the capital moving through those dreadful times and emerged, battered and worn but triumphant, when victory was finally achieved. But that, as they say, is another story.

Girls from the Charles Edward Brooke School board three 'E3' tram cars in Camberwell New Road on their way to Waterloo station to be evacuated by train, 1 September 1939. *London's Transport Museum*

Above: Early experiments with producer gas involved this Country Area ST, seen having its gas trailer filled with anthracite at Chiswick Works on 16 November 1939. *London's Transport Museum*

Below: The Officer's Mess cook of the 84th (London Transport) Anti-aircraft Regiment, Territorial Army, giving instructions to two members of the Women's Auxiliary Territorial Service at a training camp in Bude, Cornwall, 7 August 1939. *London's Transport Museum*

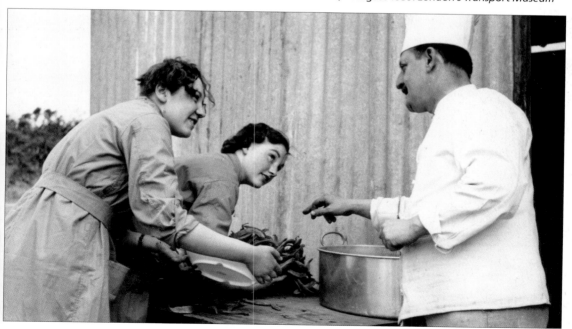

Above: An unbroken line of contemporary London buses personifies the London of the 1930s in this Liverpool Street view towards the end of the decade. Present are Chiswick-built STL and ST classes of AEC Regent and an LT-class Renown. With the onset of World War 2 London Transport would have to 'make do and mend' with these existing types and place a moratorium on the development of future models. *Ian Allan Library*

Below: A scene inside Telford Avenue depot on 24 April 1938 after the Felthams, London's most up-to-date trams, had moved in from north of the River to work the 16 and 18 routes between Embankment and Purley where their superior speed potential could be used to advantage. The six cars contrast greatly with the two ex-LCC 'E1s' in the foreground. Just visible on the far left is car No 1, the only rival to the Felthams. *London Transport Museum*

London
Transport
in the 1940s

Left: Camberwell Garage, 22 April 1940 before the Blitz. Two almost-new motorcycle combinations and their dispatch riders pose in front of one of the final design of standard STLs, still with full pre-war indicators but with masked headlights and white painted mudguards. *London Transport Museum*

Below: Four members of the London Transport Home Guard on duty at Chiswick Works, 20 March 1941. In the background are two STLs, now with restricted indicators. *London Transport Museum*

Previous page: Fleet Street, looking towards Ludgate Circus and St Paul's. Amongst the STLs are two RTs; that heading away from the camera has the white spot applied to motor buses during the blackout and which, for some reason, was painted on the early RTs, although, even more curiously, the following STL, still in wartime livery, does not have it. *London Transport*

Introduction

THERE was never a more traumatic decade in London's varied and often violent history than that which began in 1940. Following the declaration of World War 2 in September 1939, much upheaval had been caused to the lives and travelling habits of Londoners, but this was as nothing compared to that which would occur when the Blitz was unleashed upon the capital at the end of the summer of 1940.

Almost my earliest memory is of sitting under our huge, old wooden kitchen table and saying to my mother: 'It's 1940 now, isn't it?' As I was 2½ years old at the time I don't imagine the concept of years passing would have meant very much, but something on the radio, or perhaps a conversation between my parents, must have taken sufficient hold of my infant sensibilities for the passing of the 1930s to have registered.

As far as transport in London was concerned the 1930s were scarcely less dramatic than the 1940s, although marked by great progress rather than by destruction and tragedy. The London Passenger Transport Board, known to all as London Transport, came into existence a third of the way through the decade, on Saturday 1 July 1933. A curious day to choose, Saturday. Inevitably, few passengers — or anyone else in the London Transport operating area of some 2,000 square miles — would have noticed anything different about the bus, coach, tram, trolleybus or train which took them to work and brought them home again on that first day. And remember that in 1933 a great many people did work on a Saturday, usually until lunchtime. On the back of the 1937 issue of the Central Area bus map, under the heading 'Standing passengers', one reads

Tram conductors studying notices at their desks in the modernised depot at Finchley, shortly before trolleybuses were allocated there. Behind are the counters where takings were handed in and clocks showing the headway of services; similar recorders were on view to the public at London Transport Headquarters, 55 Broadway, during the tram and trolleybus eras. *London Transport*

that up to five were allowed during the morning and evening rush hours, Monday to Friday, and 'Saturday up to 9.30am [and] between 12.30 and 2.30pm'. In 1948, on passing the Eleven-plus, I found myself attending school on Saturday morning, and many schoolchildren contributed to the heavy demand for public transport at lunchtime. Later in the day, tens of thousands of fans would make their way to the many professional football clubs in the London area. My own club, Crystal Palace (well, we all have a cross to bear), despite more than once finishing at the foot of the Third Division South, attracted so many masochists like myself that I usually walked the 2½ miles to the ground at Selhurst Park rather than attempt to board a 42 tram.

Practically everyone within London Transport's 2,000 square miles would have been a customer of London Transport, on either a regular or a casual basis, for relatively few people owned cars, and, even if you did, more than one per family was unheard of, unless you were amazingly rich. In 1939 500,000,000 journeys were made on LPTB's trains, buses, coaches, trams and trolleybuses.

The LPTB had just six years to stamp its mark on the transport scene in London and the Home Counties before being engulfed by war. But what use it made of those six years! It is no exaggeration to claim that by the summer of 1939 it was probably the most advanced transport undertaking of any size anywhere in the world. This was due chiefly to two men, although many others played their parts admirably. One was Lord Ashfield, the Chairman, the other Frank Pick, his deputy. They possessed many qualities, but above all it was their vision which ensured that, in terms of design, vehicles, buildings, posters and just about every aspect of its infrastructure, London Transport led the way.

The declaration of war on 3 September 1939 drastically curtailed this wonderful, surging energy but would not bring it to a grinding halt. The consolation was that the achievements of the 1930s and the standards reached enabled London Transport to cope as well as it did with all that was to beset it, not only during the war but also during the years of slow and painful recovery which followed, through the remainder of the 1940s and into the 1950s.

Neville Chamberlain — a decent, peace-loving man who had seen at first hand between 1914 and 1918 what horrors war could bring, and who did all he could to keep Britain out of any future conflict until he realised, too late, that Hitler could not be dealt with in terms that he (Chamberlain) could understand — declared war on Nazi Germany on Sunday 3 September, 1939. The crisis of the previous year, when Chamberlain had flown to Munich and had returned with his infamous 'piece of paper', signed by himself and Hitler, promising 'peace in our time', had brought home to practically everyone in Britain the inevitability of war. There is a picture in one of our family albums of me sitting on my father's knee in the back garden with the caption '1st shelter

"Munich", 1938'. Those who had followed the maverick Conservative, Winston Churchill, who would succeed Chamberlain in 1940, knew Munich was only postponing the inevitable.

Thus London Transport was not unprepared. On 31 August 1939 — ahead of the official declaration of war — most Green Line services were withdrawn and, in an astonishingly few, short hours, the coaches converted to ambulances. The general expectation, fuelled by numerous writers of both fact and fiction and by cinema films, was that there would be immediate, devastating air attacks on British cities. Evacuation of schoolchildren and, to a limited extent, other civilians began, and by 5 September over half a million had been moved by London Transport, mostly to railway stations in the centre of the capital or the suburbs for long-distance travel onwards, but sometimes the buses or coaches would be used for the entire journey, to the coast or elsewhere. For those brought by the Underground, Edgware station on the Northern Line was the main departure point by road. When the expected invasion from the skies failed to materialise many drifted back home, but, with the fall of France in the summer of 1940, evacuation of children once again took place, this time in many cases for the duration of the war. Between 13 and 18 June 1940 111,000 London children and their attendants were evacuated in 1,300 buses, 200 trams and trolleybuses and 180 Underground and Tube trains before continuing on to their destinations in 180 steam trains.

We took ourselves off to Bognor Regis, although my father continued to work in London, but by then access to coastal towns was restricted and most evacuees found themselves experiencing for the first time in their lives the delights or otherwise of a rural existence for which very few were prepared. Children, being adaptable, often took considerable delight in all this, but many did not, either through homesickness or ill treatment by those in whose care they were placed.

Perhaps surprisingly, petrol rationing did not happen quite so quickly but was eventually introduced on 22 September 1939. Fuel supplies to London Transport were reduced by 25%, but, as there was less demand for its services, with many businesses being evacuated and others operating on a much-reduced level, this was not quite as inconvenient as it might have been. Getting on for 1,000 Central Area buses were taken out of service, and some of these were also evacuated, a number serving in the provinces for periods varying from a few weeks to several years. Conversely, once bombing raids began on London, provincial buses were drafted in, although it has been suggested that this was a propaganda move to show solidarity with the capital rather than the result of dire necessity. These buses represented a real mixed bag — some quite modern, many elderly and all very different from the standardised fleet of AECs and Leylands which had been

built up since 1933. For those who had to maintain this motley collection it must have brought back memories of the 'pirate' fleets absorbed into London Transport seven years earlier. Certainly it is odd that such a mixed bunch should have been sent for when a number of standard (if elderly) London buses were out of service and being held in reserve.

During the war many buses, trams, trolleybuses, coaches and trains were destroyed, although, given the intensity of the Blitz and the later devastation by the V1 'flying bombs' and finally the V2 rockets, perhaps not as many as might be expected. Many more were damaged, patched up and returned to service, often with windows boarded up. Staff and passengers were killed, although (if at all possible) vehicles stopped when the air-raid sirens sounded and shelter was sought. Garages, stations, depots and other buildings were also hit, but services never came to a complete halt; indeed, the staff became adept at performing near-miracles in keeping some sort of service running however devastating the damage of the previous night, for, after the initial days of the Blitz and before the final 'flying bomb' and rocket attacks, most bombing raids took place during the hours of darkness.

In September 1939 London possessed probably the largest municipal fleet of passenger road and rail vehicles in the world; there were 1,316 trams, 1,411 trolleybuses, 5,138 Central Area (red) buses, 604 Country Area (green) buses, 465 coaches and some 3,629 Underground/Tube carriages. In England, Wales and Scotland there were 90,000 PSVs all told, including taxis, meaning that around one in 10 of the country's public-transport vehicles operated in the London area. The total of cars and light vans in the UK, excluding Northern Ireland, was 2,034,000; in the 1940s the vast majority depended on public transport.

The furthest north the London Passenger Transport Board's vehicles reached was Baldock, terminus of Green Line route K1; eastwards they reached Tilbury and Gravesend, twin towns on opposite banks of the Thames, where several Green Line and Country Area bus routes terminated; in the south they could be found at Horsham, terminus of Green Line K3 and Country buses 414 and 434, whilst to the west it was a tie between West Wycombe and Aylesbury, the former the terminus of the 455A, the latter that of the 301, the 359 and Green Line B and E.

One of my most vivid memories of the 1940s is of sitting at the front — where else? — of the top deck of an Embankment-bound tram and looking down Brixton Hill. From this great height I could see two lines of trams stretching towards the horizon, which was formed by two railway bridges — one high, one low — in front of which yet more trams infiltrated and intersected, accompanied by double-deck buses, some of them six-wheelers.

Michael H. C. Baker
February 2003

· 1 ·

The Fleet

THE six-wheel buses in London's fleet at the outbreak of war were AEC Renowns, both double- and single-deck, of the LT class. The oldest dated from 1929 and were due for imminent withdrawal, but the war would prolong their lives by almost a decade. The standard London double-deck bus at the beginning of 1940 was the 56-seat STL-class AEC Regent, the last of which (STL2645) entered service from Alperton garage on 4 September 1939. (It should be explained at this point that within the STL class there were all sorts of variations, the type having originated with the General and Tilling companies in 1932/3; indeed, there would be further STLs, but none which could, strictly speaking, be called standard.) The RT, successor to the STL, was already in existence, but only the prototype was at work, the first of the production batch not entering passenger service until 2 January 1940.

We shall return to the RT — one of the all-time classic British buses — in due course, but let us first consider the STL. There was a time, in the years following this type's withdrawal from passenger service in London in 1954, when it would have been hard to argue that this too was a classic, but of late there has been a re-evaluation of its many qualities. Today the final prewar version is seen as

a fine example of the bus builder's art — from the point of view of passengers, drivers and operator as advanced a PSV as any on the road at that time. The superb restoration carried out by the London Bus Preservation Trust at Cobham of STL2377 has reminded those of us who remember the STL the first time round (or revealed to those who don't) what a magnificent vehicle it was. Interestingly it is turned out in the condition in which it appeared after its first overhaul (rather than as when brand-new) and thus exactly as it would have been at the beginning of 1940.

Concurrent with the STL was the STD — the Leyland version of the standard London double-decker. This was based on the Titan TD4 chassis and fitted with a Leyland body heavily disguised to resemble a roofbox STL; in this Leyland had done a pretty good job, although the differences were not hard to spot. There were only 100 STDs, all based at Hendon, but they were to have some influence on the RT and the postwar fleet and were a familiar sight in Central London, working the 113, which terminated at Oxford Circus, and (best known of all) the 13, which continued on to London Bridge station.

A design which might have transformed British double-deck design many years before the Leyland Atlantean did so was the side-engined AEC Q. Four were built in 1934 — two in red livery and two in green. All later worked in the Country Area but were withdrawn on the outbreak of war and never ran again in London. The single-deck version was much more numerous and successful and lasted in some numbers until the 1950s.

An example of the final version of the standard prewar double-decker, the 15STL16, STL 2624, with long radiator, is seen working out of Hanwell garage in postwar days, shortly before the chassis was rebuilt to form the basis of an SRT and the body transferred to one of the STL2014-2188 series. *Alan Cross*

An 'E3' tram and an 'H1' trolleybus meet in Woolwich. *R. Hubble*

Elephant & Castle, one of the busiest traffic intersections in London, is the setting for this prewar view including a 'Bluebird' LT, four early STLs and a long line of trams. *Collectorcard*

Above: Tram route 57 was replaced by trolleybus route 557 (Liverpool Street station–Chingford Mount) some two months before the outbreak of war. Many trams retained open platforms into 1940. Despite its archaic appearance, 'E1' No 566 was built as recently as 1930. When one considers that the ultra-modern 'Feltham' trams were under construction in 1930 one wonders what on earth the LCC was thinking of in perpetuating a design which went back to 1907, at which time many of its competitors were horse-drawn. *Alan Cross*

Above: Tram No 1370 could probably claim to be the only new tram built by London Transport. It was reconstructed in 1933 from the remains of a badly damaged 'E1' car dating from 1910, with a complete new upper deck and new seating throughout. A most handsome car, it is seen with white-painted domed roof before being renumbered 2. *Author's collection*

Right: London Transport made an attempt to upgrade the 'E1' class by rehabilitating 154 of them. Their interiors were certainly an improvement, as this view of restored No 1622, which is in regular service at the National Tramway Museum at Crich, demonstrates. *Author*

A view inside Harrow Weald garage in immediate prewar days. A mechanic is working on the rear of a standard ST. Next to it (believe it or not) is an STL; this was originally a Redline Birch-bodied bus, given a secondhand body dating from 1930. It started out with an open staircase which was later enclosed, but then, remarkably, London Transport rebuilt it with an open staircase once again and route boards instead of roller blinds. On its right is a 5Q5 of 1936, Q142. *London Transport*

The last chance for survival of the London tram beyond the early 1940s, had not the war intervened, was the magnificent 'Feltham'. Here, after transfer to south-side work, one is towed around Charlton Works by a tractor. A turntable is set amongst the cobbles in the foreground. *Author's collection*

Predecessors of the STLs and contemporaries of the six-wheel LTs were shorter-wheelbase AEC Regents of the ST class. There were many versions of both ST and LT, the oldest due for replacement; indeed, the 191 ex-Tilling open-staircase STs were in the course of withdrawal when war broke out.

The standard single-decker was the T-class AEC Regal, although, strictly speaking, no one class can be said to have had a monopoly of the term 'standard' in the late 1930s, in the way that the STL was the standard double-decker. The T also originated with 'the General', many being used on Green Line work, although others came from Thomas Tilling and a whole host from smaller operators. The newest Ts — the handsome 10T10 Green Line coaches — were little more than a year old but had already been superseded by a remarkable Leyland design, the TF. These initials signified

Green Line 9T9 coach T420c about to set off for Watford from Reigate garage. The heavily built-up front end was refined in their much more numerous and highly successful 10T10 successors.
London Country

Above: 10T10 interior. Not really a coach by long-distance standards. *Author*

Right: Now this really is a luxury coach. One of the Private Hire six-wheel LTC Renowns. *London Transport*

Left: Deep in the rural fastness of a winter day in the Surrey Hills, T599 steadily climbs a deep-set lane through the North Downs on its way to Abinger. Introduced in 1938, the 10T10s were the backbone of the Green Line network but worked as Country Area buses too. The outline of the conductor can be seen through the nearside window, a reminder that two-man crews were the norm in the days of half-cab single-deckers. *London Transport*

108

Above: C60, one of the little 20-seat Leyland Cubs, in suitably bucolic Hertfordshire surroundings. *London Transport*

Top left: One of the production flat-floor-engine Leyland Tigers: Green Line TF16c, based at Romford garage for route X. *London Transport*

Lower left: TF9, the only Private Hire TF to survive the bombing at Bull's Yard, Peckham. *Alan B. Cross*

Tiger Flat, the position of the horizontal engine pointing the way to what would become standard practice in the bus and coach industry in the early 1950s. Despite this the TF class still sported the traditional half-cab layout, thus negating one of the primary advantages of the horizontal, underfloor engine. Most TFs were Green Line coaches, but 12 had elegant Park Royal bodywork and were allocated to the Private Hire fleet; these would have tragically short lives, all but TF9 being destroyed during the Blitz in October 1940.

London Transport inherited a fascinating but impractical variety of small buses operating in both Central and Country areas, and one of its many priorities was to standardise upon a replacement. Leyland had its Cub, introduced in 1931, and a prototype — C1 — was ordered and put in service in October 1934. Its Chiswick-built body was a typically handsome version of current practice, with a strong family likeness to contemporary T and STL classes. The prototype having proved itself, 96 production examples were ordered. This time the bodies were built not by Chiswick but by Short Bros (which firm would soon concentrate on

aircraft production) and Weymann. They were divided between the Central and Country areas.

There were two further variations on the Cub theme. In 1936 eight highly distinctive forward-control buses with 1½-deck Park Royal bodywork, painted blue and yellow with black roofs, were bought for the Inter Station service. This was one of the many services abandoned on the outbreak of war, the buses (C106-13) being loaned to the Entertainments National Service Association (better known as ENSA) for the duration. ENSA's role was to put on shows for the troops and those engaged in war work in factories all over the country, and the Cubs travelled far and wide, conveying concert parties (not always, it must be said, of the highest quality) to places no London bus had ever previously visited.

London Transport was extraordinarily inventive when it came to single-deckers. Following on the revolutionary Qs and TFs, was the CR class of 49 Leyland Cubs with rear-mounted diesel engines. The prototype took up work at the beginning of 1938, whilst the production batch appeared between September 1939 and February 1940. It was an unfortunate time for an experimental design. CR18 was gone within a year, destroyed when a bomb fell on the Bull Yard, Peckham, in October 1940; the same bomb also destroyed all but one of the Private Hire TFs — Hitler must have had a particular down on unusual single-deckers. Mechanically the CRs were far from reliable — a serious shortcoming when the engineering side of London Transport was under desperate pressure. In addition there was little use for buses of such limited capacity in wartime

conditions. Some were never licensed, whilst the remainder had all been put in store by mid-summer 1942. They reappeared after the war, at a time when every single serviceable bus was being pressed into service, but soon disappeared again from the streets of London. CR14 was retained as part of the London Transport collection — the sole survivor of an unfortunate class.

One of the many compromises forced upon London Transport by the outbreak of war was a halt in the programme to convert all tram routes to trolleybus operation. However, despite this, North and East London continued to lose their trams. The West India Docks–Smithfield 77 was replaced by trolleybus 677 in September 1939, the 61 and 63 — linking Aldgate with Leyton and Ilford — gave way to the 661 and 663 in November and, just before Christmas, Highgate Village lost its tram route 11 when trolleybus 611 took over. There would be just one more tram-replacement scheme (and the last to involve trolleybuses), the 565, 567 and 665 replacing the Bloomsbury/Smithfield/Aldgate/Holborn Circus–East Ham/West Ham/Poplar/Barking tram routes 65 and 67 in June 1940. Even then, new trolleybuses to full prewar standard continued to be added to the fleet, the last of these — MCW-bodied Leyland 'P1' No 1721 — taking up work from Hammersmith depot in October 1941. It is highly likely that these final 25 vehicles were bought to fill the places of those lost (or liable to be lost) to bombing.

The only variety of the Q class which exploited its potential for having the entrance right at the front was the Park Royal-bodied 5Q5. In theory these could have been one-man-operated, but they were a generation too early for that, hence the conductor smiling for the camera as Q179 of Sidcup garage heads for home, pursued by a Morris post office van. *F. G. Reynolds*

Top left: A pair of 20-seat, one-man-operated Country Area Leyland Cubs, with C22 leading, at Gravesend.

Lower left: One of the BRCW-bodied 4Q4s, Q92, at St Albans. *Ian Allan Library*

Below: The original rear-engined Leyland Cub, CR1, as delivered in July 1938. *London Transport*

Wartime 'Make Do and Mend'

IN October 1941 the first of the wartime utility buses was shown to the press. This was vastly less well appointed than trolleybus No 1721, neither chassis nor body being up to the standard Londoners had come to expect. Wartime restrictions meant no lining to the upper-deck ceiling, no double panelling below the windows, and brown leathercloth upholstery. The chassis was the Leyland Titan TD7 and was totally unsuitable for Central London. Gear-changing was painfully slow, and drivers hated them. These 11 buses were the prelude to hundreds more utility buses, although there would be no more Leylands until the war was over. They were added to the STD class but were not a patch on their predecessors, the TD4s based at Hendon, which had all sorts of modifications to make them suitable for the demands of a life in Central

London. Despite this they spent all their lives based at the most central of all London's garages, Gillingham Street, Victoria, and managed to give 10 years' passenger service before being retired in 1951.

Next to arrive were nine Bristols, in the spring of 1942. Bristol was a make quite unknown in London, but the LPTB was desperate for new buses. They had five-cylinder Gardner engines (hence the designation K5G) and Park Royal bodies more or less identical to those fitted to the STDs. They were much less sophisticated than London's prewar AECs and Leylands, but the mechanics and drivers at Hanwell garage, where they were sent, thought better of them than did the staff at Victoria of their STDs. These Bristols (forming the B class) and the STDs were known as 'unfrozen' vehicles — many of their components were already in stock but the Ministry of Supply had initially ordered that work on them be stopped so that the factories could go over to war work, but it soon became clear that a certain number of new buses would have to be produced each year to make up for war losses and life-expired withdrawals.

Authority and the times decreed that nothing could save the tram from extinction. This is Poplar depot in May 1940, with a group of chassisless 'L3' trolleybuses waiting to enter service. Note the wartime white stripe at the bottom edge of their platforms. *Ian Allan Library*

Victoria station in immediate prewar days. Amongst the variety of STs, LTs and STLs is a new roofbox STL with gleaming unpainted radiator.
Author's collection

Metro-Cammell-bodied AEC 'H1' trolleybus No 768 passes tram No 538 on route 3, which succumbed to trolleybuses in July 1938. No 538 is an 'E' class car, predecessor of the 'E1', and was built in 1906. Apart from a single example rebuilt as an 'E1', all the 'Es' had gone by the end of 1938.
London Transport

The former ST40 in use as a tree-lopper in wartime. Originally a standard LGOC bus, it was taken out of passenger service, possibly as a result of war damage, and given a converted Lewis Omnibus Co body for its new role. *Ian Allan Library*

No 418J, an AEC heavy-emergency breakdown lorry of 1939, used to clear Underground breakdowns. Equipped with a radio, it was on 24-hour standby. *London Transport*

What the LPTB wanted most were AECs, and 34 'unfrozen' Regent chassis duly arrived between the end of 1941 and the autumn of 1942, to be added to the STL class. Chiswick produced a like number of bodies, 20 to lowbridge layout, the designers managing to adapt the standard STL look pretty successfully; internally, however (like the 'unfrozen' STDs), all fell far short of prewar standards. In the event, all 20 lowbridge bodies were mounted on overhauled prewar chassis (as was one of the highbridge ones), which meant that most of the 'unfrozen' chassis received various types of earlier, overhauled bodywork. STL2674/9 each received one of the earliest LGOC STL1-type bodies; they were destined to be the last survivors, and one very nearly got preserved. The highbridge bodies, coded STL17/1, looked very much like the last series of prewar vehicles but internally were to skimpy wartime standards. All went to work in the Country Area and I got to know them well on our local 409 and 411 routes when they were based at Godstone garage. Like the STDs the chassis were built to provincial rather than London specifications but were much better received, being well suited to Country Area work and steep hills, such as that encountered on the climb from Caterham Valley to Caterham-on-the-Hill.

These Leylands, AECs and Bristols represented something of a halfway house — or rather bus — between full prewar standards and the very downmarket full wartime version which came next, by the hundred. But first there arrived 43 trolleybuses which while not exactly 'unfrozen' (overheated?) were certainly unexpected. Intended for Durban and Johannesburg, they never made the long and potentially hazardous journey south but instead took the next-best option and settled in Ilford. Despite having Leyland or AEC chassis and MCW bodywork they were very different from anything seen previously in London (or, indeed, the UK), being

STL2666, one of the 'unfrozen' buses fitted with a highbridge body, working from Godstone garage. Seen at the Swan & Sugar Loaf, South Croydon, it has neither roofbox nor opening windows at the front. *Author's collection*

fitted with such tropical devices as full-drop windows (some of them darkened) and entrances at the front as well as at the rear. Perhaps most significantly they were 8ft wide, which caused the Metropolitan Police a sharp intake of breath, nothing wider than 7ft 6in having been permitted hitherto. Special dispensation was duly granted, and the trolleys (Classes SA1, SA2 and SA3) settled down to uneventful lives in the Ilford and Barking areas.

Completing half-finished prewar vehicles or diverting those intended for export was no long-term answer to the need for new buses, so the Government authorised a resumption of production, albeit strictly controlled.

No 1731, one of the trolleybuses intended for Durban, South Africa, but delivered to London Transport in 1941, which spent its career working in the Ilford area. *Author's collection*

Bedford supplied single-deckers — little single-deck, normal-control OWBs — but these were of no interest to London. The plan was that both Leyland and Guy should produce double-deck chassis, but in the event Leyland concentrated on other war work, so that double-deck bus chassis were available only from Guy. Neither the LGOC nor the LPTB had favoured this make, but now there was no choice, and between August 1942 and March 1946 no fewer than 435 Guy Arabs entered London service. Later Daimler was also permitted to produce buses, and a total of 281 joined the LPTB fleet, the first arriving in April 1944, the last in November 1946. Most of the Daimlers were fitted with AEC engines, which alone would have made them more welcome; drivers also found them to be more responsive than the Guys.

Passengers, not surprisingly, cared little about chassis variation. The comfort and general appointments of the interiors was their chief concern, and they were to be sadly disappointed. A variety of manufacturers — many, such as Park Royal and Weymann, well known to London, others, like Northern Counties and Massey, less so — supplied bodies, but unseasoned timber and strict instructions to cut down on what were now considered luxuries (but had in the 1930s been thought of as essential) produced a very basic, rather primitive vehicle. There were few opening windows, and rock bottom was reached when some were delivered with wooden seats. However, contrasts with standard STs, LTs and STLs were not always as marked as they might have been, for maintenance standards inevitably dropped, overhauls were long overdue, windows broken

D3 was one of the first batch of wartime Daimlers; a Duple-bodied lowbridge example fitted originally with wooden seats, it was delivered to Merton garage in May 1944. It is seen waiting at a favourite haunt of the Daimlers, the forecourt of the Northern Line station at Morden. *Alan Cross*

Having just deposited a mother and child, G145, a Park Royal-bodied Guy delivered in June 1945, waits amongst the wide open spaces of Wembley for an elderly 8hp delivery van to move out of its way.
F. G. Reynolds

by bomb blasts were boarded up, paintwork deteriorated, interior and exterior lighting was reduced, and the whole fleet became shabbier and shabbier.

One surprising aspect of the wartime world of 'making do and mend' (with ever-more-stretched engineers trying to keep buses, trams and trolleybuses on the road, despite the severe shortage of materials and spare parts) was the continued advertisement of manufacturers' products. Not only, of course, does advertising cost money but there was so little choice that one would not have thought it worthwhile. Yet, right through the war, every edition of the weekly *Passenger Transport Journal* contains slogans such as 'If trolley 'buses had a flying start they would be finished in TITANINE, the world's premier aeroplane finish', complete with a jolly picture of a pair of wings protruding from 'D2' Leyland No 456 as it skims above Wandsworth on its way to 'near Willesden Junction'. In another advertisement STL934 negotiates a snow-covered street above the slogan headed 'Dirty Work at the Cross Roads' and

Right: Heavily boarded-up STL1456 on an emergency service. *Alan Cross collection*

Below: The austere lower-deck interior of a wartime double-decker, in this instance a Guy dating from 1943. Amongst the wartime features are the low-back wooden seats, the netting over the windows (of which there's only one opening one on each side) and the heavy shades over the lamps. *London Transport*

Britain's Standard War-Time Buses

Simplified Design to Meet Present Conditions

AT the works of a well-known coachbuilding concern recently we were afforded the opportunity of inspecting the first double-deck bus produced under a war-time programme to meet urgent passenger transport requirements. This vehicle, which has a seating capacity of 56, is the forerunner of many others to be built under a comprehensive scheme at numerous coachbuilding works in various parts of the country. Simplification in design and specification, along with the standardisation of fittings, will facilitate ease of

facturers' works. It was only on closer inspection that the deletion of some of the customary frills and trimmings became apparent. It must not be thought that the new standard war-time product is lacking in comfort. In fact, to the untrained eye, it would indeed be difficult to distinguish the war-time model from the peace-time prototype. Comfort in seating has not been sacrificed, but the luxuries of the usual plenitude of drop windows, heaters, decorative mouldings, have been curtailed so as to eliminate present unnecessary fixtures and fittings.

Side view of the new standard war-time double-deck bus.

production and provide considerable economies in man hours and in the use of essential materials.

These vehicles are being built to the instructions of the Ministry of Supply and on completion they will be issued through the Ministry of War Transport to operator undertakings whose war-time requirements are most urgent. The design and specification are the work of a joint committee consisting of technical representatives of the National Federation of Vehicle Trades and the Joint Passenger Transport Operators organisation.

At first sight there appeared to be little difference in the appearance of the war-time bus from that of the normal vehicle. True, the drab grey war-time garb seemed somewhat unfamiliar when compared with the bright red, green or other such livery usually associated with a new vehicle ready to be driven away into service from the manu-

In general the bodywork complies with the current regulations of the Ministry of Transport and the seating is arranged to accommodate 26 in the lower saloon and 30 in the upper saloon. In the case of low-bridge types of vehicles, of which a number are being built for use in certain localities, a slight modification of the seating arrangements has been necessary, although 55 persons are carried—28 in the lower saloon and 27 on the upper deck.

The specification calls for body framing to be of oak, ash, mahogany or teak, with the exception of longitudinal rails, which may be of pitch pine. The framing is strengthened where necessary with flitches and gussets of steel in accordance with standard practice.

The top and bottom deck hoopsticks are of selected ash, strengthened with flitches or carlines

Left: A page from the *Passenger Transport Journal* of 14 November 1941, depicting an STD-type Leyland Titan TD7 before painting into London Transport livery. *Passenger Transport Journal*

Right: Even though it was now impossible to buy a new AEC bus, this advert, depicting a 9T9, appeared in the *Passenger Transport Journal* of 19 December 1941. *Passenger Transport Journal*

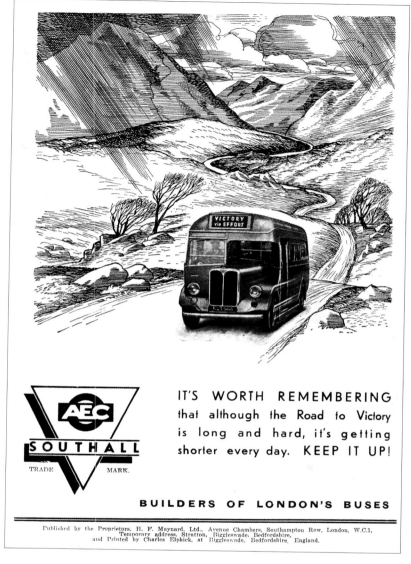

IT'S WORTH REMEMBERING that although the Road to Victory is long and hard, it's getting shorter every day. KEEP IT UP!

BUILDERS OF LONDON'S BUSES

Published by the Proprietors, H. F. Maynard, Ltd., Avenue Chambers, Southampton Row, London, W.C.1. Temporary address, Stratton, Biggleswade, Bedfordshire, and Printed by Charles Elphick, at Biggleswade, Bedfordshire, England.

emphasising the 'smooth power' of Westinghouse brakes, whilst on the same theme a group of vehicles on Westminster Bridge (including a couple of STLs, an 'E1' tram, a Morris 8 and a Humber Snipe) are supposed to persuade us of the 'greater stopping power and safer control' of Ferodo brake linings. Nobels & Hoare of Stamford Street, SE1, modestly claimed that Vincomel, the synthetic enamel was 'especially suitable for all types of new work'. However, in June 1941 we are assured that Cerrux synthetic finishes were 'the final word in finishes', and to prove it we are shown a picture of centre-entrance 'Feltham' No 331 (upon which we may still happily ride at the National Tramway Museum at Crich); I wonder if Cerrux realised that No 331 had migrated to Sunderland several years earlier?

One of the least-explicable advertisements was one placed by Leyland. A splendid full-page picture of STD33 and an Austin taxi negotiating Trafalgar Square, clearly taken before the war, appears over the slogan 'Leylands last longer', which may well have been true but was meaningless in the spring of 1941, when this great manufacturer's entire output was devoted to the war effort. No less odd is the advertisement which Leyland's great rival, AEC, published as the war was ending, in the 1945 *Passenger Transport Journal Year Book*, showing a line of vehicles headed by two six-wheel double-deckers — a Leicester Renown and a Q! Whatever AEC's production plans for the postwar years, I've never heard anyone suggest that either the Q or the Renown would feature!

119

• 3 •

Coping with War

DESPITE fears of immediate devastation in September 1939, the first air raids were a long time coming. It was not until 16 August 1940 that any damage was suffered by London Transport, when trolleybus wires were brought down by a bomb in New Malden; services were restored in just over four hours. That is the official story, although there is more than a possibility that LT260 was actually the first London Transport vehicle to suffer war damage, being caught up in a raid on Croydon Aerodrome in June 1940. Tram and trolleybus services were obviously prone to more dislocation than were motor-bus routes, which could be diverted, but the motor bus used precious petrol and diesel. The Luftwaffe initially attacked RAF aerodromes and other military installations, chiefly on the South Coast, but Hitler was so enraged by a token RAF raid on Berlin that he ordered his air force to turn its attention to London. Strategically this was a mistake, for it took the pressure off Fighter Command, which was at full stretch defending its own bases, but it meant that London — and Londoners — began to suffer fearfully.

Inevitably the area around the docks in the East End bore the brunt of the bombing, both because the raiders could easily follow the Thames as they came in over the estuary between Southend and the Kent Coast and because of its strategic importance. It was thus somewhat ironic that some of the first actual damage to LPTB property should be way over in the western suburbs, but once August had given way to September and the Battle of Britain was at its height, the bombing reached its terrifying intensity, and on 7 September 1940 a raid began around teatime and continued through to dawn the next day. Centred on the docks, the East End and the City, it consisted of incendiary bombs which totally overwhelmed the fire services. No London Transport vehicle was actually destroyed on 7/8 September, but the disruption to services was enormous, and the trolleybus network (in particular) suffered, both north and south of the river. Much of this, the routes 565, 567 and 665 along the Commercial Road and West India Dock Road had only just been introduced, in June, replacing the last of the East London trams north of the river. There were deaths and many injuries to staff and passengers, although when an raid was expected — and Britain's lead in perfecting radar gave vital minutes to prepare — buses, trams and trolleys usually stopped and passengers and crews hurried to the nearest shelters whenever possible.

It is worth quoting in some detail an article in the 14 April 1941 issue of the *Passenger Transport Journal*:

'Records hitherto considered impossible have been made by London Transport's engineers and the gangs of specially trained men who are kept ready day and night to repair interruptions caused by bombing to

An 'E3' tram emerges from the north end of Kingsway Subway and prepares to head into what has now (by 1940) become the trolleybus stronghold of North London. *B. Y. Williams*

London's trolleybus routes, which cover about 250 miles of roads. There is no waiting for instructions. The men are quickly on the spot, and their training enables them to do immediately whatever may be necessary to restore the through running of the services. Cables may be strung along trees in the street or over bushes in private front gardens, or complicated engineering work may have to be undertaken. Two examples of this work may be given.

'At a late hour one night four bombs fell on a road in North London, blowing down a number of bays of trolleybus wires and littering the road with debris. A gang was on the spot at midnight and as usual set to work immediately, although the "alert" was still on and bombs were still dropping. Whilst the linesmen replaced the wires, other men cleared the road of debris so that the first trolleybus ran through next morning at the normal time, 5.00 a.m. This is not an isolated incident. It is typical of the speed with which repairs are effected in all similar cases.

'On another night a bomb fell on a road in South London and left a wide crater entirely blocking the road to vehicular traffic. Working through the darkness, with bombs still falling, the repairmen made temporary arrangements by which trolleybuses could be run to either side of the crater, whence passengers could walk around the gap. At daylight it was decided, in consultation with the police and the

Watched by a fascinated crowd of onlookers, 'E1' No 1545, with badly damaged upper deck, is pushed home for rehabilitation. *Author's collection*

local authority, not to wait for the crater to be filled in but to restore through running of the services by erecting a wholly new system of overhead wires more than a quarter of a mile long so that the trolleybuses could be diverted along two nearby roads which had never had trolleybuses before.

'One obstacle to rapid completion of the job was the absence of any large buildings to which to attach the "span-wires" so that new poles had to be erected over the whole section. Additional difficulties were the narrowness of the roadways and six sharp corners. Trolleybuses could not pass one another at certain points and over a portion of the route two roads had to be used and one-way working instituted. Because of the presence of service mains, which abound near dwelling houses, all holes for the trolley poles had to be drilled by hand. A delayed-action bomb in one of the roads also set back the work a little.

'Despite these difficulties the detour of 500 yards had been "planted" with 43 poles, each six feet deep in the ground, complete with their overhead within a few days of the bombing. Even the white rings which distinguish the poles during the blackout had been painted upon them.'

Right: Following a raid on the Strand, LT238 is prepared for towing-away on the morning after — 10 October 1940. *P. J. Marshall*

Far right: A sturdy-looking breakdown tender waits for the call inside Riverside garage, Hammersmith, in 1948. No 219U was originally an LS six-wheel double-decker, predecessor of the LT, and was converted for this role in 1936. *M. Dryhurst collection*

The casual reference to the unexploded bomb 'setting back the work a little' speaks volumes for the wartime spirit. Which is not to say that people were not terrified and liable to panic in a bombing raid. At the height of the Blitz on the Docks, East Enders would clamber onto buses and trolleys sometimes in appalling states of shock and disarray, heading for the relative safety of further west, to be confronted by residents of the West End and beyond who refused to sit with them; some even complained to the authorities about their state.

South of the river, London's trams faced equal dangers. The 30 May 1941 issue of *Passenger Transport Journal* records the experiences of one driver. After explaining that the all-night trams had never ceased running since the war began, despite their routes' lying through some of the worst-blitzed areas (albeit having been changed or shortened on occasion), the account continues:

Left: Wartime in the East End. Workers at Silvertown board an unidentified trolleybus whilst, in the background, another (No 795A, which had been rebodied after being damaged in the Blitz) is overtaken by an impressive-looking Leyland lorry. *London Transport*

Right: Old Kent Road garage in September 1940. Originally a tram depot, it was converted for bus use as early as 1907. In this picture it houses a collection of LT double deckers, a Q single decker and an AEC lorry. The roof had to be raised when RTs replaced the LTs in 1948, the former being slightly taller. The garage closed in November 1958. *Author's collection*

'One of the drivers is Mr. Sidney Herbert Ball, of Tooting, who has been working on trams, first as a conductor and then as a driver, for 34 years. He is now aged 56, but he looks much younger. Apart from his nights off, he has driven his tram out of the Streatham Depot every night since the war began, bombs or no bombs. In the dark winter months he frequently had to walk for 45 to 50 minutes from his home to his depot, which he leaves, according to the "duty" he is on, at midnight, 12.30 or 1 a.m. His tram makes four figure-of-eight journeys between Telford Avenue and Victoria Embankment.

'Mr. Ball was on trams — then as an L.C.C. man — throughout the last war. He enjoys his work and says that it takes more than Hitler's bombs to frighten him. Bombs have fallen close to his tram on many occasions and several times he has helped to save buildings by putting out incendiary bombs. One night he saw an incendiary bomb roll under the outer door of a large building. There was just space under the door to admit the bomb, but not space for him to crawl under. He and some passengers tried to batter down the door without success and soon the building was blazing. Much worse than the bombs is the black-out. It is difficult to judge distances and in the darkness his eyes play odd tricks. Mr. Ball has often pulled up his tram, believing that a vehicle had stopped on the track, only to find what he thought was a red rear lamp was a glowing cigarette end, sticking upon the road.

'Mr. Ball takes an interest in his passengers and they take an interest in him. Before the war they were a colourful and often gay crowd — cabaret girls, dance girls, music hall performers, newspapermen, waiters, market workers and cleaners. Now that entertainments end much earlier, Mr. Ball's passengers are mostly newspapermen and soldiers on leave who have stayed in the West End as late as

possible. Mr. Ball says that during a "rough" night passengers frequently come to his cab, shake him by the hand and thank him for having got them home. This pleases Mr. Ball, who is known to many of his passengers by his Christian name of Sid. He is not always able to run as strictly to timetable as in peacetime, but he still tries to keep passengers waiting in the blacked-out and often dangerous streets as little as possible and he never leaves anyone behind.

'Mr. Ball has no nerves. He feels happier and safer in his large, Feltham-type tramcar than in a house or in the street. His passengers too, seem to be content in the car, but he has one interesting and perhaps surprising comment to make — elderly people withstand bombing much better than do young people. He has yet to see an elderly person, man or woman, give the slightest sign of being frightened.'

The 'Felthams' certainly were superb vehicles — and very strong — but were surely not impervious to a German bomb. Several were damaged during the war, although only two (Nos 2109 and 2113) so badly that they could not be repaired.

Certain old habits died hard in wartime. Passengers still managed to leave vast amounts of property behind. Apart from the usual collection of umbrellas, bags and all manner of personal belongings, in just one week in September 1940, no fewer than 3,000 gas masks and steel helmets were left on the Board's vehicles.

Bombs were hardly a laughing matter, but inevitably some of the newspaper accounts managed to find a lighter side to Blitz stories. The *South London Press*, which always devoted a whole page of its scarce newsprint to the local courts, noted that James Arthur Bastow (37), a builder from Wandsworth, was 'causing a fuss' in a pub one Saturday evening, as a result of which a policeman was called. Bastow happens to have had in his possession an unexploded incendiary bomb — we are not told why — and proceeded to try to hit the police constable with it. The next morning the magistrate enquired of Bastow if he thought hitting a policeman 'was the thing to do with a bomb' and, without waiting for an answer, fined him 10s.

Ten shillings (50p) was the value of the old-age pension in 1940. Around this time fares, which had remained unchanged for years, were raised. An elderly man boarded a bus at Camberwell Green and asked the conductor for a penny fare, explaining he was going 'to the Town Hall for me pension'. On being told that the fare was now a penny-ha'penny he replied: 'That's all right, son, you can't help it. Makes a difference, though, when you're on ten bob a week and can't walk anywhere.'

One of the most extraordinary statistics to emerge during the Blitz was the rise in the number of road deaths directly attributable to the blackout, there being many more accidents during the hours of darkness than there had been in peacetime. Mostly they involved pedestrians colliding with vehicles. Practically every issue of the London local papers during the Blitz notes deaths or serious injuries, often involving buses, trolleys or trams. Sometimes, in the almost pitch dark, people followed the tram lines in order to find their way, but this could lead to disaster. On 29 June 1940 a tram driver, Sydney Goodall, was summoned before the local magistrates following a fatal accident in Balham. He described how he had been driving at no more than 8-9mph at 11.30pm when 'a man's face loomed out of the darkness'. He slammed on the brakes with such force that his conductor was sent flying down the length of the car, but could not avoid the man, who was found lying in the road and died next day. A verdict of accidental death was recorded.

When an air raid was expected, drivers were supposed to stop their vehicles beside the nearest shelter and, before leaving, extinguish all lights, except those at the front and rear. These were fitted with shades and could

Piccadilly Circus at the height of the war. Eros has flown from his plinth, joining thousands of others in being evacuated from the capital. Private cars, no doubt all engaged on essential war work, have not entirely disappeared as an LT and four STLs — one with considerably more wood than glass in its windows — make their dignified way into or out of Regent Street. *Ian Allan Library*

be very difficult to see. Another unfortunate tram driver summoned before magistrates was a Camberwell man. His car 'crashed into the rear of a stationary tram outside Lewisham Hospital at 11.40 on the night of July 28, and drove it forward ... about 40 yards. Twenty-five persons were injured, including Driver Brewer, who was taken to hospital.' One passenger described how he jumped from the platform and 'landed on his hands and knees, covered with broken glass'. The conductor of the tram in front, having been told there was a 'red' air-raid warning, had turned off his interior lights but claimed he had left his platform lights on.

Mr Brewer said he had seen nothing and, despite being backed up by a passenger, was found guilty and fined 3s (15p), plus 17s 10d (89p) costs.

On the evening of 27 September 1940 a Poplar woman, Mrs Elizabeth Beadle, was killed by a trolleybus in the East India Dock Road whilst out shopping during an air raid. The *Hackney Gazette* of Wednesday 13 November 1940 recorded the death of a Shoreditch man who, crossing the road, was seen to 'throw up his hands and suddenly disappear under the bus, which stopped immediately ... the sirens had sounded and there was gunfire overhead.' The driver had served 31 years, had a clean licence and held the

'L3' trolleybus at King's Cross. This was delivered from Metro-Cammell with (most unusually) sliding ventilators, on 3 May 1940, the explanation probably being that wartime shortages precluded the use of the usual half-drops. No 1527 could easily be mistaken for one of the war-damaged rebuilds, which also had this type of window. *Author*

'B1' trolleybus of Carshalton depot loads up by Reeves Corner, West Croydon, on its way from Crystal Palace to Sutton on a winter's day in 1940. In the distance a Country Area STL, still with a complete route display, approaches behind what looks like one of the very last large prewar Morris saloons.
John B. Gent collection

Two roofbox STLs at Aldgate bus station in the early days of the war: Green Line STL2612, one of the final 1939 batch with long radiator and in two-tone green livery, alongside slightly older red STL2321 of 1937 (and identical to the preserved STL2377). *Author's collection*

Safety First silver medal and seven bars. 'The night of the accident was one of the darkest for some time. He had slowed down to four or five miles an hour on approaching a request stop and heard someone shout "Stop!" He applied the brakes and pulled up in a couple of yards. He found the deceased underneath the bus.' The driver was exonerated of all blame for what must have been an appalling experience, and the Deputy Coroner 'paid a tribute to 'bus drivers, remarking that it was amazing that they were involved in so few accidents during the black-out period'.

So serious was the situation regarding the carnage on the roads that the *Hackney Gazette* was driven to deal with it in an editorial in December 1940 under the heading 'Vehicles as deadly as Bombs'. It is worth quoting.

'While most people shelter from bombs, many of them continue to court danger and death on the roads to an alarming degree. It is one of the ironies of wartime existence for which there seems to be no sufficient explanation. Figures show that 19,545 civilians have been killed as the result of bombing since the Germans developed their air offensive on Britain. These compare with a total of 11,434 deaths on the roads during the fifteen months of war — an increase of no fewer than 3,141, or nearly 40 per cent., on the corresponding period immediately preceding the fateful September of last year ... As might be expected, most of the accidents occur in the hours of darkness; but a disturbing fact is that the increase is now relatively higher during daylight. Possibly the hurry and impetuosity engendered by war

conditions, as well as the larger amount of strain to which people are subjected, are mainly responsible for the rise.' The article concludes with two particularly thought-provoking observations. 'Motorists ... may allege that the more rigid limitation of vehicle lighting accentuates risks by restricting visibility and deceiving pedestrians by giving them a false idea of distance or perspective. Some of the latter may even fail to remember that Belisha crossings [named after Hore Belisha, the Government minister responsible for their introduction at the end of the 1930s] are practically valueless, from the point of view of security, in the black-out.'

Various measures were brought in to try to reduce the terrible death toll. New platform lamps, 'softly flood-lighting boarding platforms', were being fitted to buses at the rate of 1,000 a week by the end of September 1940. Earlier in the year the *Passenger Transport Journal* had noted that the Metropolitan Police was complaining that passengers were interfering with the original lampshades, fitted on the outbreak of war, in an effort to obtain more light, and that 20,000 improved ones were now on order. As people grew more used to wartime conditions the numbers of injured and killed on the roads came down, but it remained a problem throughout the war years.

• 4 •

More Tales from the Blitz

In his book *The Wheels used to Talk to Us*, Stan Collins describes an extraordinary night's adventure with a 'Feltham' during the Blitz. One suspects that the account in the previous chapter, being put out officially, was designed to boost morale, for it is difficult to believe that 'Mr. Ball has no nerves', unless he was completely lacking in imagination, but Stan Collins' account rings absolutely true, with nothing left out.

Stan has charge of a No 8, from Victoria to Tooting. Just beyond Vauxhall he is held up by debris from a bomb. 'Just at that moment another bomb fell in Higgs & Hill and the Sunnybank Laundry caught fire. I had the breeze up, I don't mind telling you. "Come on," I said to Alf [Mole, his conductor], "if he sees those fires he'll come back and bomb the hell out of us."' Stan takes a detour towards Nine Elms and is then held up by three trams abandoned by their passengers and drivers who had gone down the shelter under the Southern Railway Club ... 'So I took the hand-brakes off them all, told Alf to stand on the back of the front tram where I could see him, and pushed them all round into

Wandsworth Road. Alf put the hand-brake on the back car as hard as he could — I checked it after, because he was only a Conductor — but there was no chance of the tram running back. Then Alf pulled the points over and we turned into Nine Elms Lane.

'Just past the Dogs' Home there's a railway bridge and I thought, "Oh hell, we're never going to get under there." You see the Feltham was a little bit higher than a Standard, and it had a big base on its trolleys. Very slowly we eased underneath and I could hear the base of the trolleys scraping the bridge, but we cleared that and carried on up past the Latchmere to the Prince's Head.'

Further on, Stan encounters a regulator (inspector) who tells him: '"Felthams have never been up this road yet," ... and I told him that there was one had come up here now and what was he going to do about it? ... I wasn't staying out there all night, not with him dropping them like that. I wanted to get back to Telford.'

After a few more choice exchanges, off he goes. 'I was a bit worried about the bridge at Clapham Junction but I knew trolleybuses went under there, so I thought we'd be alright, and we were.'

Another inspector, 'very ighty-flighty and cocky', tells him to go back because he'd never get his 40ft-long 'Feltham' around the curve into Cedars Road. 'So I took it very steady, I'd got the wind up, little butterflies in my

Three 'K'-class trolleybuses from Stamford Hill amidst the warehouses of the London Docks at the terminus of the 647, a route which replaced tram 47 in February 1939. *Author*

Above: Aldgate East. In the foreground is a trolleybus approaching the Aldgate terminus of the 661; this replaced the Bow trams which had worked route 61 until 5 November 1939. *London Transport*

Below: Weymann-bodied AEC 'J2' trolleybus No 976 turns in front of Smithfield meat market. *London Transport*

stomach, and very gently we came round the curve. I'm leaning out of the near-side cab window working the controller with my right hand and the kerb's coming nearer and nearer as the front swings round … and as I came round the pilot gate just touched the kerb and then we were on the straight.'

Stan's progress comes to a halt at Clapham, where he finds himself behind a line of 10 stationary trams. 'Anyway we walked along this line of trams but couldn't see any Drivers or Conductors until we came to the café at the Plough which was open all night. By then it was getting on for two o'clock and we stuck there until the all-clear went about five that morning, and God above knows where the Drivers turned up from, but they all came up and away went the trams.'

Eventually Stan arrives back at the depot, to be told by the Depot Inspector that "You'll be on the carpet in the

morning," for taking a 'Feltham' where no 'Feltham' had ever been before. In fact, when he eventually does meet the Superintendent — 'nice old fellow, Bill Witty' — 'he congratulated me, wanted to know how I'd done it.'

One of the obvious places to shelter from the nightly air raids was down in the Tube, where one might be 60ft below ground and pretty safe from any bomb. The first such occasion seems to have been at Liverpool Street on 8 September 1940, when a large crowd pushed past LT officials and a handful of troops trying to prevent access, and found shelter on the Central Line platforms. Eventually tunnels built for the as yet unfinished extension were converted into shelters with capacity for 10,000. The *South London Press* of 20 September 1940 recorded that 'South Londoners, abandoning public overground and ground level shelters, are going underground every night in Tube stations causing the

Above: A Matilda tank on its way to 'somewhere in England' — presumably a publicity stunt, as tanks travelling any distance would be carried on special low-loaders. It is negotiating Marble Arch in the company of STL1199 of 1935 and an earlier 60-seat London General 2STL1 type. The date is 19 May 1940. *London Transport*

Left: Trolleybus No 1681, an all-Leyland 'K3', one of the last prewar-design trolleybuses. Delivered in the autumn of 1940, it is seen late in life in Holborn while working from Edmonton depot. *Author*

biggest crushes London Transport staff have ever known … public shelters are almost deserted and early every evening queues of families with bedding and food stand in line four or five deep outside. Police have had to guard the doors since crowds have tried to rush the barriers as the sirens sounded, pushing back passengers trying to emerge. "Women and children only," said the station foreman, knowing the little space available.'

A week later a reporter investigated the situation at the Elephant & Castle. 'It took me a quarter of an hour to get from the station entrance to the platform. Even in the darkened booking hall I stumbled over huddled bodies … going down the stairs I saw mothers feeding infants at the breast. Little boys and girls lay across their parents' bodies because there was no room on the winding stairs … Hundreds of men and women were partially undressed, while small boys and girls slumbered in the foetid atmosphere, absolutely naked. On every jutting beam and spike hung coats, waistcoats, shoes and shopping bags. On the platform, when a train came in, it had to be stopped in the tunnel while police and porters went along pushing in the feet and arms which overhung the line … On the train I sat opposite a pilot on leave. He looked dumbly at that amazing platform. "It's the same all the way along," was all he said.'

For a visual impression of this extraordinary period in London life, head along a few hundred yards westwards from Elephant & Castle station to the Imperial War Museum, where the drawings Henry Moore was commissioned to make down in the shelters are on display.

Ellen Wilkinson, Parliamentary Secretary to the Ministry of Home Security, describing 'some of her shelter problems', said there were large houses in Mayfair — 'whole strings of them in fact' — where people could be billeted, but they could not be persuaded to go from the Isle of Dogs to live in Eaton Square. One woman said to her: "Well, miss, whatever would I do with a flat in Eaton Square? Where do you think I should do my shopping — Harrods?"

In Southwark, local residents complained that 'foreigners' from outside the borough were moving in on their territory. 'Some evenings these treks begin as early as 5 o'clock when women arrive with huge suitcases, large shopping bags, parcels of food, milk and mineral waters.' The Mayor of Camberwell said that 'There is a tendency to stake out claims in

the shelters and regard spaces as private preserves. Because of this I have had to issue an order to wardens in charge of the bigger public shelters that no persons shall be allowed to occupy more space than one person should occupy if that space is needed by another member of the public.' Across the river, at Stoke Newington, a woman appeared in court on just such a charge. A policeman said he was on duty at Turnpike Lane station where some 1,500 people were sheltering when he was called to a disturbance. A woman had tried to reserve an extra place amongst those who had settled down for the night. Her defence was that 'because she was a Jewess some of the people did not want her there and they started pushing her and her things about'. She was fined 20s (£1) plus 8s (40p) costs.

Even in a Tube station safety was not guaranteed, and direct hits on Bank, Balham and Trafalgar Square stations caused many casualties: 56 died and 69 were injured at Bank on 11 January 1941, 68 died at Balham on 14 October 1940, and seven were killed by an avalanche of wet earth after a bomb exploded at the head of an escalator at Trafalgar Square on 12 October 1940.

The worst incident took place at Bethnal Green Central Line tube station on the evening of 3 March 1943 and, ironically, was not caused directly by enemy action but by panic resulting from what people thought was a falling bomb. The Army was testing a new anti-aircraft defence system in Victoria Park, ¼ mile from the station, and its detonation resulted in a huge bang which people not surprisingly interpreted as an air raid. I can recall vividly just how enormous such an explosion sounded, even at a distance of a mile or more. Apparently security considerations prevented people knowing what the Army was up to.

There was a rush for the perceived safety of the Underground station. It had been raining, the steps leading down were slippery, a woman fell, more rockets were fired, more people fell, those in the rear, unaware

STL2250, built in 1938 with a standard roofbox body, seen with a wartime lowbridge body. It is working the 410 from Godstone garage. *Phil Picken*

Evacuating St Thomas's Hospital, Lambeth, at the beginning of the war and carrying a stretcher case into a Green Line 10T10 based at Battersea and converted to an ambulance. *South London Press*

of what was happening at the front, pushed, and the resulting horror may be imagined. On the dimly lit steps, bodies piled upon bodies, and within a horrifyingly short time 27 men, 84 women and 62 children were dead. Alfred Morris, aged 13, told how his aunt was the last to be pulled out alive. 'She was trapped against a wall. I remember she was wearing a heavy coat, and they grabbed hold of her shoulders and pulled her free, and she left her coat and shoes behind. She was black and blue all over.' It was estimated that all the victims died — of asphyxiation — within 10-17 seconds.

Inevitably, given wartime secrecy, the event was kept out of the media as far as possible. It was only in 1993 that a small commemorative plaque was unveiled at the station.

Much easier to penetrate were the Underground stations and the surface Tube stations out in the suburbs. The worst such incident occurred at Bounds Green on the Piccadilly Line, where a bomb demolished some houses which collapsed onto the platforms, killing 19 passengers, including 16 Belgian refugees; 52 people were injured. At the newly rebuilt Sloane Square a Circle Line train was hit, causing 79 injuries on 12 November 1940.

For a while as a child I refused to travel on either the Underground or the Tube — perhaps from fear of what might happen, although I wasn't particularly worried about going down our Anderson shelter in the back garden. Later, when I had summoned up sufficient courage to travel underground, I never passed through Sloane Square on our way to visit the South Kensington museums without a shiver of fear as we entered it and a distinct sense of relief as our train pulled out unscathed. At that time many of the elderly Circle trains were not

fitted with automatic doors, and I can recall watching with a mixture of fascination and horror as the door opposite us slowly slid open as we rattled through the darkness. There were literally hundreds of other air raids all over the Underground and Tube systems which caused varying amounts of damage.

After a while the authorities realised they would have to make a virtue out of necessity: some sort of order was brought, shelter marshals were appointed, disused stations were reopened and by the end of 1940 it was said that there was accommodation for everyone. By the beginning of 1941 79 medical aid posts were operating, mostly on the platforms. A post contained an isolation bay with five bunks for the temporary accommodation of any infectious diseases, supply of water, electric heating for sterilising instruments, cupboards for surgical instruments and dressings, and bunks for the nurses. A professional nurse was in charge of each station, assisted by auxiliary Red Cross and St John Ambulance nurses, and a medical officer visited each station every night. Eight deep-level shelters were built adjacent to Tube stations, usually beneath them. Work began at the end of November 1940, but none was completed until 1942, by which time the need for them had diminished. All are still there, having served a variety of purposes (intended or otherwise) over the years, including, inevitably, settings for films and TV dramas, not least an episode of *Doctor Who*. One of the more esoteric uses saw Holborn involved in a study of

Right: RT84 in almost-new condition working from Putney Bridge garage in June 1940. *Alan Cross*

Below:
A London Transport bravery medal. *Ian Allan Library*

cosmic rays. To quote the obituary of the physicist John Barton, who led the experiments, 'The laboratory rooms were reached through a service door on one of the Piccadilly Line platforms. They were linked by an extremely narrow corridor, only wide enough for a single person, running along the edge of what had once been the platform. It was a dry and dusty environment and there were occasional problems caused by rodents chewing cables, but it was nonetheless an extraordinarily convenient site to work.'

Large numbers of LT staff joined the Forces, and by the end of 1940 no fewer than 12,167 were in uniform. By this time 72 had died on active service, but this figure was rather less than the 116 who had been killed whilst carrying out their duties with London Transport in the same period — which gives one some indication of just how much in the front line London and its population were during the Blitz.

Frank Pick, who, along with Lord Ashfield, had shaped London Transport into the magnificent undertaking it had become by September 1939, died suddenly in November 1941 at the age of 62, having retired a little earlier as Vice Chairman of the London Passenger Transport Board.

A solicitor by profession, he was one of those rare men who showed abilities far beyond that for which he was trained and, as his obituary in the *Passenger Transport Journal* noted, 'Mr. Pick was a great transport man and he was at the same time a great scholar. His activities ranged over a wide field. In art circles he was recognised as an expert and connoisseur: he had advanced views on all the problems connected with town planning and he was Chairman of the Council for Art and Industry of the Board of Trade. He was a man of immense intellectual power, and the many papers he wrote for the societies with which he was connected not only showed him as master of his subjects but able to express himself in terms of great lucidity and much literary charm. His team work with Lord Ashfield was one of the great factors in building up the LPTB. Each was the complement of the other, and history will record their partnership as one which had the most beneficent results in evolving from the chaotic traffic conditions which followed the conclusion of the last war the ordered system of transport which, although even now in many respects incomplete, makes traffic conditions in London the envy of most capital cities of the world.'

• 5 •

In the Depths of War

NOT everyone pulled together during the war: there were always those who saw their opportunity in the blackout and shortages. May Cooke, a lady conductor based at Bromley garage, worked the 47a route which passed through some of the most heavily bombed areas of East London on both sides of the river. 'I found during the late turns that people took advantage of the black-out by giving me farthings instead of sixpences for their fares, and of course I was well out of pocket. Eventually, many clippies bought small lights with batteries attached, worn on their coats at night, so they could see what money they were taking.'

'Clippie' was one term applied to a female conductor; another was 'conductorette', which conjures up images of being shown to one's seat by a young lady with a torch who might try and sell one an ice cream at the next set of traffic lights. Back in the early 1940s, Essex was clearly far less liberated than it would be 40 years later, for (according to the *Passenger Transport Journal*) the management of Eastern National, which connected with London Transport routes in the Grays and Tilbury

areas, brought in a rule early in 1941 'preventing drivers and conductresses from becoming too friendly'. No fewer than 200 Essex bus men and women threatened to strike, the 'girls contending that their work is … more efficient if they have got used to a particular driver and the driver *has got used to the little peculiarities of their conductorettes*'! (The italics are mine.)

A London tram driver commented that 'In the last war conductresses were not called conductorettes, neither were they dressed in comic opera costumes and hats, but were given proper coats and skirts and knee-length gaiters (providing their own boots), all designed to stand up against the hard and draughty work on a back platform and the perpetual climbing of stairs fitted with steel treads. Slacks made of poor material are not the solution. Wages the same as for men, as the women were doing the same work with equal skill. Women as bus drivers have not "taken on" and a recent picture in the newspapers of young women learning to drive a trolleybus did not make it clear that they were engaged only in shunting. Maybe the bus is too heavy for braking. I remember that in the last war I drove a tramcar with my wife as my conductor and I did not stop at the exact spot at which the more accomplished motormen [stopped], which caused a lady passenger to abuse my poor driving to my conductor with the words:

ARP wardens making tea in Brixton Road as a rebuilt ex-Croydon Corporation 'E1' heads south towards Purley, sometime in 1941. *South London Press*

"Cannot your driver stop when he is told?", to which my conductor replied: "He doesn't do a damn thing he's told — he's my husband!"'

London Transport employed three female clockwinders, Mrs Lily O'Loughlin, Mrs Joan Colvin and Mrs Florence Bex having taken over from men who had gone to war. Its magazine noted that their job was to 'keep 171 clocks going in 52 garages and depots ... also at 170 points along the bus and coach routes, conductors record on time-clock cards the time of their arrival.' The ladies travelled by bus around the network, but the 'two skilled fitters' who maintained the clocks had a van, and 'At a moment's notice they can dash off to Leatherhead or Luton to stethoscope a patient whose heart is beating irregularly or not at all.' On St George's Day (23 April) 1942, 12 London women conductors took part in a Battle for Freedom pageant at the Royal Albert Hall. Six worked on the buses, the other six on trams and trolleybuses. For some reason which the account chooses not to divulge, all were 5ft 9in tall — well above average height. They were selected by the Women's Welfare Superintendent, and, as they paraded across the stage of the Royal Albert Hall 'in their summer uniforms of grey-blue, and with their punches flashing, they typified the courage and resolution of the 7,000 such women who have replaced men on the

London Transport vehicles'. They were 'a credit to the Board'.

The employment of female conductors was vital if services were to be maintained. Interestingly the 12,167 employees of the London Passenger Transport Board in the Forces were still paid as though in civilian employment, the LPTB having been granted funds to make up the difference between military and civilian pay. From January 1940 wages were increased, and the rates of tram and trolleybus drivers and conductors were at last raised to equal those of bus crews. There was much resentment of the latter by the former, going way back to the LCC and LGOC days when motor buses were considered (with some justification) to be taking business away from the trams by unfair means, the trams being crippled financially with various charges not imposed on buses. Trams certainly enjoyed a renaissance following the outbreak of war, for it was recorded that in the 12 months from September 1939 'the main operating problems were the rationing of petrol and fuel oil', which meant many buses were taken off the roads whilst trams and trolleybus services were unaffected. Of course, once the Blitz began, every aspect of the LPTB's operations suffered.

One solution to the fuel problem was producer gas. A number of unfortunate petrol-engined STs and Ts had

Gas Producers for London Buses

DEMONSTRATION AT CHISWICK PRIOR TO ENTERING SERVICE

A S mentioned briefly in our last issue, a demonstration of the feasibility of running London Transport buses on gas was given on Tuesday of last week, when a double-deck bus carrying the equivalent of 60 passengers was operated under similar conditions as would be met with in actual service, with the gas producer equipment mounted on a two-wheel trailer.

has been in extensive use under comparable operating conditions.

Anthracite or specially graded coke can be used as fuel for the gas producer. The Board is at present using activated anthracite, activation being the treatment of the fuel with sodium carbonate to increase vehicle performance. When the anthracite fire is lit, the gas given off is passed from the container through cooling

Gas producer trailer fitted to a "S.T." type petrol-engine bus.

During the demonstration, Mr. W. A. C. Snook, the Board's acting chief engineer (buses and coaches), explained that the change-over from petrol to gas must not be confused with a change-over from, say, petrol to paraffin. In this case an ordinary petrol engine, to which certain modifications had been made, was being used as a gas engine with a consequent loss of some 40 per cent. to 50 per cent. in efficiency. In order to reduce this loss the compression ratio has been raised from 5-1 to 8-1 by fitting high compression pistons, thereby reducing the drop in power to some 25-30 per cent. The engine cylinders have been bored out to a larger diameter.

The gas producer unit as used by London Transport for the initial operations has been developed by Messrs. Thomas Tilling Ltd. from the Government emergency producer. Messrs. Tilling have been operating this type for some twelve months, and the Chairman of that Company has very kindly placed at the disposal of London Transport all the experience gained during that period. Fundamentally the only difference from the Government emergency type is that this producer embodies the use of a water filter instead of a Sisal filter. This filter, known as the Morison filter, was introduced and developed by the chief engineer of the Eastern National Omnibus Co. Ltd. This type of producer has been selected by the Board for the reason that for the 7.5 litre engines, as used by London Transport, it was the only one of the required capacity that

chambers into the water filter, and from there through a water separator on the trailer to another on the front of the bulkhead of the bus, then on through a mixing valve to the engine. The method of operation is as follows :

The gas producer has been serviced and properly charged, and is parked away from the bus. The bus

Showing some of the modifications made to the petrol engine to adapt its use for gas.

Above: Britannia and Hitler get admiring glances from a warden corporal as they prepare to set off in a dignified mode of transport to head a parade marking Brixton's Warship Week in 1942. *South London Press*

Far left: An article introducing producer-gas STs. *Passenger Transport Journal*

two-wheel trailers attached which were, in effect, miniature power stations. They burned anthracite treated with sodium carbonate, which produced a gas, and, after various processes this passed through a mixing valve into the engine. Efficiency was down by as much as 50%, and, to help counteract this, the cylinders were bored out to a larger diameter; any attempt to save fuel, at a time when the very continuation of the war was threatened by the huge numbers of tankers being sunk by German U-boats, was worthwhile. The buses were certainly very underpowered, but, by being confined to routes with few or no gradients, they at least kept on the move. In all, 172 STs and nine Ts operated the system between the summer of 1942 and September 1944.

Not everyone — well, possibly no-one — was able to keep a stiff upper lip and act with bravery, compassion and fortitude on every occasion throughout the war. I was sitting on the longitudinal seat downstairs on another ST one afternoon as we pulled away from the Swan & Sugar Loaf at South Croydon (not far from the bus garage) when there was an almighty bang not too far away. 'A bomb!' exclaimed a woman opposite. 'Ah well, that's a few less fares I'll have to bother about,' the conductor replied. It did not go down well with the passengers.

One of the worst consequences of a bomb blast was the shattering of glass. To minimise this risk, netting was stuck on vehicle windows. The trouble was that passengers couldn't see out and immediately began to try and pull it away; on a long journey one could virtually strip a window if one worked assiduously and avoided the conductor's gaze. The solution was to leave a small, clear diamond in the centre, and this worked pretty well. By the end of 1941, 218,400yd of the stuff had been applied — 96,000yd on bus and coach windows, 42,400yd on trams and trolleybuses and 80,000yd on Underground and Tube carriages.

You will want to know precisely how the netting was applied, so here goes, courtesy of the *Passenger Transport Journal*: 'Originally a solution of gum Arabic, plasticised with glycerine, was used but it was found to be subject to condensation and peeled off. The present method is quite satisfactory; the window is given a coating of varnish, which is left until it becomes tacky. The netting is then mounted, being first cut to size. A rubber roller is used to press it into position. It is then left overnight to dry. The next day it is given a coating of exterior quality varnish and instead of laying-off with a brush the rubber squeegee is again used. Normally the full process takes two days, but in warm weather it has sometimes been possible to get the two coats on in one day.' We then get the full instructions on how to 'cut the new standard diamond-shaped aperture', but this is altogether too exciting for those of a weak disposition, so we'll merely conclude that the exterior-quality varnish was quality indeed — so much so that, for years after the war, traces of it could still be found on bus, tram and trolleybus windows. (Maybe this would be the solution to graffiti scratched on to the windows of modern-day buses.) Windows continued to be blasted regularly and in large quantities. Glass was just one of the commodities in short supply, and throughout the war it was common to see a London tram, trolleybus or motor bus with many of its windows boarded up.

Left: Don't worry; the unfortunate chap hanging off the back of STL919 was an actor taking part in a children's road safety demonstration at Hackney Downs Secondary School on 16 April 1943. *London Transport*

Below: Workers pour out of their appropriately bucolic-looking factory and board a Watford-based former National ST, still in prewar Country Area dark and light green but with netted windows and white wartime markings. *London Transport*

• **6** •

Beyond the Blitz

FOLLOWING the triumph of the RAF at the end of the Battle of Britain, daylight raids on London were much reduced, and, whilst the Luftwaffe bombers continued to cause many casualties and much damage at night, this danger also began to reduce, such that by the beginning of 1941 the *South London Press* could claim that, 'whilst London gets routine bombing visits every night, few of them are sufficient to keep Cockneys from their beds'.

One of the delights — and pitfalls — of researching old newspapers is that one inevitably gets sidetracked. I am sure you would like to know that 'Big-Hearted' Arthur Askey and Richard 'Stinker' Murdoch were appearing at the Trocadero, Elephant & Castle — 'Europe's largest cinema' — in *Charley's Aunt*. The two were, along with Tommy Handley, probably the most popular radio comedians of the war years — a popularity that would continue for decades afterwards. The Trocadero was one of the most spectacular of all the magnificent picture palaces erected in the heyday of cinema in the 1920s and '30s. Designed by George Coles, its doors opened in 1930. It boasted a 24-rank Mighty Wurlitzer organ which rose majestically into view and was part of a complete evening's entertainment which included not only the main feature but a second feature, trailers and the Movietone newsreel. The Trocadero had seats for no fewer than 3,500 and

was extremely popular, a welcome diversion from the grim reality of life in the unemployment-hit years of the early 1930s in London's East End. (It would close in October 1963, at a time when television was not only taking millions upon millions away from the cinema but was hitting public transport equally hard, now that people preferred to stay at home and gather round the 'goggle box'.) Alice Faye was simultaneously appearing at the Odeons Camberwell, East Dulwich and Peckham. However, the silver screen was not getting it all its own way, for the Canterbury Music Hall in Westminster Bridge Road, which had been a cinema, was going to revert to variety, once the problem of 'the noise of passing trains' had been solved.

The day would come, decades ahead, when the conductor would be done away with, apart from on a few of the most heavily patronised Central London routes, but even during the depths of the war London Transport was prepared to experiment with variations on the theme of the conductor's traditional role. At this stage there was no notion of getting rid of the conductor, but rather to make the work easier and to ensure that no one got away without paying his/her fare. (The best way of achieving the latter — it pains me to confess — was to make a fairly short journey on a 'Feltham' tram: as the conductor came up the rear stairs, one descended via those at the front and alighted at the back, one's penny still intact and available for contribution towards that week's *Dandy* or *Beano*.) No pay-as-you-enter experiments were carried out on trams, but two trolleybuses and three motor buses were so adapted. In each the conductor sat at a desk and collected fares as the passengers came aboard. There remained a single entrance/exit, except in the case of STL2284, which had one of each. Four of the vehicles

'Bluebird' LT1403 of Hammersmith (Riverside) garage (R) at the Mitcham Cricket Green terminus of the 88. *Author's collection*

139

Above left: No escaping paying your fare on this 'Feltham'. Looking down the staircase of preserved Feltham No 330. *Author*

Above right: Prototype trolleybus No 61 with Chiswick-built body as converted to experimental pay-as-you-board layout in March 1945. *London Transport*

Left: Passengers paying their fare on pay-as-you-board STL1793. *London Transport*

INTER-
STATION
BUSES
FROM HERE FOR
KINGS 4 EUSTON
PADDINGTON VICTORIA

FORM QUEUE
THIS SIDE

Above: An evening scene at Waterloo station just before Christmas 1943. One of the Inter Station Leyland Cubs is caught by the flash camera of a Topical Press photographer. The caption reads: 'The first bus leaves from Waterloo station with servicemen and their wives for Paddington'. The Inter Station service was reinstated in December 1943 and was usually worked by STs. *Ian Allan Library*

Right: One of the STs repainted into Inter Station blue and cream, at Victoria station. *Alan Cross*

One of the many early STLs transferred from the Central to the Country Area and sent to Chelsham garage waits to depart from West Croydon on a summer day towards the end of the war. It retains red livery. *W. J. Haynes*

had suffered bomb damage which made the structural alterations easier. The most interesting, probably, was RT97. A number of the RT class, which had survived the Blitz when brand-new without damage, were casualties in flying-bomb attacks, the worst being RT66, whose body was destroyed in June 1944. The following month RT97 became a casualty, badly damaged when a bomb exploded close by. It was sent to Birmingham to be repaired but was brought back untouched several months later and was then converted at Chiswick for its new role. The only undamaged vehicle used in the experiment was trolleybus No 61, the prototype with a Chiswick-built body; this had a central entrance and was therefore ideal. Powered platform doors were fitted to each vehicle, a circulating space was provided (which resulted in a loss of seating capacity), staircases were moved towards the centre by the entrance, and the conductor issued tickets from a TIM machine.

The experiment failed on several counts. Although no one could get on without paying, it was difficult to check if passengers rode past the stop they had paid for. Passengers themselves, waiting to board, were not best pleased at hanging around at the stop once the bus had arrived whilst other passengers were paying their fares, and loading took longer, which meant schedules were not maintained. The trolleys and two of the buses were rebuilt to see out their days in their original configurations, the exception being RT97, which retained a number of its new features and would, as we shall see, re-emerge after the war as a prototype double-deck coach.

In June 1944 London was suddenly subjected to a new terror, known variously as the flying bomb, 'doodle-bug' or V1. Pilotless aeroplanes launched from France and the Low Countries, these wreaked terrible devast-ation. They *could* be caught by RAF fighters, but if one

got too close and was fired on then the subsequent explosion could bring down the RAF 'craft too. The most satisfactory solution was to fly alongside, put your wingtip under that of the V1 and then flick it over — something its guidance system could not cope with. It would then crash, hopefully into the English Channel or the empty countryside. It could also be brought down by anti-aircraft fire.

It is estimated that around half of all V1s launched against London were destroyed by various methods, but this meant that the other half got through. Bexleyheath trolleybus depot was hit in June 1944. Twelve trolleys were destroyed and nearly all the others damaged, so that for the rest of its time as a trolleybus depot it operated a fleet largely composed of rebuilt or rebodied vehicles. West Ham depot was hit twice, one vehicle being destroyed and over 100 being damaged. Elmers End garage suffered grievously. Seven people died when it received a direct hit from a V1, 32 buses and coaches being completely destroyed and 28 damaged so badly that their bodies were beyond repair.

Between 1939 and 1945 no fewer than 426 London Transport staff were killed, either at work or off duty. The population of Central London generally had, not surprisingly, gone down — by 650,000 — but journeys over the whole of the LT network in 1945 were within 3% of the 1939 total. It was the Country Area which had redressed the balance, its passenger figures almost doubling between 1939 and 1945.

Right: Front page of the *Daily Mail*, 8 May 1945. Two Hendon-based prewar STDs and an LT are caught up in the jubilant celebrations at Piccadilly Circus as the war in Europe comes to an end. *Daily Mail*

3 POWERS WILL ANNOUNCE GREAT SURRENDER SIMULTANEOUSLY

VE-DAY—IT'S ALL OVER

The King to speak to Empire: Victorious generals will follow Premier on radio

THE pavements and most of the roadways in and around Piccadilly-circus, including Regent-street, were jammed nearly solid for hours yesterday afternoon and evening by crowds expecting to hear VE-Day announced. These Daily Mail pictures give you a vivid impression of the immense concourse of Londoners who waited patiently—and vainly. Other crowd scenes—Page THREE.

The U.S. went ahead

'OUR VE-DAY,' ANYHOW'

From DON IDDON, Daily Mail Correspondent

New York, Monday.

THIS was VE-Day in the U.S.—official or not.

The celebrations began in New York at breakfast time, a few minutes after word came from Rheims, France, that Germany had surrendered unconditionally to Britain, the United States, and Russia.

They went on all day despite an avalanche of confused messages, lack of official confirmation, half-denials, and a barrage of rumours that the surrender was a hoax.

The American public, and particularly the New York public, this time was determined that this was the end of the war in Europe, and resolved to commemorate it.

The first reaction, and it was the same all over Manhattan, was to jab open windows, tear up telephone directories, and hurl paper into the streets.

For hours tons upon tons of ticker tape, torn-up newspapers, envelopes, letters, magazines, and in some instances hats and waste-paper baskets, cascaded down.

Tens of thousands of people abandoned work and rushed into Times-square area, shouting and singing. Motorists blew their hooters, factory whistles shrieked, and in New York Bay ships sounded their sirens.

Bands of Service men and girls paraded the avenues, waving flags, shouting and yelling, planting roadways, jumped on to the running-boards of private cars, taxis, and buses.

At first city officials, led by Mayor La Guardia, attempted to curb the jubilation.

Over the radio came a reminder that there was nothing official; that it was merely a report which had declared that war in Europe was over.

The people ignored the advice. They had heard the electrifying report over the radio; they had enormous headlines in the extras; and that was enough.

While New York took the dizzy parade, other cities lagged behind. Washington, the capital, was subdued, but the crowds that gathered outside the White House appeared to be waiting a victory fanfare.

Press secretaries said brusquely that when any news was announced it would come from President Truman.

Fanfares

In the Midwest, Chicago took the reports in its stride, did a little mild drinking and half-hearted parading, but kept its head.

These are some of the things that happened in America :

Chefs danced on the window of hotels, throwing their stocks of dine and breakfast cereals in handfuls to the crowds below.

Everyone with a trumpet or a saxophone or a trombone opened the windows wide and leaned out, playing a victory fanfare.

Housewives formed up in street parties and marched to the main thoroughfares, clashing frying-pans and saucepan lids.

PATTON 7 MILES FROM PRAGUE

The Patriot Prague radio report that advanced U.S. Third Army tank units have passed the town of Repotrye, about seven miles south of Prague.

BELGIANS TO HEAR CHURCHILL

Brussels radio announces that it is cancelling its transmission for this afternoon so that Belgians can hear Mr. Churchill's speech and listen to B.B.C. broadcasts of London VE-Day.

Nightcrowd at Palace shouts for the King

West End cheers

By Daily Mail Reporter

LONDON decided to celebrate after all. The crowds flocked back to the West End last night and made VE-Eve whoopee.

Not long after the disappointed thousands had gone home after a day of waiting, the streets were full of yelling, singing hordes.

In Piccadilly they climbed on to the roofs of buses and taxis.

Outside Buckingham Palace they massed in thousands, and stayed there for hours, chanting "We want the King! We want the King!"

Their shouting and cheering reached crescendo when a plane circled over St. James's Park, just after 10.30 and dropped flares of white, red, and yellow.

Cheer leader

A youth clambered to the head of one of the massive stone figures of one of the monuments facing the Palace, and with a foot on each ear led a cheer-party in bellowing "G-E-O-R-G-E—we want King George!"

Figures could be seen leaning forward at one of the upper windows, and later someone appeared against the balustrade of the roof. They could not be identified, though an optimistic woman did her best with a pair of binoculars.

Sports cars ran into the thick of the throng, carrying people riding on the mud-guards, radiators, and clinging to the backs. Everywhere there were rattles, squeakers, streamers, and paper hats.

A few lights occasionally flickered from the Palace windows. Whenever one was shown from an upstairs room the crowd roared again.

In Piccadilly-circus traffic was stopped. From Leicester-square a huge column, led by Scots pipers, marched to join them.

A little man climbed through the upper window of a bus and on to the roof. A New Zealand sailor made a seamanlike trip from the bonnet to join him. A soldier followed—and soon the bus top was perilously packed.

Beer sold out

Soldiers were soon climbing on to the other buses, and taxis jammed among the crowd.

At one time 20 buses were stranded in the centre of the circus.

Most of the public-houses around Piccadilly had to close by 10.30 because they had no more beer.

Cars, nosing their way through the crowds, vanished and emerged again with 20 or 30 men and women clinging to the bonnets, the sides, and the back, and others standing on top.

London's Day of Hope—Page THREE.

Lord Lascelles at the Palace

The King's nephew, Lord Lascelles, and the Queen's nephew, the Master of Elphinstone, recently freed from a German prisoners' camp, arrived in London yesterday by plane.

They drove from the airfield to Buckingham Palace, where they were welcomed home by the King and Queen and Princess Elizabeth.

Daily Mail

IN accordance with the expressed desire of the Government that workers generally should enjoy a day's holiday following the announcement of the cessation of hostilities in Europe, this Daily Mail, in common with other London morning newspapers, will not be published on Thursday.

THE WAR GOES ON HERE—
Prague bombed as SS men shoot Czechs

GERMAN bombs are falling on Prague for the first time as the war in Europe enters its last hours. In defiance of surrender orders, German forces in Czecho-Slovakia are fighting on. They are venting their last spite on the Czechs, shooting them down ruthlessly in the streets of the capital.

Refugees from Prague who have reached Allied-occupied Pilsen say that, in many cases, the S.S. went through the city driving people out of their houses into the streets.

And there other S.S. men mowed them down with machine-guns. The S.S., according to the refugees, know they will probably be executed when caught and have abandoned all normal conduct.

That the S.S. are completely out of hand is indicated in a broadcast by the German commander in Bohemia and Moravia warning his troops to respect international law.

He admitted that "breaches" had occurred along his troops.

Two columns of General Patton's tanks are racing to Prague's rescue and were last reported 15 miles south of the capital.

Pilsen kisses

PILSEN, Monday.

LIEUT.-GENERAL MAJEWSKI, commanding the German garrison of Pilsen, blew out his brains after surrendering with his staff to the U.S. forces who entered the city yesterday.

The crowds did not wait for the shooting to stop to begin their singing and dancing and to cheer the American troops. It was just like the liberation scenes in France, with wine, flowers and kisses.—Reuter.

'Evil Hitler'

The camp in which these famous people were found was a mountain affair—a group of huts around a chateau on a hillside. But behind its barbed wire, the Fifth Army men found many high officers—Greek, Russian, Hungarian—and a number of German including Dr. Schacht, former German Minister of Finance and President of the Reichsbank.

Asked if Hitler was sane, he said: "In some things no, in others he is a genius."

Someone suggested an evil genius, and Schacht said: "Yes. An evil genius ... an evil and diabolical genius."

None of the prisoners had had any charge preferred against him.

Fleet off Oslo

A Allied naval force of 48 ships has been assigned at the entrance to Oslo Fjord, says the Swedish radio, quoting reports from Oslo.

BACK PAGE—Col. SEVEN

THE WAR'S GREATEST DAY OF SUSPENSE

By WILSON BROADBENT, Diplomatic Correspondent

GERMANY surrendered unconditionally to the Allies yesterday. But there will be no official announcement of victory until 3 p.m. to-day—officially described as VE-Day—when Mr. Churchill will give the news to the world. He will follow this with an address to the House of Commons, and at 9 p.m. the King will speak to Britain and the Empire.

Mr. Churchill's private room at the House of Commons was last night "wired-up" so that if he wishes he can make his broadcast from there.

To-day's announcement will be made simultaneously in London, Washington, and Moscow. To-day, therefore, is the first of the promised two-days V-holiday for the country. Broadcasts will also be made by General Eisenhower and Field-Marshals Montgomery and Alexander.

Mr. Churchill's two statements to-day will not affect his intention to broadcast at length on Thursday night, the fifth anniversary of his assumption of the Premiership.

After the King's speech, London will be floodlighted, searchlights will fill the sky, and it is now possible that there will be a victory salvo of guns, but this point had not been finally settled at a late hour last night.

After his statement in the House of Commons, Mr. Churchill will propose the adjournment of business while M.P.s attend a special Service of Thanksgiving at St. Margaret's Church, Westminster. They will then return to the House of Commons, adjourn, and arrange to meet again on Wednesday.

STANDING BY

Until shortly before 6 o'clock last night it was fully expected that Mr. Churchill would be able to announce the news that the war was over.

He had been standing by the microphone from some time after 3 o'clock, and everything was ready for him to break into the normal programmes of the B.B.C.

Earlier in the day he had been speaking on the Transatlantic telephone to Washington, and he also had several calls to Moscow. His object was to obtain an agreed time for releasing the big news.

There had been a previous agreement that there should be simultaneous times for release. Apparently, in London, it was understood that Monday would be suitable to all concerned.

In anticipation of this important occasion, Mr.

Continued in Back Page, Cols. 4 and 5

SCHACHT SAVED BY 'FIFTH'

Niemoller, too

Daily Mail Special Correspondent

ALLIED H.Q., Italy, Monday.

SOME of the most famous victims of Nazi-ism have been rescued by the Fifth Army from the Prager Wildsee prison camp, near Obblaco, Italy.

Among them was Pastor Niemoller, head of the German Confessional Church, whose defiance of Hitler led to a seven years' incarceration in concentration camps.

A few hours after his release Pastor Niemoller, with his wife and son in the lounge of a hotel.

His text was the words of Isaiah:

For the mountains shall depart, and the hills be removed; but my kindness shall not depart from thee, neither shall the covenant of my peace be removed, saith the Lord that hath mercy on thee.

In all, the Fifth Army saved 137 hostages, including Dr. Schuschnigg, former Chancellor of Austria, who during the week-end was reported to have been executed by the Germans.

Dr. Schuschnigg's wife was also found. M. Leon Blum, former Socialist Premier of France, and his wife, were also freed.

GOEBBELS' BODY IN A SHELTER

Took poison

GOEBBELS, the German Propaganda Minister, his wife, and their children have been found dead in Berlin.

Moscow says that their bodies were found in an air-raid shelter near the Reichstag, and it has been established that all died of poisoning.

No trace has been found of the bodies of Hitler or Göring.

There was speculation in London last night whether the Nazi leaders may have fled to a place of hiding.

It was pointed out, however, that their bodies may have been destroyed in the wreckage of the burning Chancellery or some other building.

MONTY MEETS ROKOSSOVSKY

4 toasts at lunch

TWENTY-FIRST Army Group, Monday.— Field-Marshal Montgomery lunched to-day with Marshal Konstantin Rokossovsky at Wismar.

It was their first meeting, and very cordial greetings were exchanged.

Toasts were drunk to the Allied armies, Mr. Churchill, Marshal Stalin, and President Truman.—Reuter.

VE-WEATHER

Strait of Dover yesterday: Sunny weather, with hours of sunshine. Day temperature rising at dusk 57. Barometer rising.

ARRESTED POLES MAY BE TRIED BY LUBLIN

LUBLIN radio said yesterday that the Polish Provisional Government may demand that General Okulicki and others of the 16 Poles arrested by the Russians be tried both in Warsaw and Moscow for high treason.

The radio said: "Apart from those actively taking part in the military action in Poland also received with indignation the news of the action of Okulicki and his accomplices, who are accused of carrying out diversionary activities against the Red Army.

"Because the criminal activities are directed both against the Soviet forces and were also directed against the re-

born Polish State, it constitutes high treason.

"The Provisional Government reserves the right to demand that General Okulicki and his accomplices be turned over in the Polish authorities to be indicted in the courts of the Republic as well."

M. Mikolowych, former Polish Prime Minister, in London, said he understood the arrested men cannot be accused of action against the Soviet forces, as they were sincere partisans of a Polish-Soviet understanding.

War came to an end twice. The first time, 8 May 1945, was VE Day — Victory in Europe — which was celebrated the day after Germany surrendered; later in the year, on 15 August, came VJ Day — Victory over Japan — after atomic bombs had been dropped on the cities of Hiroshima and Nagasaki.

Having been evacuated to Bournemouth, I missed out on the VE Day street parties, but was back in time for the VJ celebrations. The last bombs — V2 rockets — had fallen on Croydon in January 1945. Taking the tram to the town centre on VJ night, I was enthralled by the spectacle of the Town Hall, the Tudor Whitgift alms-houses and other buildings floodlit — something I had certainly never seen before.

The most spectacular parade of all was not held until almost a year after VJ Day. This was the Victory Parade, which took place in Central London on 8 June 1946.

There were actually two parades — one of marching men and women representing all the Allies, and one a mechanical column. I would have preferred to watch the latter but Dad, despite (or perhaps because of) having driven a great variety of military vehicles all over the Middle East between 1914 and 1918, chose the former, and, with the aid of a periscope — a piece of scientific apparatus I had not previously encountered — I had a pretty good view opposite Selfridge's in Oxford Street. We did manage to catch the tail end of the mechanical parade in The Mall, which included two RTs (4 and 39) and two provincial buses (from Manchester and Halifax) which had helped out in London during the war. By this time it had been hoped that the first of London's standard postwar buses — updated versions of the RT — would be in service, but these would not appear for almost a year.

Left: Windsor celebrates the end of the war. Pay-as-you-board STL2284 waits patiently as the crowds watch a marathon which has just started in front of the castle. At the top right of the picture, spanning the street leading to the station, is a 'Victory Day' banner. *London Transport*

Above: The Victory Parade. Crowds line the route, including a servicewoman on the far right, as RT39 and RT4 pass. *F. G. Reynolds*

Brave New World

BY late 1944 it was clear that the Allies were winning the war, although no one could predict just when final victory would be achieved. The dropping of the two atomic bombs on Japan ended the war in the Far East more quickly than most had anticipated, but many preparations for the postwar world were already in hand. It might have been thought that London Transport's first priority would be to complete the tram-replacement programme. The tram had been all but swept away from North London: all that remained were the three Kingsway Subway routes (31, 33 and 35), the 34 (which terminated at the end of King's Road, Chelsea), the Victoria routes and, of course, those which ran along the reserved track on the Embankment on the north bank of the Thames. Early in 1946, 77 new trolleybuses were ordered from BUT

(a new name for the well-tried AEC/Leyland combination, the two leading British suppliers of PSV chassis having merged their trolleybus businesses). Forming the 'Q1' class, these vehicles, which had MCW bodywork and were strikingly similar to the prewar fleet, were not the precursors of hundreds more but merely replacements for the original London United 'Diddlers' and wartime losses.

Two reports which came out during the war years prophesied a Corbusier-inspired London of the future, with towering 'cities in the sky' flats and office blocks served by motorways designed for the car, where public transport would be supplied by over- and under-ground railways and motor buses. In this brave new world there would be no need for trams or trolleybuses. London Transport's annual report of 1946 stated that it was

Left: A youth pedalling a three-wheel delivery cycle leads an original STL and a 'Hendon' STD on the southern approach to London Bridge, whilst two standard STLs and an LT head in the opposite direction on 22 October 1946. *London Transport*

Below: On the same day, with headscarves prominent (although with rather less covering on male heads than in prewar days), workers hurry across London Bridge for City offices, with three STs, an STL, a brand-new Series E Morris 8 and a horse-and-cart in the background. The tower of Southwark Cathedral can be seen over the roof of the nearest ST. Also visible is a cargo steamer tied up on the south bank of the river in the Pool of London; London was still the busiest port in the world, and the Pool of London teemed with every type of vessel, including passenger ships working a regular service to Spain, paddle steamers bound for Southend and Ramsgate, as well as cargo ships, barges and lighters. *London Transport*

Many of the later North London ex-corporation cars were transferred south of the river in the late 1930s as their routes were converted to trolleybus operation. One such was No 2054, bought by Walthamstow Corporation in 1932 and seen alongside a Rover of similar vintage at Streatham Hill. These cars were one of the many variations on the 'E1' theme, easily distinguished by their windscreens. Along with the 'Felthams', No 2054 was based at Telford Avenue, some half a mile distant.
Alan Cross

Coombe Road, Croydon. Although only four years separated the building of Croydon Corporation 'E1' No 385 and 'Feltham' No 2192, in concept, appearance, performance and comfort they were light-years apart — which was one of the biggest nails in the tram's coffin. It beggars belief that until the 1930s the LCC and the various corporations could go on building cars which were essentially Edwardian; if they could have got together with the MET and the LUT and invested in fleets based on the Feltham and LCC No 1 concept, the tram would have been able to put up a much better fight.
D. A. Thompson

'essential to select a means of transport not rigidly tied to existing routes'. Any sensible planner knows that transport needs vary, and bus routes in London and its suburbs have always been under review and subject to change; what was not appreciated in the 1940s and '50s is that demand *will* remain more or less constant on certain trunk routes, which is why, in the 21st century, the tram is making a comeback. But in the immediate post-World War 2 period it was decided not only that the tram-replacement programme would continue but also that diesel buses (as opposed to electric trolleybuses) would take the trams' place.

Notwithstanding the aims outlined by LT in 1946, replacement of the trams would have to wait; although shabby and elderly, they were in basically sounder condition than many of the petrol and diesel buses. Even the STL class — London's standard type of the immediate prewar period — was in dire need of almost complete rebuilding. The London bus was not designed to last much more than 10 years, yet the LTs and the STs were well into their teens; wartime neglect meant that many were scarcely roadworthy and would have to be replaced before a start could be made on getting rid of the trams.

A scheme was instituted whereby between November 1945 and October 1949 1,106 prewar buses were overhauled and/or rebuilt by outside contractors. In the early-postwar years all manner of undertakings turned

Rebuilt and smoothed-out T32 in that favourite haunt of single-deckers, Kingston. *Author's collection*

Rebuilt single-deck 'Scooter' LT1045 of Kingston garage, at New Malden. *F. G. Reynolds*

to building and repairing bus and coach bodies in order to make up for the wartime backlog, most of these firms either reverting to their previous activities or simply disappearing in the 1950s. Mann Egerton of Norwich, hitherto unknown in London-bus circles, carried out most of the work, on 511 STLs, 262 LTs and 29 STs; it would also build completely new single-deck bus bodies on AEC Regal and Leyland Tiger chassis. Redundant wartime aerodromes, with their huge hangars, provided ideal bases for this work. There were many of these in the flatlands of East Anglia, and Mann Egerton sub-contracted much of the work to firms that leased ex-Bomber Command bases.

In most cases the renovation of the double-deckers was not particularly obvious to the casual observer, beyond the fact that they looked in good shape inside and out, and the wartime livery of red and white with a brown roof was retained. However, a number of single-deck Ts and LTs were much more heavily rebuilt by

Marshall of Cambridge, with a general smoothing-out of exterior protrusions and repainting in the new standard all-red livery with narrow cream bands around the windows. They looked rather splendid and, although they retained their original lines (by now going back nearly 20 years), did not appear dated.

There was still considerable shortage of materials, and many buses had to make do with little or no remedial work. Chiswick did a sort of 'parcels' effect, wrapping strengthening straps around members of the STL class, a bit like a mini mediæval buttress. This did nothing to beautify vehicles, but it kept them on the road until new members of the RT family could put them out of their misery. A few vehicles were disposed of, notably the four remaining double-deck Qs, (Nos 2, 4, 5 and 188). These revolutionary buses had not run since the outbreak of war and were too non-standard to justify the time and expenditure required to keep them on the road. Q3 had been damaged in an air raid in 1941 and was

149

The most dramatic rebuild of any prewar bus (in terms of appearance, at least) was carried out on LT1131, by Bush & Twiddy of Norwich — a name not readily associated with London buses.
In the distance is a Weymann-bodied TD.
Ian Allan Library

subsequently scrapped, but the others found new owners. Q2 ended its days as a snack bar, having been converted by St Helens to a single-decker, Q4 went to Blue Ensign of Doncaster, which ran it until 1951, whilst Q5 and the six-wheeled Q188 migrated (as would many more London double-deckers) to Scotland, being operated until *c*1950 by H. Brown of Garelochhead. Q188 had still not come to the end of its career, for it then re-emerged as a furniture van and continued to work in the Cheshire area until 1953. One or two other double-deck Qs lasted in passenger service but none survived to be preserved. The best we can do is buy one of the handsome Corgi models of Q2 or Q3, or make a pilgrimage to visit the preserved single-deck versions.

Meanwhile orders were put in for some 500 of the postwar standard double-decker, the RT. In fact 338 RTs, in addition to the initial 151, had been ordered at the end of 1938, but, of course, the war had put a stop to this. Chiswick Works had so many other demands placed upon it that there was no capacity to build new bodies, so the contract for these was awarded to Park Royal and Weymann. But 1946 came and went, and there was as yet no sign of the new bus. Deliveries of wartime Bristols, Guys and Daimlers were completed in that year, the last examples being rather less austere than their predecessors, and a small number of new AEC and Leyland double-deckers, to more-or-less full peacetime specification, also arrived. They were also of purely provincial design.

Bristol began bus production again in 1945 and London Transport was allocated 20 K6As. With their AEC engines and less than totally austere Duple 56-seat bodywork they were by no means the least popular of

the wartime buses. They had the elegant, low, standard postwar radiator and spent their lives working out of Hanwell garage. Upon disposal by London Transport in the early 1950s they were snapped up by the Tilling Group and, rebodied, continued at work for some years. The final 100 Daimlers were also of an interim nature. Their Park Royal bodies were almost of prewar appearance; they had full three-piece route indicators back and front (although these were never fully utilised), and their seats were trimmed with standard LT moquette. All 100 were allocated to Sutton garage, and thus the Sutton/Morden/Mitcham area became very much Daimler-land.

Twenty AEC Regent Is fitted with handsome 56-seat Weymann bodies arrived at the end of 1945 and were put to work from Watford garage in early 1946 on routes 321/351. Not all were in Country Area livery initially, but they were soon repainted and all wore the green and white with brown roof of the immediate prewar and wartime years. In contrast, 65 all-Leyland PD1s which arrived around the same time were painted in the standard early-postwar Central Area livery of red with a cream waistband and upper-deck window frames. A few worked from my home garage, Croydon, and passed the end of our road whilst carrying out their duties on the very suburban 115 route, linking Wallington with Croydon Airport. Croydon's STDs soon took themselves off northwards. The class was a familiar sight in and around Victoria, a number living at Gillingham Street garage, working the 10, 38 and 38A.

Both the Weymann-bodied AEC Regent and the all-Leyland Titan — two classic designs — could be seen the length and breadth of the land. Very little concession

Above: One of the later and very different-looking Guys, G281 was fitted with a Northern Counties body — much more rounded than other wartime designs. It arrived in 1945 and is seen here in Chingford, an excellent venue for G-class-spotters. *R. E. Vincent*

Right: G153 of 1945 seen in Prestons Road, Wembley, alongside a Bedford lorry of similar vintage. *F. G. Reynolds*

Left: One of the final group of 100 Daimlers, Sutton garage's D208, with semi-austerity Park Royal bodywork, at Morden. It is in the early-postwar livery of all-over red with two narrow cream bands. *Alan Cross*

was made to LT requirements in either case. The STLs had a basic single-piece front indicator and nothing at the back, and, whilst the STDs were fitted with a prewar STL-type full front destination and 'via' indicator with a roof-mounted number box, the actual display was still the restricted wartime standard; approaching an STL or an STD from the rear, you had to guess where it was going unless you managed to catch a glimpse of the minuscule number stencil as you steamed in pursuit. In other respects both types were a huge improvement on the austerity types with which Londoners had had to contend throughout the 1940s. There was a return to peacetime interior standards of trim and seating, and, at £2,593, an STL was actually £96 cheaper than an austerity D — a real bargain.

The year 1946 saw the reinstatement of the Green Line network. The first routes, with their new 7xx-series numbers, were the 715 (Hertford–Oxford Circus–Guildford) and the 720 (Aldgate–Bishop's Stortford), which started on 6 February, and by June the complete service was up and running and doing excellent business. The 'demobbed' 10T10s, the TFs and the Qs worked all the routes except for the particularly heavily patronised services east from Aldgate, which employed (believe it or not) 37 austerity Daimlers. Any pretence that Green Line routes were operated by what the rest of the world thought of as coaches had been well and truly abandoned.

Initially many of the Green Line coaches carried the livery of green and off-white worn by Country Area buses, but the off-white was soon replaced by a distinguishing pale green. Route boards were carried on the sides above the windows, and from 29 May distinctive new blinds were fitted front and rear, featuring black lettering on a yellow-orange back-ground, described officially as 'old gold'.

Right: The final additions to the STL class were the provincial-style Weymann-bodied Regents of 1945/6. Newly delivered STL2687 of Watford High Street garage is seen out in the Hertfordshire countryside. *Author's collection*

Left: King's Cross in 1946. In the foreground a 'prewar' RT heads westwards; behind 'B2' trolleybus No 118 is preparing to turn right to head northwards between St Pancras and King's Cross stations. In the other direction are a 'sit-up-and-beg' STL, another one of the original RTs, a CR (helping out in these days of acute vehicle shortage), a further STL and a trolleybus. *London Transport*

Below: Still in LNER territory, a newly delivered STD-class Leyland PD1 of Loughton garage waits for an 'N7' 0-6-2T to pass with a suburban stopping train. *London Transport*

9T9 T406 being restored to Green Line livery after war service as an ambulance. Livery is green and white, and the indicator has white lettering on a black background — two short-lived, early-postwar features. The 9T9s put in little Green Line work, being considered underpowered compared to the 10T10s, and saw out their days as Country Area buses. *London Transport*

Backbone of the Green Line fleet in the early postwar period was the handsome 10T10 class. T687, resplendent in the new two-tone green livery with black-on-amber route blinds, poses near Godstone for its official picture on a foggy winter morning in 1946. *London Transport*

The first single-deckers since the CRs arrived in 1946. Like contemporary double-deckers these were more-or-less-standard provincial AECs and Leylands, although all were fitted with virtually identical bodywork by Weymann. The 50 AEC Regals were, naturally enough, added to the T class, while the 31 Leyland Tigers started off a new TD class (the prewar TD class of early Leyland Titans having become extinct in 1939). All 81 were painted in the new livery of red with a thin cream band above and below the windows.

All sorts of sporting events not held since the declaration of war came back — welcome signs of peace and stability returning. Charlton, with Sam Bartram in goal, won the FA Cup, no doubt cheered on by many employees of the Central Tram & Trolleybus

D161, one of the very early postwar Daimlers used on the East London Green Line services, in this instance the 722 to Upminster, at Aldgate bus station. Two TFs are in the background. *Alan Cross*

CR47 helps out on the 88, normally the preserve of vastly bigger LTs, as it speeds across the tram tracks at Tooting Broadway. *Author's collection*

Repair Depot, and Dad and I went to watch the Boat Race. For some reason we supported dark-blue Oxford, which didn't do them any good, as they were soundly beaten by Cambridge, but it was all very exciting, especially walking back along the Upper Richmond Road to catch a 630 trolleybus home from Putney, and watching what seemed like practically half the entire fleet of original RTs pass by, each one packed to the gunwales.

T768, the final member of the 50 provincial-style 14T12s, with Weymann 33-seat bodywork of 1946, at Greenford. *Author*

· 8 ·

The Long Haul out of Austerity

AS we all know, we British love discussing our weather. Whenever it decides to do anything which we perceive out of the ordinary we complain bitterly that we've never had to suffer so much cold/wet/heat/ice/snow/sun/lack of sun/etc. We blame God/the atomic bomb/the Health Service/global warming/the state of English cricket/modern youth/etc, feel a lot better and then go about our business. Well, in 1947 we really did, for once, have cause for complaint.

For most of January there was little indication of what was about to descend on Britain; indeed, the weather was unusually mild, lulling us into a false sense of well-being. On the night of the 20th there was a frost — nothing unusual, you might think, for mid-winter, but on the 23rd it began to snow with a vengeance. From

then until 17 March it snowed every day somewhere in the United Kingdom. Central London, which is always that much warmer than its immediate surroundings (to say nothing of the polar regions north of Watford) suffered less than much of the country, but it was bad enough all the same.

February was awful. For 22 consecutive days Kew recorded no sunshine at all; when it did break through, the night-time temperatures plummeted, and in the far north of London Transport's Country Area, around Luton and Dunstable, it fell to –4°F (–20°C). Inevitably, in the outer suburbs and the Home Counties, particularly the hills of the Chilterns and the North Downs, where the snow lay deepest, bus services suffered more disruption than those closer in to the capital, but every part of the network was affected. Snow and ice penetrated the tram conduit, and services ground to a halt, although disruptions seldom lasted more than an hour. Staff worked heroically to clear a way. No fewer than 50 tram and 120 trolleybus motors suffered snow damage, and hundreds of motor-bus radiators cracked. Everywhere Britain slowed down and in parts almost ground to a halt. Coal could not get through, people stayed at home, electricity supplies were affected and production stalled, which meant the delivery of the long-promised RTs was further delayed.

March offered no respite. High winds and snowstorms meant heavy drifting, the snow reaching a depth of 10ft in the Chilterns. On 10 March it looked as if the worst was over, for the temperature began to rise as mild air came in from the south-west. In reality this simply heralded another hefty swipe from vengeful Nature: the resulting sudden thaw brought even more dramatic conditions, with melting snows and ground still frozen from weeks of frost causing extensive flooding in the Thames Valley, services around Windsor

Rehabilitated former Croydon Corporation 'E1' tram No 380 in freezing conditions on the Embankment in February 1947.
Ian Allan Library

Although this picture of 'N1' trolleybus No 1594 was taken at Paddington Green a decade or so later, it illustrates the conditions London Transport had to contend with during the winter of early 1947. *Author*

'E3' No 1927 at Hackney while working the 31, one of the three Kingsway Subway routes which continued to penetrate deep into North London in postwar days. *Author's collection*

Above: Weymann-bodied RT428 (of Leyton) and a milk cart cross LNER tracks in Leytonstone. Deliveries of bread, greengroceries and especially milk by horse-and-cart were an everyday sight in London when the first postwar RTs were new.
London Transport

Right: Park Royal-bodied RT251 of Bromley, on its way to Croydon. The route number on the lower deck (above the garage code) was a short-lived feature of the early postwar RTs.
F. G. Reynolds

and Staines being particularly hit; Watford High Street garage had to be abandoned for two days until it dried out. A deepening depression which reached southern England on 16 March brought high winds, reaching 80-90 knots and inflicting yet more (if varied) misery on the long-suffering populace, which was having to endure shortages of everything from coal to food as all forms of communication were disrupted. A final flourish was rain on an almost unprecedented scale. Camden Square recorded no less than 122 hours of it in March, making this the third-wettest month in London since records began in 1881.

Spring brought vastly happier tidings. Saturday 10 May 1947 is a significant date in the history of London's public transport, for it was then that the postwar RT — regarded by many as the finest piece of urban road transport ever — entered public service. RT402 (HLX 219) was delivered to Leyton garage and took up work that day on the 10 (Woodford Bridge–Victoria) and could thus be seen at the capital's best-known bus terminus. It was undeniably a thing of beauty and stood out from the rather down-at-heel crowd all around it. RT402 had a Weymann body; on 23 May it was joined by RT152 (HLW 139), with Park Royal body. These two manufacturers would supply the vast majority of bodies to London Transport in the next seven years. So closely did they follow the guidelines laid down by London Transport that it was virtually impossible to distinguish a Park Royal from a Weymann body; they were interchangeable, even (in later years) between AEC and Leyland chassis. It took a real rivet counter to

distinguish one from the other, and not even John Wadham or Clive Gillam — my mentors in all things London Transport in Class Five at Winterbourne Primary School — could enlighten me. The buses they replaced were the oldest, open-staircase LTs, which were almost 20 years old, having nearly doubled their expected life span. However, these did not immediately stagger off to the scrapyard, for quite a few of them were in rather better condition than their newer, enclosed-staircase brethren and even many of the later STLs, so they were sent to a variety of Central Area garages to hold the fort until the trickle of postwar replacements became a flood. London Transport was having to operate 2.6% more services (in terms of route mileage) than in 1939, and, whilst this may not sound much, given the size of the London network it required several hundred extra vehicles.

By the end of 1947 171 new RTs were in service. When one considers the size of LT's fleet — and the size of its problems in dealing with the decrepit and time-expired — this was nothing like enough. So what was to be done? Someone must have consulted the ghost of Marie Antoinette and decided that if there was no bread to be had then Londoners had better be

Right: B18, a Duple-bodied Bristol of 1945/6 at Ealing. Is that the Queen Mother, behind the lady encumbered with pram and children, about to board? *F. G. Reynolds*

Below: ST802 intrudes into Daimler land on the forecourt of Morden station. *Alan Cross*

Above: T207, one of the pioneer Green Line coaches, seen in its declining years working as a bus from Kingston garage. Behind stands a Cravens-bodied RT, which type had just replaced the original 60-seat STLs on the 65. *F. G. Reynolds*

Left: One of the many exchanges between the Central and Country Areas features once-green BRCW-bodied Q53, transferred to Kingston garage and repainted red. It is seen being pursued through Kingston by a refurbished T17. *D. W. K. Jones*

offered cake, as luxury coaches were now provided for the lucky few to take them to work and fetch them home again. Others had to make do with a wartime austerity normal-control Bedford OWB or a relic from the 1920s in the shape of a Gilford or a very early Leyland Tiger — or perhaps even a Midland Red-built SOS, which certainly looked like a relic from a bygone age, even if these looks were slightly deceptive.

What the LPTB decided to do was hire in several hundred vehicles from coach operators in the Greater London area. Not surprisingly, only two years after the end of the war these varied enormously, from brand-new Duple- and Harrington-bodied Leyland Tigers, AEC Regals and Dennis Lancets to second-, third- and umpteenth-hand representatives of practically every variety of PSV produced in the UK over the previous 20-odd years. The latter even included some ex-London Transport buses and coaches disposed of but now temporarily returned to mother, among them the prototype Leyland Cub (C1) and Leyland Tiger (TF1). In the middle of October the vehicles were brought to Chiswick for inspection, and the engineers must really have got their skates on, for by Monday 27th 325

coaches were ready to take up work. Many of these were far from suitable for Central London bus duties, but they were better than nothing. Two faults were common to most vehicles — limited capacity and coach-type seating. Getting in and out was not easy, but many of them were rather more comfortable than a London double-decker, and if one was travelling a fair distance — in from the suburbs to Central London to work, for instance — then such a journey could be a distinctly pleasurable experience. The scheme must have been considered successful, for the original contracts were extended beyond 1947 and throughout 1948, not finishing until August 1949. In all some 550 coaches took part, with their owners providing the drivers.

A fascinating pair of coaches helping out London Transport's vehicle shortage at Victoria, with an RT and a G behind. On the left is a Gilford 168OT of Elms, Phillips & Brown of Tottenham, dating from 1933; next to it is a Leyland Tiger TS1 of 1930, re-registered and fitted with later 'Covrad' radiator, of Vineys, also of Tottenham. *Alan Cross*

· 9 ·
Nationalisation

RTL501, the first of its class and the only one to be built with a roofbox body, heads westwards towards Hounslow in an area which was gradually becoming dominated by the ever-expanding Heathrow. *Author's collection*

ON 1 January 1948 London Transport, along with the four main-line railway companies, was nationalised. Lord Ashfield, who, with Frank Pick had put London Transport at the forefront of innovation, had quit as Chairman in October 1947 to join the British Transport Commission. He died before the year was out. The legal lettering on vehicles now read 'London Transport Executive', but, as far as the travelling public was concerned, very little changed. Behind the scenes, the world *had* changed, however, for London Transport no longer had the freedom it had enjoyed under Ashfield and Pick, and the BTC was responsible for major decisions.

Rationing would persist right through the 1940s, and there would be shortages of all manner of items — not least Hornby train sets and Dinky Toys — but the world was gradually recovering from the terrible years of World War 2. The unemployment of the 1930s was replaced by the opportunity for every able-bodied member of society to help produce for a world eager for virtually anything Britain could make. 'Export or die' was the cry, and the slogan 'Britain can make it' was often modified or added to by a workforce which looked

longingly at all the consumer items it now had the money to buy but which were whisked off to earn much-needed foreign currency. Petrol was still rationed, and most new cars were shipped off to the Empire (or Commonwealth, as it was now starting to be called), as well as Europe and (in the case of high-powered sports cars) the USA. On 1 June 1948 petrol, although strictly rationed, became available to the private motorist. Dad was at last able to get our 1932 Lanchester 10 (which he had bought from the front garden of a house on Brixton Hill for £3 10s in 1943) on the road. Our first expedition was to Reigate Heath, where I watched Qs and STLs pass on the A25 and a brand-new Southdown Leyland Tiger PS1 arrive on an evening excursion from Brighton. The Lanchester would be sold later when my twin sisters arrived — 'Can't afford all three,' as Dad put it — but the boost to private motoring heralded a world where the ownership of a car would become the norm for most families, with all that would mean for public transport.

AEC and Leyland were at the forefront of the export drive, but by 1950 they were able to satisfy many home needs. Production of the RT soared, and in June 1948 the Leyland version appeared in the shape of RTL501.

Above: Outside the impressive Horniman Museum in Forest Hill, 'HR2' No 1859 heads for the steep, four-track section at Dog Kennel Hill, Dulwich, on one of the hilly routes for which these ex-LCC cars were specifically designed. *Author's collection*

Right: Most of the Croydon Corporation 'E1s' spent their entire careers on home territory. No 393 stands at the Purley terminus of the 16/18 — the most southerly point reached by London trams. The conductor keeps a watchful eye as his passengers alight in the middle of the road whilst a Ford V8 Pilot waits to pass — one of the hazards of tram travel, and a powerful argument at that time for its abolition. The indicator is already set for its return journey; the conductor will shortly lower the far pole and raise that at this end, after which No 393 will set off back to Croydon behind the RT. *A. W. V. Mace*

This curious number was arrived at on account of its being intended that the first 500 should be 8ft wide, unlike the hitherto-standard 7ft 6in.

It will be recalled that 8ft-wide trolleybuses had been diverted from South Africa to London during the war, and now a batch 8ft wide and built to London specification arrived. These were the 'Q1s', ordered in 1946. Aside from their extra width (which gave them a somewhat tubby appearance) and the five- (instead of six-) side-window layout, they were otherwise remarkably like the last standard prewar 'P1' trolleys. The 'Q1s' were sent to Fulwell and throughout their careers were associated with the Kingston area.

The first production batch of RTLs comprised buses

No 1838, one of the 1948 delivery of 8ft-wide 'Q1' trolleybuses, at Tolworth — an area always associated with these vehicles. *Author*

not to the promised 8ft width but to the previous standard, and had bodies identical to the latest RTs. Right through the 1930s no one seemed to be quite sure how route indicators should be arranged — or maybe it was that several people had very definite ideas, and each was allowed to try his out. At any rate, a standard seemed to have been reached with the newest STLs. In these the number indicator was in the roof, and the destination was above the 'via' point. The 'prewar' RTs continued with this, but the first postwar examples had the destination below the 'via' indicator. Even this was not the final variation, however, for RT852 appeared at the 1948 Commercial Motor Show with the number

STLs, a 'Hendon' STD and a 3RT3/1 without roofbox in Trafalgar Square in 1949. *Alan Cross*

indicator removed from the roof and placed alongside the 'via' display, to its right (identical to the rear layout of the standard STL), the body being designated RT3/1. One reason for this change was said to be that the roof was weakened by the roofbox (although, to my knowledge, no owner of a preserved STL or RT with this arrangement has ever detected any problem). Henceforth the new layout was adopted as standard, and the Park Royal bodies on the first production RTLs perpetuated the RT3/1 design.

No fewer than 1,200 new buses were expected in 1948; in the event there were 755 RTs and RTLs. By the standards of any other undertaking, even this would have been quite enormous, but it wasn't sufficient to satisfy London Transport's needs. Prewar buses were falling by the wayside in unsustainable numbers, and so

on 7 December 1948 five extraordinary, brand-new apparitions materialised in the shape of lowbridge ECW-bodied Bristol Ks — three red and two green. Like London Transport, Bristol and ECW were part of the British Transport Commission, and thus 180 Bristol double-deckers, instead of being delivered to their Tilling Group owners, were sent to London.

The Bristol Ks were tough and well-built (if a trifle unsophisticated by London standards), their chief disadvantage in London, where there were few constraints on vehicle height, being their lowbridge layout. There were a few highbridge examples, intended for Brighton, Hove & District and for Eastern Counties, but the great majority were 55-seat lowbridge examples with four seats abreast upstairs (making the conductor's work more difficult) and a sunken gangway on the offside, which projected into the lower deck and was skilfully designed to catch the head of any unwary passenger larger than a dwarf. All in all these were not the most popular vehicles ever to have been foisted upon London's travelling public. Of course, to schoolboys like myself they were a fascinating variation on the norm, and for me brought back the days when I used to travel on Hants & Dorset examples in 1944 and early 1945. Indeed, some Hants & Dorset AEC-engined K6A buses did run in London, and Corgi makes an excellent model of TD895 (HLJ 44) with blinds set for working the 336 from Chesham to Watford.

Above: RT683 passing Tottenham Court Road tube station, followed by a wartime Daimler. *Ian Allan Library*

Top right: This lowbridge ECW-bodied Bristol K (Eastern National 4007) looks as if it only just fits under the bridge at Waterloo, but of course there was (and remains) sufficient clearance for normal-height double-deckers. *Alan Cross*

Lower right: A highbridge ECW-bodied Bristol K6A destined for Eastern Counties finds itself working from Potters Bar garage in 1949. *Ian Allan Library*

I once had a ride on a highbridge example based at Croydon garage on the 68 — the only one I can remember. Records state that they also worked the 166 and 166A, but I rather doubt this, for these routes passed the top of our road. I was a regular user of both and would surely have remembered any journey on such an unusual bus. But then again, memory can play tricks.

The final total of Tilling buses, purloined from their rightful owners, was 45 highbridge examples (all from Brighton or Eastern Counties) and 135 lowbridge, all being in service by 16 June 1949. They were due to pass to their rightful owners between the end of 1949 and the middle of 1950, which was more or less what happened, although the dispersal rate was somewhat slower than originally intended — another indication that wartime depredations were not yet overcome.

Not even 550 coaches and 180 Bristols could totally satisfy London's desperate need for buses — in 1948 London Transport carried 4,675,000,000 passengers, its greatest total ever — and in 1949 three almost-new Daimler CVG6 doubledeckers were hired from Maidstone Corporation and 17 prewar AEC Regents from Leeds.

Top left: One of the few vintage double-deckers hired by London Transport was this centre-entrance, Brush-bodied AEC Regent of 1931, owned originally by Burnley, Colne & Nelson Corporation. *Author's collection*

Lower left: T769, one of the final examples of the many varieties of the T class, the 15T13 of 1948, does excellent business at Hemel Hempstead. *F. G. Reynolds*

Right: One of the Brush-bodied Daimlers borrowed from Maidstone Corporation at work from Sutton garage under the trolleybus wires — as it would have been back home. *Author's collection*

Below: Sent to ease London's chronic shortage of buses in the immediate postwar years, a new ECW-bodied Bristol K, destined for Hants & Dorset but working from Godstone garage, finds itself at Bromley about to set off for Biggin Hill, Westerham, Oxted, Redhill and Reigate. Unlike most of the lowbridge Tilling Group double-deckers, this one was appropriately employed on a route normally worked by lowbridge STLs. *Alan Cross*

• 10 •

Ends and Beginnings

T HE need for vehicles from unlikely sources was driven by the very poor condition of the prewar fleet. Buses were regularly inspected and, if they failed to pass a roadworthiness test, were marked with the inscription 'PSV71' and had to be withdrawn and sent for scrap. Bodywork was usually the determining factor; no London bus was intended to last more than 10 years, yet here they were struggling on way beyond this. Many mechanical parts were also being expected to last much longer than normal.

The year 1948 also saw the delivery of London Transport's last half-cab single-deckers. The final members of the T class, nearly 20 years newer than the original members, were 30 Regal IIIs, of the 15T13 variety. Painted green and (anachronistically) white, they were put to work in the Country Area. They were immediately followed by 100 TD-class Leyland Tiger PS1s; these were given the new standard livery of all-red with a cream line above and below the windows and were sent to a number of garages, enabling a few (but not many, there being a shortage of single-deckers) elderly members of the T and LT classes to be withdrawn. The new Ts and TDs all had Mann Egerton bodies, identical except that the Ts had sliding passenger doors and the TDs none. Mann Egerton had never previously built bus bodies for London but had built up vast experience of refurbishing STs, LTs and STLs. Although officially stated to be of provincial design, these single-deckers always seemed to me to incorporate many Chiswick features, and I know of no others in service outside London. There are preserved examples of each type, so the reader can judge for him/herself.

As part of the planned extension of the Northern Line beyond Edgware, a large depot had been built out in the country at Aldenham. The extension had not yet taken place (and in fact never would), so the depot was 'temporarily' adapted to deal with buses. This arrangement would soon become permanent: a production line was set up, and all heavy body repairs and overhauls were transferred there away from the garages and from Chiswick. It became as much a Mecca for enthusiasts as Chiswick — and equally difficult to enter without permission. The best most could do in later years was to sit through endless replays of the Cliff

Above: Rehabilitated 'E1' No 1422 has the streets immediately south of Southwark Bridge virtually to itself, the curve of which can be seen in the distance, with the façade of City offices beyond. Even today, Southwark's is much the least-used of all the London bridges. Commencing its journey on the north bank of the river, the 46 wended its way through South East London before ending up back beside the Thames at Woolwich. *D. A. Thompson*

Far left: Among this fascinating collection of vehicles in the Holloway Road are four 'E3' trams, at least two STs, two STLs, a lowbridge ECW-bodied Bristol and a trolleybus. *Ian Allan Library*

Left: An 'E3' tram with an RT in the distance amongst the shoppers on a sunny day in Woolwich in 1949. *R. Hubble*

Right: A group of time-expired STs and one STL at Epsom Racecourse for the 1949 Derby. Military uniforms are still prominent. *Author's collection*

Below: Members of the Lebanese Olympic team alight from a CR at Wembley in the summer of 1948. *Ian Allan Library*

Richard & the Shadows film *Summer Holiday*, wherein an RT was taken on a European excursion and featured an extensive musical sequence where the bus (several, actually) is prepared for immortality as it is taken through the various stages of overhaul at Aldenham.

Within the weather — not as ferocious as the previous year — there still lurked a vicious streak, heavy snowfalls towards the end of February 1948 closing a number of roads across the North Downs and causing several days' disruption to Country Area services worked by Chelsham and Dunton Green garages.

Once spring arrived there was great demand on the Green Line and Country Area bus routes — places such as Whipsnade Zoo, Windsor and the Surrey Hills proving very popular — and 141 buses were borrowed from the Central Area. Ken Glazier, in his book *Routes to Recovery* (Capital Transport, 2000), recalls that on Easter Monday it was 3pm before all those wishing to leave Victoria Coach Station for Windsor could get away. Demand was even greater with the warmer weather and longer evenings of Whitsun. Central Area buses increased their revenue by 15% over the same period in 1947, Epping Forest and the Thames at Richmond and Hampton Court being particular favourites, whilst there was a similar situation further out into the rural Home Counties, where Country Area buses were doing equally well: Green Line takings were up by a staggering 25%. London Transport would never have it so good again. Not surprisingly, many of the coach operators which had lent their vehicles to London Transport wanted them back. Over 100 were returned but only 63 were obtained from other operators. None was used by London Transport at weekends; although they would have been ideal for such work, there was an agreement that LT would not use them to compete with their owners.

Having clearly got the bit between its teeth, the weather had yet more surprises in store and on 14 June unleashed thunderstorms of such violence that 37 East London trolleybuses had to be taken out of service on account of flood damage.

To help deal with extra seasonal demands a 'Special Events' fleet was formed, consisting of some 50 more-or-less time-expired buses — principally STs and LTs — which, whilst not fit for regular daily passenger service, could just about stagger up the hill from Morden or Epsom station to Epsom Racecourse on Derby Day or from Wimbledon station to the All England Lawn Tennis Club; a number of driver-training buses also remained licensed for such work.

In the summer of 1948 London hosted the first postwar Olympic Games. Although this put huge demands on an already stretched transport system the event was generally welcomed, for it was a very visible sign that the world was returning to normality after the horrors of the war. The main venue for the Games was Wembley Stadium, but events took place at football and

LT91 of the Special Events fleet waits outside Wimbledon station for customers for the Lawn Tennis Championships in June 1949. *Alan Cross*

sports grounds all over the London area. London Transport simply didn't have the capacity to lay on many extra vehicles, the exception being the 662 trolleybus route from Paddington to Wembley, which was boosted to 10 trolleys an hour using vehicles displaced by the new 'Q1s'. The Underground carried most of the traffic, whilst some 30-odd single-deckers, mostly LTC six-wheeled coaches and the unreliable CR-class 20-seat rear-engined Cubs, were provided for competitors. At the peak of the Games, double-deckers — a mixed bag of due-to-be-retired LTs and STs and brand-new RTs — ferried competitors to and from Wembley.

The first RTs to be delivered to the Country Area took up work in the northern area — on the 301 from Tring and Two Waters (Hemel Hempstead) garages — on 21 July 1948. Numbered in the 5xx/6xx series and with HLX registrations, they were known to us bus spotters only from the Ian Allan 'ABCs', and we longed to see a real one for ourselves. They first reached the southern area at the end of the summer, when three

Left: A 3RT3 leads an ST and an STL around Trafalgar Square in 1949. *Author's collection*

Below left: ST16 of Alperton garage stands outside the Empire Pool, Wembley, in 1948. *Author's collection*

Above: A shiny new Country Area RT650, devoid of adverts, seen in Watford in 1948. *Author's collection*

Below: At London Bridge in 1948, brand-new 3RT8 RT1118 prepares to set off for the northern extremities of the Central Area. *Author's collection*

Top left: LTs were still working the 38 when this picture was taken at Victoria in May 1949, but the new RT alongside LT285 indicates that the latter's days were numbered. *Alan Cross*

Lower left: An outside-staircase LT, looking pretty good despite its 19 years, awaits business behind a Tilling ST. *Forever Amber — Blue Peter* material today — was considered scorching, red-hot stuff in 1948. *Alan Cross*

Above: An LT and a standard STL meet their end at a scrapyard in Rainham in June 1949. Although the Fox Photos caption describes STL2028 as 'ancient' it was actually a mere 12 years old, having been delivered to Holloway garage in March 1937. *Ian Allan Library*

went to Leatherhead. This garage had a share in the 408 and the 470, which served our part of the world, but for a while the new RTs kept well away, on the 418. Eventually, just before the year was out, we got our first sight of these (for a few weeks) advert-less beauties, when more were delivered to Leatherhead and to Reigate. By now JXC and JXN registrations had taken over from the HLXs.

STs and LTs were now disappearing fast. Old, faithful friends and (in the case of the LTs in particular) full of character though they were, they compared very badly with the magnificent new RTs and RTLs. LT1, dating from August 1929, whilst certainly not the first to go, was taken out of service in November 1948, and a few other open-staircase versions lasted into 1949. London Transport, more than any other transport undertaking, was aware of its heritage, and LT165 and ST821 were put aside for preservation. They were stored for a number of years at Reigate garage, where we spotters naturally converged in the hope of catching a glimpse of these and other hidden-away veterans. It would be a long time before they appeared permanently in public.

Above: Part of tram route 12 was converted to trolleybus 612 in 1937; the intention was that the entire route should be operated by trolleybuses once the south-side tram routes were replaced, but the war intervened and the 12 continued to run between Wandsworth and the Borough until 1950, when both it and the 612 were replaced by motor-bus route 44. This is 'D3' No 514 of Wandsworth depot. *Author's collection*

Left: On loan to the Country Area, red ST374, one of 10 built with this type of route indicator, heads through South Croydon for Redhill in the summer of 1949, performing one of its last duties before withdrawal. *Author's collection*

Above: A pair of STLs in the red and cream standard in postwar years until all-red became the norm. STL1780 leads STL1243 at Redbridge station. *R. E. Vincent*

Right: One of the many variations in the LT class was this one, seen at Victoria shortly before withdrawal. The indicator is mounted directly over the driver's cab, but above it is provision for a board with further details and illuminated at night by the lamp set into the upper-deck central window frame. Board and lamp were taken out of use in the early years of the war and never reinstated. *Author's collection*

179

· 11 ·

RT Triumphant

BY 1949 the tide was turning. The oldest classes of double-deckers — STs and LTs dating from 1929 — were now nearing extinction. I made my last journey in a double-deck LT — an Elmers End example — in September 1948 on route 194 from my new school, Whitgift Middle, in the centre of Croydon to our playing fields at Shirley. Elmers End garage operated nothing but LTs and thus was an early candidate for RTs. By the end of September our Wednesday- and Saturday-afternoon journeys to learn the secrets of the strange oval ball game played by public schools would be undertaken in an RT which was so new that it gave off that rich aroma of fresh paint and upholstery unique to the RT family. Who could resist such a vehicle? But I was sorry to see the end of the LT, with its six wheels (very impressive) and its variety of architectural styles, ranging from the outside-staircase versions — a

throwback to the horse bus — through the inevitable variations on the theme of route indicators, to the impressive-looking 'Bluebirds' which, back in 1930, had heralded the future. One achieved a sort of immortality by being driven around Brooklands race track at speeds far in excess of what were normally required of it in a Will Hay film. Neither the first nor the final versions of the LT were normally seen in Croydon, which made them more exotic, and I had to venture to Victoria to get a ride on an open staircase 38A or Mitcham for a 'Bluebird' 88 and see Dad play cricket and receive personal tuition on how to spin a googly from a former Surrey Second XI player — not that it did me much good as wicket-keeper for the 3B Second XI. My very last sight of an LT was of one of Hammersmith's heading along Buckingham Palace Road for Liverpool Street on London's most famous route, the 11.

STs too disappeared from the streets of Croydon, replaced both by RTs and by standard STLs drafted in from elsewhere. I was less put out by this, for the ST came in only one variety, and that a shortened version of the least interesting LT and minus a couple of wheels, to

Right at the end of their careers several former Tilling STLs migrated to the 'far north' and ended their days in Country Area green livery, like STL115 seen in Watford in 1948. *Author's collection*

Above: A rather woebegone single-deck LT based at Croydon (TC) garage waits at the Wallington terminus of the 234A in 1945. *Author's collection*

Left: No 2, London's newest tram, and Metro-Cammell-bodied RTL765 at Eltham church. *R. Hubble*

boot. It looked as if just one of each would survive in preservation, but later Prince Marshall found Tilling ST922 mouldering away in a scrapyard and had it beautifully restored. The official preserved ST was not, as it happened, ex-General but rather one from the National fleet. This was almost standard but had a smaller front indicator and looked a little odd when repainted into red and first put on display, many years later, at the Museum of British Transport in the former bus garage at Clapham. Tending to be the sort of people who go into terminal decline if, having counted nine million and three rivets, they find they are one short, some enthusiasts got very hot under the collar about this, but ST821 eventually reverted to London Transport postwar green, and peace and harmony once more reigned. Decades later, LT165 was joined by the newly rediscovered remains of a couple of single-deck versions ('Scooters') and, as I write, restoration of that belonging to the London Transport collection has been completed.

The single-deck LTs lasted rather longer than did the double-deckers, 60 being rebuilt by Marshall in 1948/9, enabling me to ride into the rural fastness of Riddlesdown on one on Croydon's 234A route in late 1949. To all intents and purposes the ST also disappeared by the end of that year; a few just lasted into 1950, while six lowbridge examples in the Country Area

Right: It is difficult to imagine the fashionable King's Road, Chelsea, and the workaday tram co-existing, but the junction of Beaufort Street and King's Road was the terminus of the 34. After crossing Battersea Bridge its route took it through Clapham, Brixton and the Elephant & Castle before terminating back on the north bank of the Thames at Blackfriars. A typical Thompson night-time shot of an 'E1' beside the river.
D. A. Thompson

Below: An 'E1' tram and RT1147 of Croydon (TC) garage on the Embankment in September 1949.
A. W. V. Mace

Left: A contrast in styles between tram No 96, an ex-East Ham car built in 1928 to an Edwardian design, and a very Transatlantic-looking brand-new Vauxhall Wyvern and an RTL, both of 1950.

Below: ST141, one of only eight members of its class to survive beyond the beginning of 1950. All eight were lowbridge examples, and ST141 once belonged to the National Omnibus & Transport Co. Although in Country Area livery, it is seen working the Central Area 230 from Harrow Weald (HD) garage. *Author's collection*

were needed for a little while longer. A curious late phenomenon to be seen in the streets of Croydon was an ST adorned in blue and yellow, having been employed on Inter Station duties between 1943 and 1946. The last of these returned to normal duties, initially without being repainted, in 1947, when some of the Leyland 1½-decker Cubs built specifically for Inter Station work were returned from the Railway Air Service and once again ran between the main-line stations.

I know of no ST or LT which passed to new owners and was operated as a PSV (although in some cases the chassis saw further service), but the STL was virtually the first London type to go on to carry passengers after London Transport had dispensed with its services. Relatively few were fit enough so to do, but this nevertheless marked the beginning of a trend which would see ex-London buses take up work all over the world.

A curious arrival at the end of 1949 was G436. Guys, despite their poor bodywork, had impressed a number of operators which had been forced to buy the make during the war years — one thinks particularly of Southdown and Chatham & District — and they were selling well in the late 1940s. A solitary Arab, with a very powerful 10.35-litre Meadows engine and air-operated preselector gearbox, was sold to London Transport in

November 1949. It had a standard Park Royal body and looked as if it had taken a wrong turn upon delivery to Midland Red or East Kent. The intention was that a second chassis adapted to take the Park Royal or Weymann RT body, should follow it, but this never happened, and G436 remained unique in the London Transport fleet.

Remarkable survivors right through the 1940s were examples of the NS class. Of almost prehistoric aspect, these ancient objects, dating from 1923 and the link between the horse bus and the modern double-decker, had last run in passenger service in 1937. However, 12, including one single-decker, were converted to mobile canteens, in which form they popped up all over the London Transport area, being particularly useful during the war in keeping hard-pressed crews fed and watered in emergencies, when their own garage canteens were out of action. One NS was withdrawn in 1944, and most of the others had gone by the end of the 1940s, but two lasted into the 1950s. One of these was the former NS2295 (No 39H in the service fleet). I paid a visit to Chelsham garage early in 1950 to admire the new KXW-registered RTs which had just been delivered. I was particularly intrigued by the 2499-2521 series, all of which worked through Croydon, for the bus-spotters' grapevine had it that RT2500 was going to be the last RT. How wrong could we be? Parked to one side of the garage, in stark contrast to the gleaming, dark-green, state-of-the-art RTs, was an extraordinary apparition.

G436, the solitary Park Royal-bodied Guy Arab of 1949, at Peckham. *F. G. Reynolds*

Painted a drab shade of leaf green, it had minimal mudguards, a radiator which was wider than it was tall, a towering driving cab much higher than the rest of the lower deck, a four-piece front window on the upper deck and many other features I associated with a long-vanished era. Just visible on the panels where 'LONDON TRANSPORT' would normally be was the legend 'STAFF CANTEEN'; below was the wording 'LONDON TRANSPORT EXECUTIVE' — there were very few NSs which lasted long enough to become part of the nationalised industry. A short while later, having defied Old Father Time for over a decade, NS2295 finally met its end and was sold to a dealer in April 1951 and broken up. Whenever I visit the London Transport Museum at Covent Garden I always take a look at the sole surviving NS (NS1995) and reflect that I came across such an antiquity which just made it into the second half of the 20th century.

Six Tilling STs were converted to mobile canteens in 1946/7, but these were only a stopgap. However, one of these — ST922 — kept going until 1955 and (as already described) was eventually preserved by Prince Marshall. Many years later, in the 1970s, it returned to passenger service, operating tourist route 100 in Central London, and lives today at Cobham, still roadworthy and often seen out and about. More permanent replacements for the NS canteens arrived in 1947/8 in the shape of purpose-built vehicles. These were based on Scammell chassis and had semi-trailer bodies built, very much in the Chiswick stylistic tradition, by Spurling of Hendon. They were hauled by petrol-engined Bedford tractor

units — one of the classic designs of all times and the most popular commercial vehicle of the early postwar years. There were 10 of these, numbered 700-9B (HLX 480, JXC 1-9). These, in turn, were withdrawn between 1959 and 1967. Bedford No 702B (trailer unit No MC11) is still with us, having passed into preservation and is yet another resident of the Cobham Bus Museum.

No fewer than 1,592 new double-deckers entered service with London Transport in 1949. Extraordinary as this total was, it would be exceeded the following year. Nevertheless 1949 is highly significant in the history of London Transport not only for the volume of new vehicles but also for the introduction of three new varieties within the RT family.

The RT is rightly remembered as one of the all-time classic PSVs, yet two of the varieties introduced in 1949 were short-lived failures. The more unusual (and a one-off) was RTC1. Strictly speaking this wasn't a new vehicle at all, being a rebuild of war-damaged RT97, but it certainly looked completely new. Intended to be the forerunner of a class of double-deck coaches, it was a striking-looking vehicle and was tried out on a number of Green Line routes. A great deal of thought had gone into its planning. A new suspension system was fitted, lighting was by fluorescent tubes, there was air

Above: Men in long, brown mackintoshes stride purposefully across Piccadilly Circus as a Battersea-based RT on route 19 passes Eros. *Author*

Right: A graphic illustration of just how appalling the London fogs of the 1940s and '50s could be. The bus is an RTL. *London Transport*

RTC1, the handsome if unsuccessful double-deck Green Line coach, originally RT97. Although it was deemed a failure, many of its features would be incorporated in the successful Routemaster coaches of a decade later. *London Transport*

conditioning, and the 46 seats were the result of a survey of passengers' preferences. Sadly RTC1 was not a success. The suspension gave rise to many complaints, there were no overhead luggage racks, and mechanically it was not very reliable. After nine months it was relegated to bus work and was eventually withdrawn in 1953. However, it was an experiment worth carrying out, and much of the experience gained would be put to good use with the production Routemaster coaches of the 1960s.

The SRT arose from the fact that production of RT bodies was running ahead of that of chassis, it being decided that 300 of the latest prewar STL chassis should be refurbished — remember that it was the bodies which were wearing out quicker than the chassis — and fitted with RT bodies. The STL chassis in question came initially from buses of the FJJ- and FXT-registered batches; their bodies were not broken up but were transferred to earlier (mainly DLU-registered) members of the class, whose Park Royal all-metal bodies of 1937 were in a very sorry state (although, ironically, one or two of these would still be in passenger service when the last SRT was withdrawn). The problems with the SRTs soon became apparent and stemmed from the fact that they were a good deal heavier than the STL yet retained the STL engine, so that performance was sluggish. Perhaps even worse, their brakes were unreliable. Not surprisingly drivers hated them. They were kept off hilly routes, and, although their brakes were modified, the problem was never solved. The various modifications included lowering the radiator, so that, in just about

every respect, an SRT looked exactly like an RT; the only clue that it was a pussycat pretending to be a tiger was the retention of the original registration number. Latterly a few of the earlier, DLU-registered STLs were converted to SRTs, but the intended total of 300 was never reached, production ending at SRT160.

The final 1949 variation on the RT was perfectly satisfactory. The 500 Leylands intended to be RTL1-500 eventually emerged as RTWs, which, like their prewar Titan predecessors (STDs) of 1937, were entirely of Leyland manufacture. The STD was not a bad attempt at copying the contemporary STL, but the resemblance was far from perfect; with the RTW Leyland got it just about spot on. Apart from the extra 6in width it looked 98% like an RTL, inside and out. The earlier examples had the characteristic up-and-down Leyland rainstrip above the rear window, and all had black rubber-mounted route indicators, but otherwise even the most dedicated rivet-counter would have been hard-put to spot the difference. Because of their 8ft width the Metropolitan Police insisted they stay in the suburbs, like London's other eight-footers, the 'SA' and 'Q' class trolleybuses. However, they were most needed on the busiest Central London routes, where their extra width made ingress and egress that much easier. Indeed, several of the suburban routes upon which they were originally employed were just as narrow as any to be found in the City or the West End, but the ways of the Metropolitan Police in public-transport matters were always eccentric and generally backwards-looking. In 1950 it agreed to trials in Central

London, and from then on the RTW became a familiar sight in Oxford Street, around Trafalgar Square and elsewhere in the heart of the capital. However, no 8ft version of the RT was ever produced, and a number of garages had to have structural alterations before they could accommodate the RTWs.

Within the RT class itself two further variations appeared in late 1948. From the outset it was clear that production of the chassis would outstrip that of the bodies by Park Royal and Weymann, and various other builders were approached. After much negotiation, contracts were signed with Cravens of Sheffield and Saunders on the faraway Isle of Anglesey, the latter firm being yet another better known for its aircraft activities. The two took a very different approach to the task. Saunders produced a body (classified RT3/3) which was virtually pure Chiswick down to the tiniest detail; the Cravens version (RT3/4) most certainly wasn't. The first Saunders to appear locally was RT1155, which was delivered to Croydon garage in March. It had a roof-mounted number box and looked exactly like one of the final Park Royal or Weymann roofbox varieties.

The first 27 Cravens-bodied RTs went to the Country Area — the only non-Weymann RTs delivered new in green — and it was May 1949 before the first red examples arrived. These were sent to Nunhead and Elmers End garages and thus brought yet more brand-new buses to the streets of Croydon, on routes 12 and 194. The cab area was standard RT, but the rest was quite different. Perhaps the biggest variation was the five-bay window design. There was no inward taper, making the Cravens RT look rather ungainly from the front, whilst the rear was much more curvaceous than the standard version. Internally the seats and some fittings were standard; others were not. The general opinion of the bus-spotting fraternity was that they were an interesting variation but not as good as the real thing.

The Cravens RTs had fairly short lives with London Transport but were snapped up when they appeared on the second-hand market in the mid-1950s. Thirty were bought by Dundee Corporation to replace trams, the rest mostly going to independents which couldn't believe their luck in getting such beautifully maintained buses at a bargain price. The Saunders RTs were treated as totally standard. No Cravens bodies ever left the RT1402-1521 series, but Saunders bodies were readily exchanged throughout the RT fleet. None ever appeared on an RTL, but for a time the highest-numbered RT (RT4825) had a Saunders body. The very last roofbox RT in passenger service was Saunders-bodied RT1903, which was withdrawn from Battersea garage in March 1971. Examples of both Cravens and Saunders RTs have been preserved. In all there were 300 Saunders and 120 Cravens RTs.

Left: RTWs 164 and 263 pass at Kensington, proving that 8ft-wide buses could operate successfully in the heart of London. *Ian Allan Library*

Below: Close to the Bank of England, RTW47 makes its stately progress through the narrow streets of the City of London. *Alan Cross*

Right: In the postwar years Morden Northern Line station forecourt was a haunt of Daimlers from Sutton and Merton garages, but you could also be sure to see a 'prewar' RT from Putney on the 93, a route which extended deep into Country Area at Dorking, the southwestern extremity of the vast LT empire these pioneer RTs normally reached. RT71 is on a short working to Epsom. *Alan B. Cross*

Below: An official photograph of Weymann-bodied RT3066, taken before the bus entered service in 1949. *MCW*

The year 1949 was the last in which the South London tram network would remain intact, for the final demise of the London tram — or so everyone thought — would begin with the replacement of the Wandsworth and Battersea trams in the autumn of 1950. Work began in 1949 on the rebuilding or replacement of a number of tram depots.

Many consider that the summer of 1939 marked the zenith of London Transport, but an equally strong argument can be made for the final days of 1949. Huge reliance was still placed on the Executive's bus, trolleybus, tram and railway services, by Londoners and those served by the Country Area buses and Green Line in the Home Counties. Much of the ground lost

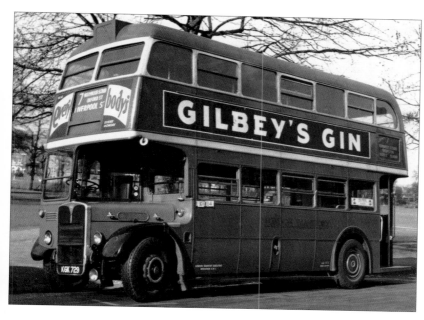

Left: Cravens RT1470 of Middle Row garage, Kensington (X), takes a breather at Acton Vale before heading back to the West End and the City in 1949. *S. L. Poole*

Below: Park Royal-bodied RTL521 at home in Barking garage before setting off on an excursion to Whipsnade Zoo. In the background is a selection of Gs and further RTLs. *D. A. Jones*

between 1939 and 1945 had been made up. The trams, seen by most (but not all) as old-fashioned and time-expired, might still have been with us, but production of the RT, built by AEC (the firm for ever associated with London Transport), and Leyland's RTL and RTW equivalents, would soon sweep them away. These classic double-deckers had already replaced much of the prewar bus fleet and by 1954 would reign supreme. The trolleybus fleet — the world's largest — had been boosted since the war, although its long-term future was already in doubt. Full employment, television and private motoring, which would have such an impact in the coming decade, were considerations for the future.

By the end of 1949 the stock totals of London Transport's enormous fleet of buses and coaches looked like this:

Trams
E1	491
E3	133
HR2	90
ME3	2
Feltham	91
Bluebird	1
TOTAL	**808**

Trolleybuses
A1/A2	10
B1/B2/B3	76
C1/C2/C3	251
D1/D2	152
E1/E2/E3	100
F1	100
H1	147
J1/J2/J3	148
K1/K2/K3	325
L1/L2/L3	172
M1	25
N1/N2	115
P1	25
Q1	77
SA1/SA2/SA3	43
X1/X2/X3/X4/X5/X6/X7	7
TOTAL	**1,773**

Buses
Double-deckers
LT	74
ST	146
STL	2,191
STD	176
B	29
D	281
G	436
RT	1,812
RTC	1
RTL	550
RTW	213
SRT	149

Single-deckers and coaches
T	451
LT	120
Q	231
LTC	24
TF	76
C	74
CR	47
TD	131
TOTAL	**7,212**

GRAND TOTAL 9,793

Of these, the LTC class, used exclusively for private hire, and the CRs were not officially scheduled for regular service. It will be seen that the STL class was still the largest numerically, although would not be for much longer: in 1950 it would be decimated, over a thousand being taken out of service, whilst the RT/RTL/RTW classes would increase by more than 1,500.

Another view of the unique LT1131, this time in rural outer-suburban Kent. The LT class, in its various forms, would serve London Transport throughout the 1940s, the last examples surviving until 1953.
F. G. Reynolds

London Transport

in the 1950s

Above: Two chassisless AEC/MCW 'L3' trolleys, with 1474 leading, head through Islington towards Central London. *Michael Dryhurst*

Left: STL510, nineteen year old but still looking in excellent condition in the red livery introduced in 19 and with full route indicat restored is still on front-lin duty on 22 June 1953, working route 22 through the heart of the City of London and the West End. Behind is RT657, dating fro February 1950 and still wit restricted indicators and cream upper deck window frames. A year later, the la STLs would finish passenge service in the Central Area, followed two months later by those in the Country Area, all displaced by the vast RT family. *Alan B. Cro*

Previous page: An RT and a RTL outside the National Gallery in Trafalgar Square c1951. The RT has almost completed its journey to Ludgate Circus, but the RTL has far to go to the Croydo suburb of Addiscombe. *London Transport*

Introduction

IN one enormously important sense the 1950s was a vast improvement over the previous decade: the War was over. Rationing finally came to an end, although not until 1954, and much of the visual damage caused by World War 2 had, by 1960, disappeared. In its place were TV, teenagers, rock-and-roll and the seeds of that extraordinary decade of the 1960s when youth would become eternal, the world its oyster and peace — except for the minor inconveniences of Vietnam, the Berlin Wall and a thousand other conflicts — would prevail.

For London Transport the decade ended with a good deal less optimism than it had begun. The dependence of almost all Londoners (and their cousins in the inner Home Counties) on public transport, which had been a fixed certainty for 50 years and around which bus, tram, trolleybus and train timetables, plans and predictions could be plotted, had gone.

Electricity — that clean, modern, invisible power source — also fell out of fashion (although this would prove to be a temporary aberration). By the summer of 1952 trams had gone from the streets of London, seemingly for ever, and the only present Santa Claus could offer the trolleybus for Christmas 1959 was a one-way trip to the scrapyard. However on the Underground electricity was in no danger, new designs of rolling stock were appearing, and at the end of the decade work was well in hand for the replacement of steam on the Metropolitan Line beyond Rickmansworth out to Amersham and Chesham. This did not prevent the purchase of a fleet of elderly Swindon-designed pannier tanks from British Railways to work engineering trains.

The 1950s was the decade of the RT and the Routemaster, the two longest-lived types in the history of the British double-deck bus. To this distinguished duo should be added the RF; although the single-decker has always played a secondary role in London, the presence of 700 RFs — enough to constitute a substantial complete fleet in provincial terms — must be

Left: Trams still played a significant role in London when the decade opened. In this suburban scene one of the former Croydon Corporation 'E1'-type cars, No 399, heads away from Thornton Heath town centre on local route 42 along one of the several stretches of interlaced track to be found on Brigstock Road, which connected Thornton Heath station with Thornton Heath Pond, where the depot was situated. *D. A. Thompson*

acknowledged. While they monopolised neither Central Area nor Country Area operations, they took over all Green Line duties save those worked by RTs and became a familiar sight in the outer suburbs and in the countryside beyond.

Production of the RT family (though not its entry into service) ended in 1954, and withdrawal of standard versions began four years later. However, withdrawal would be a protracted affair, spread over 21 years and in a sense still not (and perhaps never to be) completed. The Routemaster, contemporary of Leyland's rear-engined Atlantean, was already considered old-fashioned by some when it went into production in 1958. Yet when the 21st century dawned many hundreds

Below: A pair of ex-Metropolitan Railway veterans, 0-6-2T No L50 and L45 — one of the classic 4-4-0Ts used to haul passenger trains beneath the heart of London — stand outside Neasden shed in October 1958. Just visible inside the shed is L53, a Peckett 0-6-0ST built for the railway in 1897. *H. C. Casserley*

were still at work in Central London, and one could see virtually nothing else, other than taxis and the odd shopper, in Oxford Street.

I hope the impression left with the reader when he reaches the last chapter is not one of regret for a golden past. An historian is bound to have his own agenda, his view coloured by his own experiences, good, bad and indifferent. But he sells his readers short if he does not at the same time try to step back and view his subject with as much objectivity as he can muster. Was there ever a golden past? Perhaps, somewhere, sometime, for somebody. But in general it was not London and its suburbs and countryside in the 1950s. There was much to recommend life in the 1950s, and much that needed changing. We sometimes forget how buttoned-up and repressed society could be, how limited, for instance, career options were for women; there were no women in senior management positions in London Transport. In an era of full employment London Transport actively recruited workers from the Caribbean but only to

jobs which white Englishmen were unwilling to take on, largely because of unsocial hours and/or low pay. They were expected to be grateful and know their place in society. Many landlords felt no shame in stipulating 'no coloureds' in their adverts.

Abroad, Stalin continued his reign of repression and fear until his death in 1953, and surveys regularly showed that most people expected that sooner or later we would be engaged in a nuclear war with Soviet Russia. National Service continued right through the 1950s. CND had huge influence, especially amongst young people, most of whom left school at 15 and went out to work rather than on to college or university. Each Easter the anti-nuclear march from Aldermaston arrived at Trafalgar Square, disrupting bus services, just as did ceremonial occasions each year such as the State Opening of Parliament, although they also created business carrying participants and spectators. Mods and Rockers, mostly resident in the London suburbs, fought each other beside the sea on bank holidays, although just how widespread this was is difficult to judge, for the newspapers, then as now, saw no need for restraint when it came to castigating the sins of feckless youth.

High-rise flats and New Towns were seen as the answer to slum clearance and rebuilding after the devastation of World War 2. The politicians, planners and architects meant well, even if the results were a mixed blessing. London Transport took account of

these changes in society and living habits but by the end of the 1950s found that it had been far too optimistic in providing new buses and routes for a society which was rapidly turning towards the car as its prime means of transport. Living in houses with gardens but no garages, the residents of Crawley and Stevenage parked their Ford Anglias and Morris Minors on both sides of their (not very wide) estate roads, allowing little or no room for a bus — even a small one-man GS — to squeeze between them.

Only a relatively small handful of enthusiasts, regarded with amused unconcern by the decision-makers, campaigned to keep trams and, later, in even smaller numbers, to retain trolleybuses. Some of these

Above: Night-time at Piccadilly Circus. Newly built RT1545, still with wartime reduced destination display and with cream upper-deck window surrounds, heads for Victoria. *Author's collection*

Left: Recently delivered Metro-Cammell-bodied RTL864 at the Sidcup terminus of route 51. It is in all-red livery but still sports the wartime-restricted route indicators. *F. G. Reynolds*

Above: RTL1318, RT2765 and RT473 await the 'off' at Trafalgar Square in March 1955. *Author*

few (but by no means all) made the point that electrically powered street vehicles caused a great deal less pollution than did the motor bus, but this argument carried very little weight 50 years ago.

The visitor's image of London is no doubt dominated by the City and the West End, the famous landmarks — St Paul's, Parliament Square, Regent Street, Tower Bridge and so forth. Yet, paradoxically, the heart of the London Transport network could be said to be not here but in the suburbs. This was where the garages (with the sole exception of Gillingham Street, Victoria) were, where the Underground and Tube depots could be found and where the overhaul, building and repair works — Chiswick, Charlton, Fulwell, Aldenham and Reigate — were situated. The suburbs were where most of the customers lived, and it was through the suburban streets that most bus, tram, trolleybus and Green Line routes ran and behind (or, quite often, above, but relatively seldom under) which the Underground and Tube trains operated.

It has long been fashionable to dismiss the suburbs as dull, dull, dull, a vast, sprawling mass of un-distinguished architecture, row upon row of 'little boxes' inhabited by those who ideally would prefer to live either in a penthouse in the West End or deep in the countryside with roses around the cottage door and a BMW in the half-timbered garage. Certainly, as a teenager and then, from 1958, as an art student, I was almost ashamed to admit I lived in suburbia. How short-sighted, how very wrong.

Only recently my wife Maeve and I took a number 29 to the Nag's Head, Holloway, keeping an unsuccessful lookout for Humph and the team as we passed Mornington Crescent. Even though I scorned suburbia 40 years ago I had enough sense to see the beauty the intricate network of overhead wires at this busiest of trolleybus junctions created, and drew them more than once together with the mix of architecture all around. From the Nag's Head we walked past the beautifully cared-for art-deco Odeon — still a cinema — to Archway, noted the latest Routemaster route, the 390 (well, I did), climbed to the top of Highgate Hill where the 271 — the only former trolleybus route still keeping exactly to its trolleybus termini — ends opposite a very French, very popular restaurant where you are encouraged to sketch on the paper tablecloths, a few hundred yards from the scarcely changed setting for 'Work', Holman Hunt's famous Pre-Raphaelite painting, and gazed between the houses way across London to St Paul's and the Manhattan-like skyline further east before continuing past Highgate Wood to Muswell Hill Broadway. There we sat in the warm sun at a pavement café — can you imagine doing that in the 1950s? — watching the

199

frequent and well-patronised 102s, still based at Palmers Green as they had been in the 1950s, pass by.

Our walk had taken us past a bewildering variety of buildings — scarcely any two identical, even in the row of semi-detacheds opposite Highgate Wood — encompassing early-Victorian London-brick villas, restaurants serving food from the four corners of our planet, mobile-'phone emporia, schools, university departments, blocks of flats (of varying quality, from the dire to real between-the-wars gems) and the smiling, slightly smug but nevertheless endearing perfection of Highgate Village. As we returned to Central London on a well-filled 134 I couldn't help reflecting on the diversity to be found in the capital and on how times have changed since the dawning of the New Elizabethan Age some 50 years ago.

Michael H. C. Baker
April 2004

Above 'H1' and 'L3' trolleybuses head past the Nag's Head, Holloway — the busiest trolleybus junction on London Transport's entire network and thus possibly the busiest in the world. *Author*

Left: A London Transport icon of the 1950s, the bus-overhaul works at Aldenham was converted from an unused Underground depot on the abortive Northern Line extension to Bushey Heath. This official view was recorded in November 1956. *London Transport*

• 1 •

Setting the Scene

THE second half of the 20th century began with several hundred buses from London Transport's predecessor, the LGOC, as well as Thomas Tilling and some of the independents, still at work, although not for long. There were also the trams, all of which, with the possible exception of No 2, predated London Transport. Ten years was generally considered the lifespan of a bus in the 1930s, which meant that even the very latest of the prewar standard STLs would normally have gone by 1950, particularly in view of the minimal maintenance — or, to put it another way,

neglect — they had received during the war. But, of course, the war had reduced production of new buses to a mere trickle, and most of those which did come London Transport's way were non-standard Bristols, Daimlers and Guys. If neither their chassis nor their engines were sophisticated by London standards, their bodies were positively primitive in terms of design, fitting-out and general standard of workmanship, and all would leave London Transport ownership before the last prewar STLs.

The oldest buses in the fleet were the STs and LTs. The former were, like the newest, AEC Regents, albeit the earliest form of this superb Rackham design and petrol-engined. They had LGOC bodies and, with their many-stepped front end with the cab protruding well ahead of the upper deck, looked exactly what they were

Below: RT549, a Weymann-bodied RT3 of 1947 allocated to Chelverton Road garage (AF) in Putney, circumnavigates Eros in Piccadilly Circus alongside a prewar taxi and ahead of RT415, another RT3, *c*1950. *Ian Allan Library*

— a left-over from a bygone age. As in all prewar London buses the driver sat high up in his door-less, instrument-less cab, by turns frozen by icy winds (blowing in not only through where his door should have been but also through the many gaps in the floor) and cooked by the engine thundering away inches from his left knee. Power steering was far in the future. The best that could be said of his lot was that it was better than that of the tram driver, who was even more exposed to the elements and suffered them standing up; indeed, it was only nine years since trams without windscreens had finally quit the streets of London. Neither did half as well as the trolleybus driver, often an ex-tram man, with his seat, door and almost silent vehicle.

Yet in those days the bus driver still had status, as (to a slightly lesser extent) did the conductor, whilst the ornate insignia of the inspector marked him out as a superior, somewhat intimidating personage. The inspector wielded considerable power, over both staff and

passengers; Blakey in the TV comedy series *On the Buses* was not all that far from reality. Uniforms were much more frequently seen than nowadays on the streets of London, and, with World War 2 only five years distant, their wearers were generally afforded respect. This extended even to cinema commissionaires, postmen and milkmen, most of whom were likely to be ex-servicemen. I'm not sure about callow youths doing their National Service, although I always found it easier to get a lift back home on a 48-hour pass wearing my RAF uniform than in 'civvies'. By the 1960s uniforms were more likely to be seen adorning students on their way to a 'hop' or happening, or worn on a record cover by four young gentlemen from Liverpool.

National Service loomed large in the lives of my generation, *i.e.* youths reaching the age of 18 in the 1950s. The reader may wonder what directly this has to do with London Transport. Well, it often postponed career decisions until one was almost 21, and by that age, having been wrenched from home and all that was familiar and thrust into two years of the rough-and-tumble and trauma of serving Her Majesty, quite possibly in some far-flung outpost of the Common-wealth, one was a very different person from what one had been at 18, let alone 16. It also gave my generation a wanderlust, and increasing prosperity allowed us to indulge this. A safe and secure career on the railways, which I had contemplated, or with London Transport and the prospect of steady promotion became just one

Below: Two 'E1s' stand outside New Cross depot on 13 June 1951; the gap in the row of early-Victorian terraced housing is the result of a World War 2 bomb. The leading car is No 562, one of the final batch of 'E1s' built in 1930 and mounted on trucks recovered from Kingsway Subway single-deckers. Construction of such an antiquated design (dating back to early-Edwardian days) as late as 1930 goes a long way towards explaining why the tram was considered such an anachronism. *R. Wiseman*

Right: Looking down Fleet Street towards Ludgate Circus and St Paul's. In the foreground is a Tilling ST seeing out its days on driver-training duties. *Author's collection*

FLEET STREET & ST. PAUL'S CATHEDRAL LONDON.

of many possibilities. And, instead of confining ourselves to seaside holidays in England and days out by London Country bus, we were inclined to go much further afield. Of my three close bus- and train-spotting school friends, one was taught Chinese by the RAF and sent to Hong Kong to listen in to Red China and went on to pursue his gift for languages, a second did finally take up a career with London Transport after graduating from Cambridge, whilst the third turned up at RAF West Malling one breakfast time, having been invalided back with a tropical ailment from Aden, and also pursued a career in transport in a manner of speaking, first as a steward with BOAC and later as a pilot with the Fleet Air Arm.

Although there was very little unemployment and people were generally better-off than they had been in the 1930s, clothes were vastly less stylish than they are today and had to last longer, men's clothes in particular being infinitely less colourful; people also bathed less often, and few showered. In short, it was a dirtier, shabbier world. Thus passengers were less inclined to remark on the careworn condition of the trams and older buses, although they certainly welcomed the pristine, superbly designed interiors of the RT family. Bomb-sites still existed throughout London in their hundreds (if not thousands), and many of the undamaged buildings,

Below: New Cross c1950, and a relic from LCC days, even though the trams have gone, with a couple of RTs and an early-postwar Maidstone & District AEC Regal coach, probably *en route* from the Medway Towns to Victoria. *Author's collection*

particularly in the inner suburbs, hadn't seen a lick of paint for the best part of 20 years. On the positive side, there was less graffiti — the technology ('magic markers', spray cans etc) to produce it hadn't been developed, and what there was usually got washed away during the next shower of rain. Don't imagine, however, that vandalism didn't exist; British Railways was so worried about it that as early as 1950 it banned train-spotters (some of whom were among the culprits) from certain areas and from some stations altogether.

London Transport was beginning to be affected by the number of private cars on the roads, both in terms of congestion and of falling receipts, in a trend which had begun in 1948. Perhaps reflecting the affluence of outer suburbia and beyond, Green Line services were hardest hit, carrying 6.6% fewer passengers in 1950 than in 1949. This decline was not, perhaps, taken too seriously, and possibly no-one quite foresaw the forthcoming enormous increase in car ownership or the effect that television would have on people's travelling habits, particularly in the evenings and at weekends. Until September 1955 there was only one television station, the BBC, serving the country; in that month ITV began to broadcast in London.

Figures for the number of passengers carried during the morning and afternoon rush-hours barely declined, reflecting the tiny percentage of those who motored to and from work, whilst the number of children who were taken to school by car was so small as to be insignificant. The school run in a four-wheel-drive vehicle almost high enough off the rutted, rugged terrain of Purley, Hampstead Garden Village or Thames Ditton for the occupants to see into the upper deck of an Olympian was many decades away. Far more common motive power was the sturdy three-speed BSA or Hercules, with a saddle-bag for the homework and packed lunch and a melodious bell attached to the handlebars — just why are bells considered so 'uncool' by present-day cyclists?

Petrol rationing ended in May 1950. Bus services were not put under threat overnight — sufficient petrol had been allocated for pleasure motoring long enough for a decline in demand to be already noticeable on bus services serving popular country beauty spots and attractions such as Hampton Court, Kew Gardens, Hampstead Heath etc — but from now on the graph of the increase in private motoring began to climb steeply. In 1950 cars represented 48% of total traffic on the roads; 50 years later this had risen to an astonishing 81%. The Statistical Survey noted that buses and coaches nationwide, 'from being the dominant mode' in carrying passengers in 1952, had declined to a mere 6% by the end of the Millennium, although the actual numbers of journeys made had remained roughly the same. The total number of passenger vehicle journeys had risen from 218,000 million in 1952 to 728,000 million by the end of the century.

• 2 •

The Veterans Disappear

FIFTY-THREE of the highly distinctive six-wheel double-deck LTs remained on the payroll on 1 January 1950. Six-wheeled buses had enjoyed a brief popularity in the late 1920s and early 1930s on account of their being allowed a longer wheelbase than four-wheelers and thus able to carry more passengers, but in 1932 changes in Construction & Use Regulations wiped out this advantage. One extraordinary vehicle seated 104. This was an ADC802, with an LGOC body, which entered service in the summer of 1927 and was

Below: One of the impressive six-wheel LTs — a variation with separate number, destination and 'via' displays (not used postwar) — at the end of its career in the summer of 1949. *Alan B. Cross*

used as an AEC works staff transport; as no fare-paying passengers were carried normal Metropolitan Police rules did not apply. A few LSs, seating between 66 and 72 passengers, did enter ordinary service, lasting until 1937; even then, four refused to give up the ghost and were converted into what were probably the most comprehensively equipped (if rather slow) breakdown lorries ever owned by London Transport and lasted in this form until 1951, thereby just entering our period.

New six-wheel buses continued to enter service in different parts of the country until 1939, including 24 petrol-engined LTC touring coaches for London Transport. (It could, however, be argued that any bus which has double rear wheels is really a six-wheeler, but we'll only hurt our brains if we get into this area, so

Right: The Royal Forest Hotel at Chingford, a familiar setting for generations of London buses until the 1960s. Seen here with a wartime Bedford OWB is an ST from Muswell Hill garage. *Author's collection*

Below: Two old London General double-deckers, ST522 and STL20, await their end in a scrapyard. The lower-deck half-drop windows of the STL look ready to drop of their own accord! *Ian Allan Library*

we will just note that London owned far more genuine six-wheelers than the rest of the UK put together.) I, like many other impressionable spotters, was much enamoured of the LT because it looked a lot more impressive than the short-wheelbase ST, which it resembled in many respects. Upton Park, out in the mysterious east, was the final home of the LT, working suburban routes 86A and 40, the latter ensuring that the type was still seen in the City of London at least for a few days in the second half of the century, running as it did between Wanstead, Camberwell Green and Herne Hill. It is not recorded how these final survivors felt about the trams with which they shared the streets of the inner South London suburbs, some of which were 20 and more years older and would outlast them by up to two years.

Although the single-deck variety would go on for another three years the last day in passenger service for

Above: STL2328, one of the classic, standard-roof examples of the class, heads towards the West End on 4 February 1950 on the 25B, one of London's busiest routes. *Alan Cross*

the double-deck LT class was 11 January 1950. Shortly afterwards, on 23 February, the Special Events Fleet, used to provide transport for such events as the Derby, the Wimbledon tennis championships and so forth, was disbanded and so got rid of its LTs, as well as STs and STLs (of which more anon). A handful of LT double-deckers continued for a few weeks as trainers, but even this duty came to an end in March. The very last on London Transport books was LT379, which served as a tilt bus, growing ever more battered, until put out of its misery in October 1950. Virtually all were sold for scrap. The lucky odd man out was LT165. Put into service in January 1931 it served exactly 19 years, being one of the LTs which was still at work from Upton Park on 11 January 1950. Originally fitted with the first type of enclosed-staircase body, it ended its days with a later, more curvaceous variety which had route details in a box which slightly overhung the driver's cab. Selected for preservation in the London Transport collection, it was duly despatched to Reigate garage for storage. One would like to know just why this particular bus was chosen to be the sole survivor of this distinctive class; presumably its condition had something to do with its achieving immortality.

The standard STs ended passenger service very soon after the LTs, on 26 January, when the last four in Country Area service at Northfleet, Watford High Street and St Albans came off the road; Central Area passenger activities had finished the previous day. As always there were exceptions, eight lowbridge STs being

needed until 1953. As with the LTs, practically all the STs went for scrap. However, double the number survived into preservation. The example chosen by London Transport was ST821 — a slightly eccentric choice, being a Country Area bus with a rather smaller front indicator than that fitted as standard to Central Area examples, yet when eventually put on display at the Clapham Museum in the early 1960s it was painted red. As is their wont, a lot of enthusiasts were annoyed by this, and there were suggestions that whoever was responsible should make a one-way journey by river to the Tower of London, entering through Traitor's Gate. Eventually several pots of authentic dark-green paint were discovered, and ST821 now glories correctly attired for working the 301 from Watford High Street, where it lived throughout the 1930s and '40s.

The other surviving ST has an even more remarkable history. Back in 1946/7 six Tilling STs had been converted into mobile canteens, replacing NSs which had fulfilled this vital role throughout the war. These were joined by 13 trailers, powered by nine Bedford lorry-type tractors, built between 1947 and 1949. The last Tilling ST dispensed its final London Transport cup of tea from Stockwell in November 1954; this was 693J, formerly bus ST922. It duly moved on, still dispensing nationalised comestibles but now courtesy of British

Road Services, at Tufnell Park goods station. All good things must come to an end, however, and this vehicle duly made what was expected to be its final journey, to a scrapyard. But then, lo and behold, far into the future a fairy stepfather saw its sad remains and, undeterred by cries of 'impossible!', waved a magic wand consisting of equal parts of dedication, skill, hard graft and quite a lot of money. And so today, thanks to the late Prince Marshall, ST922, complete with outside staircase, petrol engine and mid-1930s livery, can often be seen out and about on excursions from its home at Cobham.

Which brings us to the STL class. Although not yet 12 years old, the first diesel-engined standard example, STL1837, deemed fit neither for rebuilding nor even for patching up, had been withdrawn in January 1949, and throughout the remainder of that year oil-engined STLs replaced petrol-engined LTs and STs in the trainer fleet. However, the great majority (2,191) of what was then still London Transport's largest class remained in stock on 1 January 1950. How different was the picture one year later, by which time more than half — 1,207, to be precise — had gone. Add to this the withdrawal of several tram routes and one trolleybus route, all of which needed replacement motor buses of the RT family, and one thinks: 'Golly [if one is stuck in 1950s-speak], what a lot of new buses must have been needed!' Absolutely — 1,828 in all, comprising 18 SRTs (not *strictly* new buses), 299 RTWs, 455 RTLs and no fewer than 1,056 RTs.

Never matched before or since, 1,828 is a *Guinness Book of Records*-type figure — 'the greatest number of new buses ever put into service in London in a single calendar year' — and, I dare to predict, one unlikely ever to be surpassed. However often I come across this figure it always brings me up with a start. It was more than the entire fleet of Midland Red, Britain's next-biggest bus company, which covered an area from Preston Bissett in Buckinghamshire — just eight miles from the edge of London Transport's Country Area — to the Welsh Border northwest of Shrewsbury, over 150 miles away.

It was around this time I gave up collecting numbers, although this seems to have been less widely documented. Well, if it wasn't a member of the RT family then it was an STL, and most of my 'cops' of the latter type had disappeared anyway, whilst the 'ABCs' couldn't keep up with new deliveries of RTs and RTLs and they had to be handwritten around the edges and it all looked rather a mess.

Below: An Essex scrapyard, with a Tilling STL, LTs and STs in the background and the chassis of STL33 — one of the original 1STL1s — centre stage. Some 24 early STL chassis were used as the basis for a variety of vehicles in the service fleet (two of which are preserved). STL33 was not among them, being withdrawn in November 1948 and broken up two months later. *Author's collection*

• 3 •

New for Old

Left: Tilling STL121 stands at the Bromley terminus of the 119 while driver and conductor take a break before returning to Croydon.
Author's collection

JUST one petrol-engined STL was still in the fleet on 1 January 1950, and this — Tilling STL43 — departed from Bromley garage on 12 January. I was always slightly surprised that Bromley didn't have trams. After all, Croydon — the next county borough to the west and similar in some respects — still had three routes and 20 years earlier had several others, two of them replaced by trolleybuses. Perhaps it was because Bromley has always had a tendency to give itself airs and graces and trams were not considered a particularly upmarket form of public transport. Richmal Crompton, who in her incomparable 'Just William' stories perfectly captured comfortable middle-class life in the first half of the 20th century, lived in the countryside just beyond Bromley and during World War 2 worked in the town in civil defence. The nearest trams got were Downham and Grove Park, which was pretty close. But not close enough, so Bromley's streets remained innocent of any

form of electric traction other than milk floats; it had to make do with electric trains, of which it had lots. Surface ones, that is, for the Underground was even further away than the trams.

Mabel, an elderly cousin of my father's who lived in Bromley, used to recount travelling as a schoolgirl by horse tram to visit her father, who worked for the Crown Agents in Downing Street. Her mind was as clear as yours or mine to the day she died, and she certainly knew the difference between a tram and a bus, whatever its motive power. The nearest horse trams got to Bromley was Rushey Green, Catford, which wasn't very far away. These lasted until 1906, so presumably Cousin Mabel would have taken a horse bus (or perhaps walked this far) and then boarded the tram which would have taken her to the south end of Westminster Bridge, whence it was a short walk to Downing Street.

Being, like Croydon and Catford, an ex-Tilling garage

with lots of elderly petrol-engined STs and STLs, Bromley acquired some of the earliest postwar RTs, and when the Metropolitan Police at first refused to let the 8ft-wide RTWs work through the centre of London, it also got some of those, which it put on the 119, a route which terminated in Croydon. Perhaps it did this as another demonstration of its superiority over its rival! Croydon saw RTWs only at the very end of their London career, when they worked from Brixton on the tram-replacement 109s.

But we are getting ahead of ourselves. At the beginning of 1950 the trams were still with us, although their end was nigh. Three acres of land at Charlton, near the works, were set aside to gather together all the cars as they were withdrawn, and this was where they would be broken up. Not all would come to such an end, however; Leeds, which still saw a future for trams, had agreed to buy the entire surviving 92-strong fleet of 'Felthams', and in September 1949 the first, No 2099, had headed north (joining three 'HR2s' which had been sold before the war) to see how it took to living in Yorkshire. In July 1950 'E1' No 1322 made a very different journey, to the Penhall Road, Charlton, scrapyard, to see how it took to being burned — or, rather, how the nearby residents felt about having red-hot trams as neighbours. A group of trams was stationed on one of the 32 tracks to act as a fire-screen, and this proved satisfactory. The trams on routes 12, 26, 31 and 34, having returned to their depots at Wandsworth, Clapham and Camberwell for the last time on the evening of Saturday 30 September, were duly despatched, the 'E1s' to the scrapyard, and the more modern 'E3s' to other depots, where they mostly replaced other 'E1s', although at Telford Avenue they took over from 'Felthams'; some of the supposedly better 'E1s' — and there were drivers who claimed that a good 'E1' was better than your average 'E3' — also went to Telford Avenue. Whatever the crews might have thought, we mere passengers considered it nothing short of an insult to have foisted upon us such far-from-pristine antiquities after the noble 'Felthams'. These latter also went to Penhall Road, but only as a temporary measure while they were prepared for the long journey up the A1 to Leeds. Ex-LCC tram No 1 accompanied the 'Felthams' to Yorkshire, which may account for its eventual preservation.

Although some 'Felthams' remained, they disappeared virtually overnight from the 16 and 18 routes which passed the top of our road by Thornton Heath Pond, and with them something departed from my life; it was one of those events which brought home to me the understanding that that which had always been might not be there in the future. The 'Felthams' were truly magnificent cars, favourites with crews, management and passengers, way ahead of their time, and even when Leeds scrapped them nine years later they were still up to date and more comfortable than most contemporary buses. Had they managed to survive into the 1990s — fanciful, I know, but look at the longevity of the Routemaster — it would have been a seamless progression into the present generation of smooth-running, articulated single-deck cars plying the streets of Croydon, Manchester, Birmingham and other British cities today.

The Wandsworth tram abandonment also saw the end of a trolleybus route, the 612. This had been created

Right: Shortly before the withdrawal of route 31 in the autumn of 1950 'E3' No 1960 of Wandsworth depot heads for home past Lambeth Palace and one of the most easily recognisably locations on the entire London tram network. The 31 was one of the three routes which worked through Kingsway Subway. No 1960 has come from Islington Green, for the previous 10 years the isolated, most northeasterly extremity reached by London trams, all other routes in the area having been converted to trolleybus operation. *Author's collection*

Below: 'E3' tram No 1921 at the Archway terminus of Kingsway Subway route 35, surrounded by 'H'- and 'J'-type trolleybuses, in 1950. *Author's collection*

back in 1937, when tram route 12 had been cut back from Mitcham Fair Green to Wandsworth, and the intention had been to restore through working in the fullness of time, when all the southside tram routes had been converted to trolleybus operation. Of course, the war intervened, and, although restoration did come about in 1950, it was as motor-bus route 44.

A curious addition to the fleet in 1950 was the RLH. London had always had a need, mostly in the Country Area, for a very small number of lowbridge double-deckers — a need which would disappear in the 1960s with the arrival of high-capacity single-deckers, making the RLH the last of this (for London) peculiar breed. The motley collection of lowbridge buses in service at

Above: Early days in the scrapping programme at Penhall Road, Charlton. Despite their extensive refurbishment in the 1930s the 'E1Rs' lasted no longer than those members of the class which remained largely unaltered. Rebuilt and unrebuilt 'E1s' stand in the foreground awaiting their fate, while stretching into the distance is a long line of 'Felthams' ready to head north to Leeds. *Ian Allan Library*

Below: A 'Feltham' on the long, straight 16/18 road stands all alone at the traffic lights at Coombe Road, South Croydon, on the last leg of its journey from the heart of London to the (almost) countryside of Purley. *D. A. Thompson*

Above: A somewhat woebegone-looking Country Area ST1101 with square-edged cab, seen shortly before withdrawal at the Watford terminus of route 346. This was one of 48 AEC Regents bodied by Ransomes, Sims & Jeffries of Ipswich; it had been delivered to East Surrey, a subsidiary of London General, in 1930. *Author's collection*

Below: Lowbridge STL2292 of Addlestone garage basks in the summer sun at the Staines terminus of the 436 on 3 June 1950. The bus comprised a wartime body fitted to an earlier chassis, and although it looks very much like a lowbridge version of the standard Chiswick product austerity conditions meant that internally it was not up to usual London Transport standards. *Alan Cross*

Above: STL1127 in the far southeastern reaches of the Country Area at Sevenoaks bus station, which London Transport shared with Maidstone & District. *Author's collection*

Below: Red RTL1090, borrowed from the Central Area, waits at the Bromley terminus of the 410 before setting off on a short working to Biggin Hill and Westerham. Behind is a lowbridge STL which will be able to make the entire journey, beneath the low bridge at Oxted, through to Reigate. *D. A. Jones*

the beginning of 1950 consisted of eight STs, 12 'Godstone' STLs (buses dating from 1934, fitted with more-or-less standard provincial forward-entrance Weymann bodies and based at Godstone garage for the 410 route), 20 prewar STLs, with bodies built to wartime specification in 1942/3, and 10 wartime Daimlers of the D class.

The fact that there had been a 'standard' lowbridge version of the STL — or at any rate one that looked from the outside like an STL, even if it was not up to usual Chiswick standards internally — led to the assumption that there would be a lowbridge RT. One was indeed on the drawing-board, but it so happened that Midland General, recently taken into the British Transport Commission fold, to which the London Transport Executive also belonged, had already on order 20 lowbridge Regent IIIs which it did not now require. London was offered them and decided to accept, presumably because the chassis was similar to that of the RT. Visually there was no resemblance at all, for the

Above: Newly delivered RLH1 speeds past an advert for one of Humphrey Bogart's most celebrated films on its way to the Chesham terminus of the 336. In the distance is one of the postwar STLs. *Author's collection*

Left: The very un-London-like upper deck (apart from the upholstery) of an RLH. The single-skin roof and sliding-vent windows contribute to its provincial appearance. *Author*

Above: D5, a lowbridge Daimler, painted in all-red livery and shortly before replacement by an RLH, at Morden. *F. G. Reynolds*

Below: A red Central Area RLH, originally green, stands at a wet Stratford Broadway on route 178. *Author*

radiator was much higher and the body of standard Weymann design — a less handsome version of that fitted to the postwar STLs mentioned above. Like them the first 20 RLHs were painted green and allocated to the Country Area. With their sliding-vent windows, one-piece front destination display (and none at all at the back), provincial-type seats and quite different décor they could certainly not be described as a lowbridge version of the RT. However, they adequately fulfilled the role for which they were purchased, and in 1952 a further 56 (with MXX registrations, the first 20 being KYYs) were bought. The final 24 were painted red for Central Area use, and by the end of 1952 all the remaining ST-, STL- and D-class lowbridge buses had

been withdrawn. None survived into preservation. By the end of the 1950s there was scarcely sufficient work for the class, despite the creation in 1959 of a new RLH route, the 178, which was worked by Dalston garage and replaced the single-deck 208A (and which was destined ultimately to be the last route on which the class operated).

• 4 •

How Stands the Underground?

TO a Thornton Heath resident like myself Tube and Underground trains were very much associated with Central London, but this view would not be shared by those living on the north bank of the Thames. One has only to look at a map to be struck by the relative absence of below-the-surface railways south of the Thames, as compared with north, west and east. A variety of historical reasons have brought this about, not least the rapid expansion of a tightly knit and extensive network of surface railway lines in Victorian times by the London & South Western, London, Brighton & South Coast, South Eastern and London, Chatham & Dover companies. Morden, southern terminus of the Northern Line, was the nearest the Tube got to home, and I would cycle over there — more, I confess, to sample the variety of buses (chiefly wartime and early-postwar Daimlers) than the trains themselves. This was not quite the end of the line, for the rails

extended under the road and emerged, dazzled, beneath sparkling suburban skies at the end of the longest tunnel on the Underground and Tube network, to fan out into a large depot. Well, even on a grey November or February day Morden could seem pretty sparkling after 17 miles and 528 yards without daylight; indeed, for many years this was the longest railway tunnel in the world.

There had been plans to extend even further south, to the vast LCC housing estates at Rose Hill and St Helier and on to Sutton, but in the event the Southern Railway, in agreement with the Underground, occupied this territory with its line from Wimbledon by way of Wimbledon Chase, South Merton, Morden South (within sight of the Tube depot), St Helier, Sutton Common and West Sutton, which opened in 1930. This makes it just about the newest surface suburban line in the London area. It is known locally as the Wall of Death, but don't get too excited by this title. One doesn't wish to be uncharitable to what I'm sure is a railway line beloved of its regular passengers, but I have to say I've never found a ride around its bends and twists particularly thrilling, passing as it does through deepest suburbia, and certainly it bears little resemblance to the

Below: Class F5 former Great Eastern Railway 2-4-2T No 67200 propels the 10.16 Epping–Ongar near North Weald, 3 August 1953. British Railways would shortly hand over working to Central Line Tube trains. *Brian Morrison*

only 'wall of death' performance I've ever seen. (This was at the back of Kennard's store in Croydon, where I watched spellbound after school one day in 1950 as a leather-clad daredevil raced a very noisy motorbike of mid-1930s vintage round and round his creaking, shuddering wooden drum, rising nearer and nearer the top until I wondered whether he might not shoot over the edge and scatter the stalls of cabbages, apples and oranges, plus stallholders and customers, all over Surrey Street below!)

The Northern Line may never have achieved its territorial ambitions, but elsewhere the Tube continued its extension once World War 2 was over, and between 1946 and 1949 the Central Line reached eastwards to Stratford, Leytonstone, Newbury Park, Hainault, Woodford, Loughton and finally Epping, much of this being over former LNER tracks. As in the 1930s some highly adventurous architectural ideas, inspired by the Bauhaus movement in Germany and by the best transatlantic practices, went into the design of the new stations. After the excitement of the immediate postwar years, typified by the Festival of Britain (at which Thomas Bilbow, London Transport's architect, won an award and at which we will shortly take a look), things went into a decline. Too many British architects — and those who commissioned architecture — seemed to lose

Above: Pre-1938 Central Line train bound for Epping. The driver is about to put the rear red oil lamp in place — an archaic touch. *Ian Allan Library*

Below: A Northern Line train of 1938 stock emerges from the tunnel at Hendon Central, bound for Central London and Kennington. *London Transport*

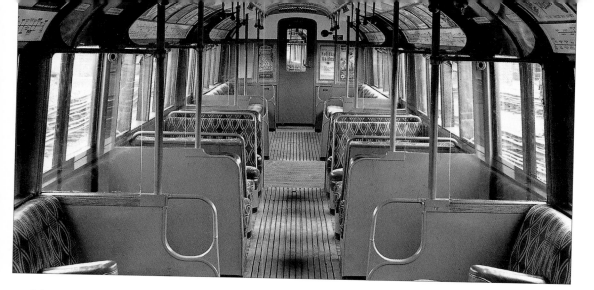

confidence, resulting in the dull timidities and *pastiches* of the subsequent decades, revival coming only towards the end of the 1980s and in the 1990s, London Transport once again leading the way with the inspired design of stations on the Jubilee Line Extension.

Westwards on the Central Line co-operation with the LNER and the GWR meant that the main-line companies had completed much of a planned extension of the Tube from North Acton by 1939 but had then had to take up the rails for emergency use elsewhere. Work started on re-laying and completion once the war was over, and Tube trains to Greenford commenced in June 1947, running alongside the GWR's expresses to Birmingham, Shrewsbury and Birkenhead and the LNER's to Sheffield and Manchester. A year and five months later the Central Line reached West Ruislip, and there were plans to carry on through the Chilterns deep into the stockbroker belt

Above: Interior of a 1938-stock trailer car. *London Transport*

Below: A Watford–Elephant & Castle Bakerloo Line train of 1938 stock at Carpenters Park, with a BR London Midland Region Watford Junction–Euston EMU alongside. *C. R. L. Coles*

to Denham, but restrictions on building meant that sufficient traffic never materialised to make this viable. Similarly the extension of the Northern Line from Edgware to Bushey Heath was halted in September 1949, even though extensive civil-engineering works had already been carried out. Among this work was a depot at Aldenham, out in the Hertfordshire countryside, which would presumably not now be needed. However, London Transport's main bus works at Chiswick had more work on its hands than it could possibly cope with, and vacant Aldenham presented an opportunity to transfer bus overhauls there, so between

Right: The driver resets the trip-cock on his 1938 Bakerloo Line set at Hatch End on 7 October 1957. *G. M. Kichenside*

Below: A Metropolitan Line train of elegant Metadyne stock at Harrow, bound for Baker Street. *G. M. Kichenside*

1952 and 1956 this was transformed into what was arguably the most up-to-date such facility in the world.

Work on improving the design of both Underground — District, Metropolitan and Circle lines — and Tube trains never ceases, and throughout the 1950s renewal of the trains continued. At the beginning of the decade the most up-to-date trains on the Tube, the 1938 stock, numbered no fewer than 1,121 cars. To these were added carriages converted after the war from a group of experimental trains introduced in 1935. A further 91 cars were built in the late 1940s, known as 1949 stock but, be warned, a date does not always mean this was when the carriages entered service, for they might not appear until several years later.

This huge group of vehicles was of a classic design. To be found on the Northern, Bakerloo and Piccadilly lines, they were the first to have a completely flat floor and flush roof contours, features permitted by advances in motors and electrical equipment. Originally the window frames were painted cream, but by 1950 all-over red had become standard. With flush-fitting windows and simple, uncluttered lines these trains were blessed with arguably the perfect shape for a train to operate within the narrow confines of London's Tube network.

Presaging the superb lines of the 1938 Tube trains was the Metadyne stock of 1937, designed for use on the District and the Metropolitan lines. Rather more stylised, with flared-out sides and glass vanes above the main windows (a form of top-light), 365 carriages of this design, also known as the 'O' and 'P' stock, were built between 1937 and 1940. After the war 143 very similar-looking cars of 'R47' stock were put into service,

although (and I did warn you) not until 1949. Another variation was the 'Q38' stock: although virtually identical in appearance to the 'O' and 'P' stock, this had rather different electrical equipment and couplers, on account of being designed for District Line service and thus intended to work with older vehicles; there were 25 driving motor cars and 183 trailers.

Next came the 'R49' stock. These 84 carriages were also built along the classic lines of the original 1937 stock, but once again there were differences, chief amongst which was that the bodies were constructed of aluminium. This would herald one of the biggest visual changes in either Underground or Tube trains for many years: 'R49' NDM (non-driving motor car) No 23567 entered service in May 1952 bereft of paint, and eight months later a complete train of eight unpainted 'R49'

vehicles took up work. Shock, horror! Weren't London Transport trains (and buses, trams and trolleybuses) supposed to be red? Very well, District Line compartment stock was brown, but such trains were really more like main-line stoppers than real Underground ones and didn't really count. The experiment was considered so successful that in 1956 a red 'R'-stock car was repainted aluminium to match the unpainted cars, to be followed by four more in 1957. In the following decade the decision would be taken to repaint all the 'R' stock from red, and subsequent new deliveries would all be aluminium. Personally I never liked this livery, and in the 1990s some degree of red was reintroduced, being generally welcomed.

We'll look at developments deep down in the Tube in a later chapter, so don't go away.

Above: A Hammersmith-bound Metropolitan Line train departs Paddington as 'Britannia' Pacific No 70024 *Morning Star* arrives with the up 'Red Dragon' from South Wales, 20 March 1958. *Author*

Right: An eight-car rake of 'R' stock at the District Line's Upminster depot, all in unpainted aluminium save for the leading car, which is an 'R38/3' painted to match (almost) the others. *London Transport*

• 5 •

Time to Rejoice!

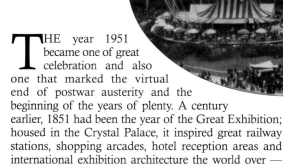

THE year 1951 became one of great celebration and also one that marked the virtual end of postwar austerity and the beginning of the years of plenty. A century earlier, 1851 had been the year of the Great Exhibition; housed in the Crystal Palace, it inspired great railway stations, shopping arcades, hotel reception areas and international exhibition architecture the world over — as well as giving its name to a GREAT football team.

As World War 2 was drawing to an end thoughts turned to a commemoration of the Great Exhibition. But it would be much more than a look back; it would look forward to a brave new, peaceful world where science and the arts would contribute to a better life for all.

At the inaugural meeting of the Council of the Festival in May 1948 none other than Princess Elizabeth (as she then was) stated that: 'The 1851 Exhibition laid special emphasis on promoting the arts and sciences . . . and it should be our object to do the same in 1951 . . . then the Festival may prove to be not simply an end in itself but a beginning of many good things.'

As with all such events a great many people were involved in the Festival's organisation, but perhaps its driving force was Herbert Morrison. A prominent London

Labour politician (the prototype for Ken Living-stone, if you will) for most of the century, he became Deputy Prime Minister under Clement Attlee.

Max Nicholson, who worked with Morrison on the Festival, looking back at the end of the century, remembered: 'Above all because Herbert Morrison was in it, he wanted the British people to have fun. He wanted it to be a fun thing, which made it unique I think among all the great exhibitions. He wanted the people to participate in it, he didn't want it to be a "them and us" affair.'

And fun it was. And although Morrison 'wanted the teaching side of it, which was about science and so on, to be played down', that too was fun. Science was not my thing. Yet despite much of the contents of the Dome of Discovery (in which the science exhibits were displayed) being beyond my understanding, they were presented in such a way — bathed in a mysterious green light — that the future was made to seem an exciting world where anything was possible and of which one wanted to be a part.

Now what does all this have to do with London Transport? A good deal. The main site was on the South Bank of the Thames, between Waterloo Bridge and County Hall. In its six-month duration the exhibition hosted 8,455,863 visitors, and nearly every one of them arrived by public transport. In addition 8,031,000 went to the Festival Pleasure Gardens at Battersea, and they too used buses, trams, trains — and river boats. This is not the place to discuss why the Festival of Britain was such a success and why the Millennium Dome exhibition was not, although the majority view of those who actually visited the latter, rather than having the media form their

222

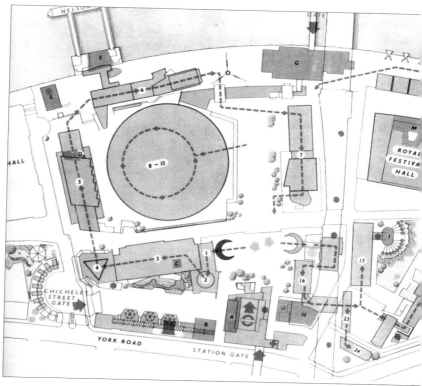

Upper left: An event which more than any other signified that the days of austerity and rationing following World War 2 were coming to an end was the 1951 Festival of Britain. This is the view looking west past the Festival Hall (right) and over the Waterloo East–Charing Cross railway line towards the Dome of Discovery. *Deane Clark*

Lower left: London Transport played a full part in the Festival celebrations based on the South Bank and in Battersea Park and as usual produced much excellently designed publicity material, of which this visitor's map is an example. *Author's collection*

Right: Plan of the South Bank site of the Festival of Britain. *Author's collection*

Lower right: A London Transport advertisement from the official guide to the Festival of Britain. *Author's collection*

opinion, felt that it was more good than bad. Like the 1951 exhibition it was imaginatively sited on the South Bank of the Thames, its main building was much admired and a committee of largely gifted and intelligent people planned it. It too was a compromise between fun and instruction. And both featured RT1702!

London Transport had a prouder design record, probably, than almost any other large transport undertaking worldwide, and in a paper read at the Festival to the International Design Congress, its Chairman, Lord Latham, paid tribute to Lord Ashfield and Frank Pick, the former giving 'the fullest freedom to the genius of [the latter] . . . who had the vision and courage to plan for the future'. He ended with these brave words: 'There will be times when one of our new designs for a station or a vehicle will surprise you, and perhaps one of our new posters will shock you. We do not mind. We are never so happy as when fifty people write to us in angry criticism, because by the same mail we always find at least fifty others who write to us in generous praise. You can only be in tune with contemporary tastes, bold in venturing into new modes of expression, and never shy of experiment.'

Transport was one of the themes of the South Bank exhibition. One of British Railways' contributions was new 'Britannia' Pacific *William Shakespeare*, and amongst the road exhibits was a Southdown Leyland Titan. On 11 May 1951 four RTs which had toured

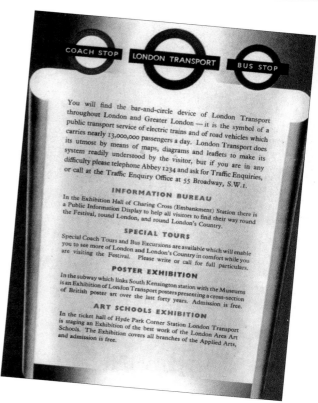

Above: Seven of the London Transport employees who took
RT1702 (now preserved) and three others on a 4,000-mile
tour of Western Europe in the summer of 1950 to publicise
the Festival of Britain. *Ian Allan Library*

Right: 'Sit up and beg' STL462 outside the South Bank site of the Festival of Britain prior to setting off on service C for the Festival Gardens at Battersea Park. *Author's collection*

Europe the previous year to publicise the great event, Nos 1692, 1702, 3070 and 3114, inaugurated the Circular Tour of London. For 2s 6d (12½p) you could take part in what nowadays is almost *de rigueur* for tourists but then was a real innovation — a tour of the sights of the City and the West End in a double-decker, with the conductor using a public-address system. Some 49 years later the by then preserved RT1702 became an exhibit in the Millennium Dome.

The 'Round the Town for Half a Crown' was one of nine services, lettered A to J, introduced for the Festival. 'A' ran from South Kensington to Battersea Park Gardens, 'B' from Sloane Square Underground station to the Gardens, 'C' linked the Gardens with the South Bank site, 'D' connected with a river-bus service, 'E' ran from Victoria Coach Station and the Green Line stops at Eccleston Bridge to the South Bank, 'F' from a special Festival coach park on Clapham Common to the Festival Gardens, whilst 'G' and 'H' were what we would now call park-and-ride services, the former linking the South Bank exhibition with various nearby car parks, the latter serving the same purpose for the Festival Gardens. 'J' was the circular tour itself. It is significant that services 'G' and 'H' generated practically no business at all and were quickly abandoned — a sure sign that very few people were in a position (or cared) to travel by private car to the Festival.

All these services, other than the tour of London, were worked by STLs (183 in all), based at a number of garages. One might have thought that new RTs would have been put on these prestigious services, if only to impress country cousins and foreign tourists unused to exotic double-deckers, but presumably they could not be spared. All the STLs had been recently overhauled and were therefore in pretty good condition, and as the duties were not particularly onerous they were considered suitable. No-one knew quite how well the Festival services would be patronised; in fact London Transport had rather overestimated their popularity, and a number of the STLs were used to operate short journeys on various Central London routes, whilst

others were sent elsewhere, notably to the Far East (Barking and Upton Park, not Hong Kong) to hasten the demise of the wartime Guys.

Despite abandonment being well underway, trams played their part in getting visitors to and from the Festival. Until it finished on 10 July one could travel by route 68 to its terminus at Waterloo, within a few hundred yards of the South Bank, whilst Westminster Bridge and the Embankment continued to be strongholds of the remaining routes right through 1951. For several months in 1950 a new section of track — a siding into Addington Street, beside County Hall — had been under construction in connection with roadworks for the Festival. It was claimed, no doubt correctly, that this was the last piece of new conduit track built anywhere in the world. London swans, especially, regretted the abandonment of the conduit system. We know this because on 21 December 1951 the *Middlesex Chronicle* recorded that a swan, 'flying over London Road, Isleworth, on Sunday, fouled the trolleybus wires near the fire station and fell to the ground, badly shocked. Fireman H. A. Peckham carried the bird into

Left: Tram No 1, which the LCC had hoped would be the precursor of a fleet of up-to-date cars, swings round off Blackfriars Bridge and heads along the Embankment on a short working of route 18. *Author's collection*

Below: The Embankment seen from Charing Cross Bridge. Heading east are two 'E3' trams, while approaching in the distance is an RTL on a tram-replacement service. For the first time buses were allowed on what had been reserved tram track; other road vehicles, including a well-loaded ERF and an elderly Ford truck of similar vintage to the 'E3s', keep well clear. *Ian Allan Library*

the fire station and gave it first aid.' An RSPCA inspector was called, examined the bird and, declaring it recovered, put it in his car, drove down to the river and released it. One would have liked to be told just how the inspector enticed the swan into his car — did it sit on the back seat while the inspector discussed the state of the economy, the lack of tune in modern music and the ever declining moral standards of present-day youth/cygnets?

The South Bank site closed on 30 September 1951 and the Festival Gardens five weeks later. These latter would reopen the following Spring and continue to attract the crowds throughout the 1950s, but the Festival itself was over, the only permanent building on the site being the Festival Hall. Of the visitors 36.5% had come from London, 56% from outside the capital, and 7.5% from abroad, 15% of these bringing precious US dollars

· 6 ·

Trams No More

THERE were four stages of tram abandonment in 1951. In the depths of winter, on the night of 6/7 January, Clapham depot closed to trams entirely and Telford Avenue partially. Routes 2, 4, 6, 8, 0, 20, 22, 24 were replaced by motor buses — RTs and TLs — working routes 60, 57, 57A, 95, 104, 155B/W, 89, 189A and 287. The B and W suffixes indicated whether the bus was going by way of Blackfriars Bridge or Westminster Bridge; in tram days separate route numbers had been used, and the suffixes served only to confuse and were soon abolished. No more trams clattered over the crossings at Tooting Broadway, leaving the 630 trolleybuses as the only representatives of electrically powered public transport there. The Tooting route had been the very first to be electrified by the CC, in 1903. Although a few 'Felthams' lingered on

from Telford Avenue on the 16 and 18, most were replaced by run-down 'E1s' — a very bad exchange.

The 'E1s' were put out of their misery three months later, on 7 April, when the 16, 18 and 42 routes were all abandoned. This meant the southernmost extremity of the London tram network, Purley, was gone, and with it the long, straight run through Croydon and down the Brighton Road along which one could enjoy an exhilarating sprint in a 'Feltham', if the driver was so minded, easily outpacing any competing STs, LTs, STLs and even RTs. Thornton Heath depot had already been razed and replaced by a new bus garage, and the trams had spent their last months in the old depot at Purley, which, for most of the time I had known it, had been used to store unwanted cars, including some of the last un-vestibuled ones, which were not scrapped until

Left: 'Feltham' No 2134 emerging from its home at Telford Avenue depot. The overhead was used within the depot, but outside current was applied by way of the conduit; the gentleman on the left is about to fork a plough underneath the tram. A neat line of ploughs can be seen on the right of the picture. *Author's collection*

Above: RT816 of Croydon garage squeezes alongside 'E1' tram No 1596 at Streatham. *Author's collection*

Below: Thornton Heath Pond. A newly overhauled 'Feltham' waits outside the soon-to-be-demolished erstwhile head office of Croydon Corporation Tramways as an 'E3' (right) turns off the main road into ... no, not the 'Timber Building Material Depot' but the tram depot next door.

The hut alongside the upmarket saloon — is it a Bentley? — and the 'Feltham' is home to the inspector who works the point lever for trams turning towards the camera (and Thornton Heath High Street) on route 42. This was a postwar luxury; before 1946 point operators had to brave whatever the weather threw at them, just as until 1940 many tram drivers had to do without windscreens. *Author's collection*

sometime after 1945. Purley depot eventually passed to Schweppes, which kept its fleet of Bedford delivery lorries there, parked over the tracks, although, not surprisingly, the inspection pits had been filled in. Later in the 1950s I had a holiday job a few doors down the road as a builder's labourer, clearing out and repainting the gutters on the Red Deer pub; having absolutely no head for heights, I would stand trembling atop a ladder, eyes closed and arms outstretched, feeling along the gutter, as RTs on tram-replacement route 109 thundered past beneath me.

As with most abandonments, there was much ceremony, and Croydon & Purley Chamber of Commerce decorated the last tram. Passengers were charged 5s (25p), and the money went to the Infantile Paralysis Fellowship, a further £22 being collected along the route. Two horses were 'harnessed' to the tram at South End and 'pulled' it through the centre of Croydon — a reminder that the original trams were thus powered. The ceremonial last tram really ought to have been one of the ex-Corporation 'E1s' but was actually rehabilitated 'E1' No 839. Although the rehabilitated cars (two of which *were* ex-Croydon) were supposed to be a great improvement internally on their unrebuilt brethren, I could never see it myself. Readers can prove me wrong by comparing the original 'E1' at Covent Garden with the wonderfully restored 'E1R' at Crich, which, of course, one can also ride on.

As the *Croydon Times* commented, it was an evening of mixed emotions. 'The crowds cheered and waved — older people as a grateful gesture for over 70 years of unflagging and unfailing service, younger people to herald another spoke in the wheel of progress.' One who was definitely of the former persuasion was Edwin Lilley of South Norwood, a winner at the 1948 Model Engineer Exhibition, who was pictured with two of his

'five detailed model trams on the miniature track he has built in the garden of his house'. The article goes on to reveal that the 'seats are reversible, the doors slide open and shut, the platform even lets down, and each tram has hanging straps for standing passengers. They are fitted with electric light, but the bulbs work loose as the trams jolt about on the track and provide a recurring problem for Mr. Lilley.' I wonder what happened to these splendid models? There is a fine model of an ex-Croydon Corporation tram in the town museum; could this be from Mr Lilley's collection?

The third tram abandonment of 1951 was relatively low-key, involving just two routes — the aforementioned 68 and the 70. The latter terminated at Tooley Street, by London Bridge. Both served Greenwich. Even today, such is the atmosphere in streets around Greenwich that one would not be totally surprised to hear the sound of an 'E1' clanking away in the Deptford direction.

Finally (as far as 1951 was concerned), on the night of

6/7 October, Camberwell depot closed, and its 99 trams, working routes 36, 58, 60, 62, 66 and 84, were replaced by 109 buses. Camberwell was always associated with the 'HR2' class, designed to scale the heights of Dulwich and elsewhere, hence the designation ('Hilly Route'). Being relatively modern vehicles, many of these moved on rather than being scrapped, and yet more 'E1s' went to the Penhall yard, from which there was no escape — unless one was a 'Feltham'. The bodies of the 'HR2s' were identical to those of the 'E3s', with which they were contemporary, and, although no 'E3' has survived, 'HR2' No 1858 was bought by a Mr P. J. Davis. For a time it stood at the entrance to Chessington Zoo but nowadays resides at the East Anglia Transport Museum at Carlton Colville, near Lowestoft. So also do several London trolleybuses, such that it is possible to travel on a London tram, alight, change to a trolleybus and then reverse the process as often as one likes as long as the museum stays open — Heaven indeed, and considerable is our debt to the dedicated preservationists who have made this possible.

At the start of 1952 there were still 13 daytime tram services operating. But not for long. On the night of 5 January day routes 48, 52, 54, 74 and 78 and all-night route 5 ceased, Norwood depot losing 21 trams, New Cross 88. The 54 was the last surviving service to Victoria, deep in the West End, the last journey being worked by 'E3' No 1920; from 6 January buses and coaches would have a monopoly there. William Gould, who had been in charge of the first tram across Vauxhall Bridge to Victoria in 1907, stood beside driver H. Mayo as he took No 1920 away from the boarding platform by the Victoria Palace. A year or so late

Right: A southbound 'E3', No 1908, at Holborn station, deep inside the Kingsway Subway. *Ian Allan Library*

Below right: Two young ladies descend into Holborn tramway station. *Ian Allan Library*

I watched the Crazy Gang perform the play scene from *Midsummer Night's Dream* there (the Victoria Palace, not the tram terminus) — straight, Bottom, Titania and all — and prove once and for all that Shakespeare can reduce a modern audience to helpless laughter.

All my home-town trams — the ex-Croydon Corporation 'E1s' — had now been withdrawn, as had many more ex-LCC 'E1s'. 'E1' No 1025 must have been greatly surprised to find itself turning not into the scrapyard at Penhall Road, but into Charlton Works, whence it would be transported to Reigate garage as the official survivor of this most numerous and long-lived of London tram classes. It would be a long time before it went on public display, but today it resides at Covent Garden.

In March I took what would be my last ride for several decades on a London tram. Journeys to school and elsewhere in Thornton Heath and Croydon were now all by bus, or occasionally trolleybus, but one March day when visiting Central London on a train-spotting expedition I found myself walking along the Embankment and watching the 33s and 35s entering Kingsway Subway beneath Waterloo Bridge. And so I made my one and only journey through the famous tunnel. A few days later, on 4 April, it closed. With the end of the 33 and the 35 routes trams had gone from North London and the last North London tram depot, Holloway, was given over entirely to trolleybuses, 127 of them, to be precise, making it the largest trolleybus depot in town.

The Kingsway Subway represented one of the very few attempts in London to give trams an advantage over other traffic by keeping it out of their way. Years later the southern half was converted for the one-way use of

Right: 'E3' No 2001, displaying 'LAST TRAM WEEK' poster, at the Woolwich changeover pit for route 40.
Author's collection

Below: Nine London mayors (none of them called Ken Livingstone) wave to the crowds from 'E3' No 1952 outside New Cross Gate depot to mark the end of the first generation of London's trams on the night of 5/6 July 1952.
Ian Allan Library

Right: Snowbroom 022 and an 'HR2' car at Penhall Road scrapyard. Converted from an LCC 'B'-class passenger car, the snowbroom survived the end of London trams; meticulously restored to its original condition as an open-top LCC double-decker, it can regularly be sampled at the National Tramway Museum at Crich in Derbyshire.
R. Hubble

motor vehicles, but no bus or trolleybus, an abortive experiment aside, ever operated through it. The northern half of the tunnel has served all sorts of purposes, some of them (so it is alleged) secret and mysterious. Most poignant of all, the double track leading up the slope out of the subway into Bloomsbury still exists, set into cobbles behind the locked iron gates.

The final tram abandonment came on Saturday 5 July. For seven days previously trams had carried the 'Last Tram Week' poster, and many regulars, visitors and enthusiasts came to pay their respects. There was much affection for the trams but probably a greater hope that with their demise traffic would flow much more easily and London streets would become safer. The final routes were the 36, 38, 40, 44, 46 and 72 (which terminated at Southwark Bridge) making a circuit of the Embankment, which for my generation will always be associated with the tram. Much film, still and cine, was exposed, the best known of the latter being the British Transport Commission's *The Elephant Will Never Forget*, which contains a rather charming sequence of a sprightly elderly couple making their last journey on the upper deck of an 'E3'. It plays every day at the Covent Garden museum.

Huge crowds gathered as dusk fell, and in the early hours of 6 July Lord Latham, Chairman of the London Transport Executive, made a speech at New Cross depot as his deputy drove the official last tram, 'E3' No 1951, in off the street. No fewer than nine mayors were present, alcohol was consumed, fireworks were ignited, songs sung, car horns hooted, souvenirs removed, and finally, sometime after 3am, the last batch of cars, with 'E3' No 1931 at the rear, entered Penhall Road scrapyard.

It took a long time to dispose of the sad ranks of the condemned lined up at Penhall Road, the last to be burned being 'E3' No 179 on 29 January 1953. It took

even longer for the last vestiges to disappear from the streets of London. Traffic was disrupted for years whilst the rails were removed, although some were simply covered by tarmac and gradually, like the ribs of abandoned hulks at low tide on the Thames marshes, re-emerged. As late as the 1980s they could be seen in Beresford Square, Woolwich, and in the forecourts of surviving depots such as Fulwell and Brixton Hill. What to do with the tracks inevitably caused controversy. A correspondent to the *Croydon Advertiser* berated the local council for temporarily filling in the tracks within the borough, at a cost of £7,000, which would inevitably be followed 'at some unspecified date by the removal of the tracks at a further cost of £180,000'. Another correspondent claimed that 'it's a pretty safe bet that none of the money will be recoverable from the L.T.E.' — a prediction which would prove basically correct.

Of the trams themselves, a few precious examples remain. Static exhibits include West Ham Corporation four-wheeler No 290, the aforementioned 'E1' No 1025 and MET 'Feltham' No 355 in the official London Transport collection at Covent Garden. LCC No 1, intended precursor of a fleet which never materialised, is on display but not yet operational at that wonderful museum up on the Pennine heights at Crich, whilst another 'Feltham', No 2055, lives across the Atlantic at the Seashore Trolley Museum in Maine, USA; this too is not operational. Of those one can ride on, 'HR2' No 1858 lives with several London trolleybuses and at least one RT in a rather extraordinary London enclave at Carlton Colville, where one can catch a whiff of the ozone blowing off the North Sea a couple of miles away. Even further away, at the National Tram Museum at Crich, are No 106, an LCC four-wheeler dating from 1903 (and the oldest survivor), and 'E1' No 1622, restored as rehabilitated in the mid-1930s. Both have

Above: A wonderful re-creation of the way London used to be, in the unlikely setting of Carlton Colville in Suffolk in September 2002, commemorating the 50th anniversary of the end of London's trams (first time around): 'HR2' No 1858, an Austin taxi and AEC/MCW 'C2' trolleybus No 260, with all-Leyland 'K2' trolley No 1201 behind. *Author*

Left: The astonishingly authentic restoration of rehabilitated 'E1' No 1622 at the National Tramway Museum at Crich in Derbyshire. *Author*

needed a vast amount of work spent on conversion and restoration to make them as wonderfully authentic as they are. Also at Crich is experimental central-entrance 'Feltham' No 331, quite the finest of them all.

The trams were replaced by a huge fleet of RTs and RTLs, and, notwithstanding any regrets one might have had, it could not be denied that there were no finer buses to be found anywhere. Overhauled every three to four years, each bus emerged from Aldenham virtually new. Their design had a considerable influence on the bus industry, and although the RT chassis had few takers outside London this was because of cost, while provincial style Leyland, Park Royal and MCW bodies clearly showed aspects of the RT design. Time proved that, expensive though a complete bus might be, compared with its provincial counterpart, the RT was a remarkably sound investment, and its longevity became legendary.

The changeover went pretty smoothly on the whole. Local papers reported that 'office workers have enjoyed the comparative quiet of the streets . . . and the comfort of the new vehicles has been commended'. The *Croydon Advertiser* reported that despite fears 'that the buses' smaller carrying capacity might leave travellers waiting at the stops . . . there have been few complaints'. M

Right: Replacing the 36/38 trams, 'prewar' RT40, temporarily based at Peckham garage until New Cross is ready, speeds alongside the now redundant tracks on route 177 from the Embankment to Abbey Wood.
Author's collection

experience was that it was indeed possible to spend longer waiting. On the first tramless Monday morning three RTs on the 109 and the 190 sped, full up, past my request stop. No tram had ever done this. But anecdotal evidence is hardly conclusive, and it probably is true that generally a slightly greater number of buses ensured there was little extra waiting time.

A factor which somewhat dampened our ardour for the new order was that many of the RTs allocated to Thornton Heath and Brixton garages were not new at all but second-hand specimens from Wandsworth, which had become an all-Leyland garage equipped with RTLs. However, we fared better than the folks further east, for when the last tram had departed New Cross it and its companions had been replaced by, *inter alia*, a motley batch of STLs. No fewer than 48 of these veterans, representatives of a class which would disappear altogether in two years' time, were allocated to tram-replacement routes 163 and 182 and worked them

for several months. The oldest, STL442, dated from 1934, making it only a couple or so years younger than the 'E3' and 'HR2' trams it had ousted. It is true that the tram-replacement STLs had been especially overhauled, but they still showed their age, particularly STL442, which retained red-and-white livery. All the STLs were given full route displays, but the rear number aperture was never used again, nor was it on the 'prewar' RTs; postwar RTs, of course, were never so equipped.

Some very curious additions to the fleet, albeit very temporary, arrived at the end of September 1951, when the Country Area took over 13 routes in the Grays area worked hitherto by Eastern National, together with 28 buses. Some of these, still in Eastern National livery, had 'LONDON TRANSPORT' glued over their original fleetnames. Many were replaced immediately by STLs, and gradually they were all withdrawn, new RTs being drafted in by the New Year.

Right: An early-postwar ECW-bodied Bristol L type of Eastern National borrowed by London Transport following the takeover of its owner's routes in the Grays area in 1951. *Ian Allan Library*

What to Do
with a Redundant Tram Depot

SOME tram depots were demolished and replaced by new bus garages erected on the same site, others were adapted to take buses instead of trams, at least two were sold off, and still others were demolished and the replacement bus services worked from existing garages.

Abbey Wood, a tram depot since 1910, continued to serve, in much rebuilt form, as a bus garage, although reconstruction had not been completed when the trams moved out. It was initially equipped with RTLs, then from 1955 with RTs, which had a very long reign, the last not being withdrawn until 1977. It closed in 1981, being replaced by the new Plumstead garage, built to serve the expanding Thamesmead.

Rye Lane, Peckham, opened in January 1952, operating some of New Cross's former tram routes, and initially housed not just RTs but also some of the STLs which worked route 163 for a short while. When it closed in 1969, handing its duties on to Peckham and Camberwell, it was also home to Routemasters.

Walworth, which until 1950 was known as Camberwell tram depot, was heavily rebuilt to take on its role as a bus garage from October 1951 but was not completed until 1954. Initially equipped with RTLs, it was the first tram-replacement garage to receive 8ft-wide Leylands, RTWs being allocated there in 1958 for routes 45 and 176.

In tram days Telford Avenue, famous as home to the 'Felthams', was officially located in Streatham, but upon

Left: RT4128 gets an all-over wash and scrub inside Peckham garage. *Ian Allan Library*

Above: Thornton Heath garage, in a view looking out towards the Whitehall Road entrance. It was built on the site of the tram depot, which had its entrance in London Road — an inconvenient, traffic-delaying arrangement, as the picture in the previous chapter makes clear. *Ian Allan Library*

conversion to a bus garage it found itself 'moved' into Brixton! Throughout the 1950s it operated RTs, although RTLs and RTWs took over for a couple of years in the mid-1960s before the RTs returned. The garage was the last operator of RTWs in London, and, decades later, the last operator of 'normal' Routemasters in London. Brixton Hill depot, a few hundred yards to the north, was sold off but rather remarkably came back into the Transport for London fold, complete with tram tracks.

Norwood had both a tram depot and a bus garage. Some of the Festival of Britain STLs actually shared the depot with the trams in 1951. The tram depot was not replaced, its replacement bus services being worked from various garages including, not surprisingly, Norwood.

Thornton Heath depot, closed some 18 months before the trams which lived there were withdrawn, was demolished and replaced by a completely new garage with the entrance around the side in Whitehall Road rather than inconveniently in the busy main London Road. RTs took up residence there and stayed for well

over 20 years. The trams moved to Purley depot, which was sold after the tram abandonment.

Clapham became very famous after closure as a tram depot, for the bus garage which replaced it lasted in this form for only eight years and in March 1961 became the Museum of British Transport. As such it rapidly came to rival Compostella and St Peter's, Rome, as a place of pilgrimage. Several anorak sellers in the vicinity of Clapham Common became millionaires as all those enthusiasts who for years had tried to peer into Reigate garage (where the London Transport collection had been housed) converged on it. London trams once again took up residence in the form of the preserved former West Ham four-wheeler, the 'E1' and the 'Feltham', which shared the company of *Mallard* (the world's fastest steam locomotive), a GWR buffet car, various London buses and all manner of other historic road and rail vehicles. Now it is a supermarket.

Wandsworth, having lost its trams in September 1950, also became the first London trolleybus depot to go over to motor buses, 75 RTs taking up residence that year

Above: RTs 271 and 3839 on the forecourt of Thornton Heath garage. Neither is working a tram-replacement route, highlighting how useful this space was (and indeed still is) as a turning and resting place for buses on a number of routes. £75,000 for one old penny was a fortune by anybody's standards in the 1950s! *Author*

in the new building, although they were replaced in 1951 by RTLs. Today it houses Arriva's 'Original London Sightseeing Tour' fleet, which means there's always something interesting to see from trains passing on the Clapham Junction–Richmond line overlooking the garage.

Holloway, the one North London tram depot to survive into the postwar era, became 'Highgate' in 1950, perhaps to avoid confusion with the women's prison, perhaps not. (There was also a Holloway bus garage; when this closed in 1971 the erstwhile tram depot became 'Holloway' once again.) It was once the largest tram depot in London, in its heyday home to no fewer than 336 cars. Trolleybuses arrived in 1938, but trams and trolleys lived (one assumes happily) together for 14 years, until the Kingsway Subway 33 and 35 routes were abandoned. Its initial motor-bus allocation consisted of RTLs and RTs, Routemasters arriving in 1960.

Holloway and New Cross may some day have to resort to an arm-wrestling contest, for each can claim to be London's largest bus garage. Like Holloway, New Cross has accommodation for over 300 guests, although full advantage has never been taken of this. As a tram depot it will be forever associated with the very end of London's trams and the accompanying celebrations/wakes. Rebuilding being incomplete in July 1952, another three months would elapse before buses started to work out of it. Amongst these were STLs and 'prewar' RTs, but by 1956 postwar RTs had a monopoly.

Over the years a huge variety of buses has worked from New Cross, to say nothing of the many vehicles which have taken advantage of its ample accommodation to rest up while awaiting disposal or reallocation.

Among the new garages built to house tram-replacement buses was that at Stockwell, completion of which was delayed until April 1952. On the whole — and perhaps understandably — bus garages don't figure high on guided tours of a town or city's architectural gems. Stockwell is the exception to this rule. Its soaring reinforced-concrete arches have sometimes been compared to a Gothic cathedral, and if, for some, a devotion to bus-spotting is akin to a religion, then Stockwell is surely the equivalent of St Peter's, Rome or the Blue Mosque, Istanbul. Shortage of materials prevented the use of steel, the preferred material; had this not been the case, Stockwell would have been far less dramatic in appearance. The nine arches amount to a length of almost 400ft and together span an unobstructed floorspace of 73,350sq ft, capable of accommodating around 150 RT-type buses. Now belonging to London General, Stockwell garage is a listed building.

Above: A sneaked view of the Museum of British Transport at the former Clapham bus garage before it opened to the public. Prominent are a B type, a Green Line T and an ST. *Author*

Left: Tram-replacement RTL841 stands over the tram tracks at the entrance to Clapham depot. It carries the short-lived 155w route number, the w indicating via Westminster Bridge (as opposed to Blackfriars). This suffix soon disappeared. *Author's collection*

Above: A 'J3' and three 'L3' trolleybuses inside Highgate depot. *Author*

Below: New Cross, some 20 years on from its rebuilding as a bus garage. A group of redundant RTs await their fate on the forecourt, among them RTs 2980, 1773, 2385 and 985. All were eventually scrapped. *Author*

Above: A 1953 view of the interior of 'the most beautiful bus garage in the world', Stockwell. *London Transport*

Below: A line of RTLs — and a solitary RT — dwarfed by the soaring arches of Stockwell garage. *Author's collection*

· 8 ·

The RT Family Reigns Supreme (Almost)

NOT only was the RT family replacing the trams during the period 1950-2, but the wartime non-standard and unloved Daimlers, Guys and Bristols were also being got rid of, as were the last of the ex-LGOC AECs — the STs, the LTs and the early STLs — whilst huge inroads were being made into the standard STLs as well. Thus an unprecedented influx of shiny new double-deckers, red and green, could be seen right across London and the Home Counties, from Luton to Crawley, from Slough to Tilbury.

One of the most convenient methods we bus spotters (I cannot say whether this was uppermost in the minds of 55 Broadway) used for categorising this enormous fleet was by registration marks. In the early days there had been two Hs and two Js, but in mid 1949 the first Ks appeared, and there were no fewer than five of these — KGK, KGU, KLB, KXW and KYY. What I am about to write will read as very silly indeed to those who are not rivet-counters or number-crunchers, but I never liked KYY-registered RTs, simply because they were the first group to abandon completely the pale-cream upper-deck window surrounds. The first bus denied this feature had been RT1679 (KXW 329), which was sent to Catford in April 1949 and therefore made my immediate acquaintance, coming regularly into Croydon on either the 54 or the 75. A shiny new RT looked handsome in any livery, but over the years London buses had become plainer and plainer — a steady

decline from the quite beautiful prewar red and white with black lining and mudguards and silver roof. Now the only relief was a single pale-cream thread-like adornment, not wide enough to be called a cummerbund, around the middle. This applied not only to red buses but also to a vast fleet of (nearly) all-over-green RTs which took to the streets of Croydon around this time, being allocated to practically all the many garages which operated routes through my home town. And if this wasn't enough, the diktat went out (not always to be obeyed instantly) that the cream window surrounds were to be painted over on those that still had them long before overhaul and general repainting was otherwise necessary on, for instance, Chelsham's fleet of KXW-registered RTs in the 2499-2521 series. These were particular favourites of mine, and I bitterly resented this minor desecration. At a time when Senator McCarthy was being beastly to anyone in the USA who exhibited any sort of left-wing tendencies, and when Communists were scarcely more popular over here, this totalitarian approach by London Transport to any attempt at deviation from the norm surely warranted some sort of investigation.

In truth LT's tight control had much to recommend it, ensuring economies of scale and a visual uniformity, and was exactly what was needed in the 1950s; a couple of decades later, when the world had moved on, London Transport found itself in deep trouble locked into a mindset which was no longer relevant, but that need not concern us for now. Returning to liveries, perhaps the greatest visual impact made of a London bus was — indeed, is —

Above: Green Line Weymann-bodied RT8/1 RT3256 of Romford (RE) garage, ready to enter service in August 1950. Although the Green Line RTs featured some attractive visual modifications, there was nothing internally to distinguish them from normal Country Area buses. *London Transport*

Below: The superbly designed lower saloon of an RT. *Author's collection*

Above: Weymann-bodied RT3115 in all-over green livery but still with restricted indicator display, stands on the forecourt of Dorking garage while working from Reigate garage on the long 414 route from Southdown/Aldershot & District territory at Horsham to West Croydon. The present 414 is worked by red double-deckers and goes nowhere near any of those destinations. *A. M. Wright*

Right: Trainer RT5, then the second-oldest motor bus in service with London Transport, heads through Chiswick on a wet afternoon in September 1959, having just emerged from Chiswick Works. *Author*

made by its advertisements. From horse-bus days manufacturers had realised what a wonderful opportunity was presented by a vehicle which travelled all over London, and the bus rapidly became a mobile billboard, practically every spare inch not displaying route or ownership details being so utilised. The RT family carried on this tradition. Advertisements were displayed either side of the route indicators at the front and at the rear, along the sides (between the decks) and beneath the rear platform window downstairs; they were also to be found inside. Their brilliant colours did much to counteract the uniformity of the all-over-red livery.

Some adverts have become famous, the *Picture Post* eyes of the 1940s and early '50s being perhaps the best known of all. Newspapers, particularly the tabloids, have long seen the London bus as a wonderful method of persuading readers to find out what naughty vicars and indiscreet stars of stage, screen and radio have been up to. Brewers of alcohol, tea and coffee, biscuit and bread makers — all love London buses, while photographic suppliers obviously decided that the back of an RT, over the registration plate and below the platform window, was quite the best place to promote their services. The huge expanse along the side of a 'Feltham'

Above: The rear aspect of the RT was rather upright but elegant nevertheless, as shown by RT1214 (left) with Saunders body and RT244 with Park Royal (though not its original) at Golders Green. *Author*

Right: The two RTs and the RTL which toured North America in 1952, seen with their Leyland Comet tender in the hold of the Cunard liner *Parthia. Ian Allan Library*

Below: The famous *Picture Post* eyes prepare to help STL2323 find its way from Victoria to Ladbroke Grove. *D. A. Jones*

tram offered sufficient space for two full-size adverts and for a time promoted my very favourite breakfast cereal, Force, featuring a curiously dressed jumping character. Now, alas, neither moving 'Felthams' nor the cereal can be savoured south of Milton Keynes.

Studying the advertisements is quite the best way of pinpointing when a picture of a London bus, tram, or trolleybus was taken, particularly if, as is often the case, a film or stage show is featured. For a time, in addition to collecting fleetnumbers, I used to see how often the most popular film posters cropped up, and for some inexplicable reason my memory has dredged up the fact that around 1952 I counted 23 buses along Oxford Street within half an hour featuring a film (the title of which escapes me) starring Burt Lancaster and Pier Angeli. One day someone will write a book on the subject.

With the end of the K registrations came, not unreasonably, the Ls, of which there were also five — LLU, LUC, LYF, LYH and LYR. Significantly, as RT-family production passed its peak, there were only two Ms (MLL and MXX), three Ns (NLE, NLP and NXP) and, finally, just one O (OLD).

Strictly speaking the L registrations should perhaps number only four, as the LYH series was applied to the very last trolleybuses put into service in London. These were a batch of 'Q1s', identical to the first series introduced in 1948. There were 50 of the LYH 'Q1s',

numbered 1842-91, needed to replace various prewar trolleybuses which were no longer fit for service. Generally speaking, the trolleybuses had survived the war years in much better shape than had the motor buses, perhaps because of the absence of the vibration, although many other concerns which operated both diesel and electrically powered vehicles got much the same mileage out of each. Whatever, the new vehicles were allocated to Fulwell (home of the original 77), Isleworth (which used to be called Hounslow) and Hanwell depots. Sharing the Fulwell and Isleworth routes with their slightly older, identical brothers, they worked the two Hanwell services — the 655 (Acton Vale–Hammersmith) and 607 (Shepherds Bush–Uxbridge) — with the 'F1' Leylands, built between March and December 1937; the 607 passed the AEC works at Southall, just by the bridge which carried the Great Western main line over the trolleybus route. Although the 'Q1s' were officially BUTs (Leyland and AEC having amalgamated their trolleybus marketing postwar), in reality they were little modified from AEC's prewar design. Fitted with Metro-Cammell bodies, they were nevertheless generally considered the finest trolleybuses to have operated in the UK and, had different environmental priorities applied, might well have been the forerunners of a fleet still serving London today. Ironically the 607 replaced tram route 7, operated by ex-LUT 'Felthams', of which the same could be said.

Above: In what appears to be a posed publicity shot, new RT2873 stands in an almost deserted Parliament Square in 1952. Where have all the tourists gone?
Author's collection

Right: Shepherd's Bush Green. 'F1s' 661 of Hammersmith depot and 691 of Acton flank *× Hanwell depot not Acton.* 'Q1' 1875 of Isleworth, one of the final delivery of trolleybuses to London.
Author

• 9 •

Up in the Air

THE 657, worked from Isleworth depot, was the nearest London trolleybuses got to Heathrow Airport. Before World War 2 Croydon was London's official airport, but so small were prewar airliners and so relatively infrequent the flights that London Transport played no part in providing road services to and from it. After the war, with very much larger transport aircraft having been developed by the USA between 1940 and 1945, a new generation of Douglas, Boeing and Lockheed four-engined airliners, capable of flying the Atlantic, entered service. Croydon's runways were too short for these relative giants, and the growth of suburbia all around its perimeter made expansion impossible, so although smaller DC-3s and other types continued to fly to and from Europe its

Below: Sunny Isleworth depot after the postwar 'Q1' trolleybuses had taken themselves off for a working holiday in sunny Spain, to be replaced by 'K1s' and 'K2s'. *Author*

importance steadily declined until it closed at the end of 1958. Its splendid terminal buildings and control tower survive, however, and until only very recently 'Croydon Airport' was still displayed on terminating buses.

British European Airways flew for a time out of Northolt, but Heathrow, out to the west, was destined to become not just London's premier airport but the world's busiest. As such it would grow into a medium-sized town, employing thousands of people and generating vast economic activity; today some 100,000 owe their employment to Heathrow. British Overseas Airways built a West End terminal at Victoria, over the railway station and opposite the London Coastal Coaches long-distance one, and initially operated a fleet of normal-control, one-and-a-half-deck coaches to and from Heathrow. British European Airways established a terminal on the Festival of Britain site, later moving to the Cromwell Road, and contracted London Transport to operate similar vehicles for it; however, air travel —

Above: One of the normal-control Commer Avenger 1½-deck coaches used in the early 1950s by British Overseas Airways Corporation to ferry passengers from its terminal in Buckingham Palace Road (opposite Victoria Coach Station), seen on the tarmac at Heathrow alongside a Lisbon bound Douglas DC-3 airliner. *Commer*

and the size of airliners — grew like Topsy (a well-known 'clippie' of the period), and by 1950 it was clear these dinky little vehicles could not cope.

The underfloor-engined AEC Regal IV had been adopted as London Transport's standard single-deck chassis, and BEA decided to follow suit. The airline commissioned Chiswick to come up with the goods, and the result was a one-and-a-half-deck vehicle, based on the RF chassis, with seats for 37 passengers and plenty of luggage space under the raised rear section. It was classified by London Transport as 4RF4, although this was never shown on the vehicles, which remained the property of the airline. The 4RF4s took up work between May 1952 and the middle of 1953. Like their Green Line counterparts, they were officially regarded as coaches, although in reality they were rather upmarket buses. Painted in the airline's colours of blue, cream and grey, they displayed such faraway destinations as Manchester, Athens, Paris and so forth, although these became meaningless as frequency of airline services increased and flights took off every two or three minutes.

The original batch comprised 50 vehicles, and although they were distinctive their Chiswick origins were very obvious, and mechanically they shared many features with the RT/RF family. They shared their MLL registrations with RTs, RTLs and Green Line and Central Area RFs, being registered MLL 713-62. Fifteen more, registered NLP 636-50, were added to the fleet between August and October 1953.

In 1955 I was working for a firm of commercial and industrial photographers based in Croydon, and we were asked to photograph a new terminal at Heathrow. At that time there were still plenty of temporary huts dotted around the airport — and very little security — and as it was stipulated that the pictures should be taken at night (to show the fancy new interior to best

advantage) and this was mid-June we couldn't start until gone 10pm. We wandered around unchallenged, in and out of the buildings, and noted that a number of the Weymann-bodied TDs of 1946/7, made redundant by the RF class, had been hired out by London Transport to ferry passengers out to the aircraft from the terminal buildings, although by this time they were all lined up for the night, flying having more-or-less finished until next morning. Eventually we got to work, setting up our whole-plate, wooden Gandolphi camera. No shutter was used; it was my job as assistant to fire off flash bulbs whilst the photographer, Brian, removed the lens cap, counted in his head however many seconds his Weston Sangamo exposure meter decreed, and then replaced the cap. The results were almost always excellent. The firm had been founded way back in 1861, and we had an amazing collection of 12x10in and whole-plate glass negatives dating back to the 19th century of such subjects as Rennie Macintosh's Glasgow Art School, the interiors of Clyde-built liners, construction work on buildings, churches, cathedrals, power stations, dams and so forth all over the UK. The firm folded at the end of the 1960s, and most of the negatives were destroyed. Seems impossible to believe now, but that's what happened in those days.

Despite the excellence of its photography, business-wise the firm was still firmly in the 19th century. Our vehicle was a very nice, very run-down Bradford van of 1947. Heading home around 3am the tail light (there was only one) gradually faded away, so I sat with a torch

Above: A British European Airways 1½-deck coach, designed by London Transport at Chiswick and based on AEC Regal IV chassis similar to that used for the RF class, beside one of the airline's Elizabethan-class Airspeed Ambassadors on the tarmac at Northolt Airport in July 1952. *BEA*

Below: Four of BEA's recently delivered '4RF4' coaches lined up at the airlines Central London terminal at Waterloo. A temporary facility opened in May 1953, this would be replaced in 1957 by the West London Air Terminal in Cromwell Road, South Kensington. *Ian Allan Library*

pressing a piece of red paper against the rear window as we rumbled across a silent and deserted (except, I suspect, for a few courting couples) Mitcham Common, until this too gave up the ghost (the torch, not the courting couples). The local police were all either safely tucked up in bed or drinking cocoa in their police station, and anyhow dawn was breaking as we arrived back home. The other principal photographer didn't have a driving licence so travelled to his assignments by London bus, with his whole-plate camera in one hand and box of plates in the other, and looked slightly taken

aback when meeting rivals who zoomed around in Triumph Heralds and MGAs.

Living in the vicinity of Heathrow was — and still is — a mixed blessing. The *Middlesex Chronicle* of 27 January 1950 commented, tongue in cheek, that 'having an important international air terminus on our doorsteps, so to speak, is no doubt a high honour and privilege . . . but disadvantages are the wiping out of flourishing farms and valuable building land, the noise of planes, the risk of crashes, the need for housing airport employees . . .' As more and more people came to live and work in the area, so bus services were expanded and developed. In 1950 London Transport was desperately short of buses and hired in vehicles from wherever it could find them. The *Middlesex Chronicle* noted that 'most of us have become thoroughly acquainted with the green-painted buses which operate on the Hounslow and Twickenham routes and which are still on loan to London Transport.

Above: Sand carrier 015 climbs away from Clapham Junction. London Transport never made any concessions of sissy windscreens on its fleet of service trams, and the driver stands erect, braving whatever nature cares to throw at him. 015 is pursued by a wartime Daimler and is passing a Bradford van identical to the one used by Bedford Lemere, the photographers for whom the author worked in the 1950s. *Author's collection*

Left: RTL1081 about to set off from Clapham on an excursion to watch the planes at Heathrow. Present-day concerns over security and the vast growth in air travel have put an end to this practice. *Ian Allan Library*

by provincial companies. Passengers on the top deck have learned by painful experience to duck their heads . . . but how the children love these buses. What a wizard plunge they can take on a vacant seat upstairs — far better than on the lower deck, which is hardly any different from the ordinary vehicles . . . One wailing and weeping little girl, aged five years or thereabouts, complained to her parent: "Daddie, why can't we go on a green one?".'

One would not have needed to go very far west on a green Country Area bus to encounter lowbridge Thames Valley buses working westwards out of Slough. Most adventurously, Thames Valley operated an open-top bus service beside the Thames through Maidenhead in the 1950s, when open-toppers, other than beside the sea or occasionally in Central London, were unknown.

From the start there were concerns about access to Heathrow from Central London. George Bennie, inventor of the rail-plane which ran experimentally in Scotland in the 1930s, gave an interview to the *Middlesex Chronicle*. '[The rail-plane] can reach a speed of

Above: Country Area RT4476 of High Wycombe garage alongside an ECW-bodied Bristol LS of Thames Valley.
M. G. Webber

Below: A prewar Green Line coach ending its days as a bus — 9T9 T423, complete with bumper (most unusual on a London — or, for that matter, any other — bus), amid the rather bleak landscape beside Heathrow Airport.
London Transport

200mph. It would be only an 8-minute trip between London Airport and St. Paul's Churchyard, London, over the Great West Road. The government's planned arterial roads from Earls Court to serve the airport would cost £37 million . . . My railplane will cost £5 million to St. Paul's.' The *Chronicle* reported that the project was being considered by the Lord Mayor, Scotland Yard and the Ministry of Transport but reckoned that 'Cranford Residents' Amenities Association . . . [would] probably have something to say'. Alas, as there is still no Bennie rail-plane to Heathrow, we must assume they did.

· 10 ·

Under the Ground and Down the Tubes

THE Golden Jubilee of the Central Line was celebrated in 1950. The *Middlesex Chronicle* recorded: 'On June 27th, 1900 the Prince of Wales, later King Edward VII, officially opened the line and Mr. Charles Hewitt of Hounslow, immaculately dressed in white boiler suit and white gloves, drove the crimson and gold special train.' Now aged 79, Mr Hewitt 'will be a guest at a special tea party being held by Lord Latham, chairman of London Transport, on August 9th'.

Four years later another Hounslow resident, Mr Priestly, celebrated his own Golden Jubilee and was still working for London Transport, as Chief Mechanical Engineer of the Underground Railways at Acton Works. According to the *Daily Mirror* of 8 October 1954 he 'began his career on the District Railway as an office boy at Lillie Bridge yard in December, 1903, when steam trains were still running on the District . . . Well known as a member of the Hounslow Operatic Society . . . he helped to found London Transport's T.O.T. (Trams, Omnibuses and Tubes) Philharmonic Society — now the London

Transport Players . . . Today he is the longest serving District Railway employee with London Transport.' Across the page was an advertisement for an epic 'at your leading local cinema next week', starring Humphrey Bogart, Jose Ferrer, Van Johnson and Fred MacMurray; based on Herman Wouk's Pulitzer Prize-winning novel, *The Caine Mutiny* was described as 'A Film to Rave About'.

By the mid-1950s the pre-1938 Tube stock was well past its sell-by date. A new design, similar in appearance to the 1938 trains but with a flat (and therefore less attractive) front to the driving cabs and, most importantly, finished in unpainted aluminium, was put in hand. Three seven-car units entered service in 1957/8 on the Piccadilly Line, where the oldest units predominated. Their interiors featured fluorescent lighting and blue upholstery. Known as the 1956 stock, each unit was built by a different manufacturer — one by Metro-Cammell, one by Birmingham RCW and one by Gloucester RCW. They proved successful and resulted in an order being placed with Metro-Cammell

Left: A train of 1956 Tube stock bound for Uxbridge on the Piccadilly Line. *Ian Allan Library*

Above Right: A train of 1959 stock approaches Woodford on the Central Line. *G. M. Kichenside*

Right: The 1959 stock first entered service on the Piccadilly Line, replacing pre-1938 stock such as that visible on the left of this scene, recorded at Rayners Lane. *London Transport*

or 76 production units, identical to the prototypes xcept for a few minor alterations. Known as the 959 stock the first actually managed to be true to ts title (just), entering service on the Piccadilly Line n December 1959. For the sake of completeness we ought to record that no fewer than 619 further carriages of this design were ordered, 169 coming from British Railways workshops at Derby, the rest from Metro-Cammell. Known as 1962 stock and intended for the Central Line, they were delivered in a continuous run once construction of the 1959 stock had been completed.

A small but noteworthy retrenchment on the railway network in 1959 was the closure of the Line branch between Acton Town and South Acton, which had been worked by a single car; the two 1923-stock cars that had been converted for this duty in 1939 were scrapped. Nevertheless, there were plenty of pre-1938 cars still at work, many of them with clerestory roofs — the last instance of this once familiar feature still to be found in normal service in the UK.

Left: One lady and a dog about to board one of the 1923-built 'G'-stock cars converted in 1938 to work as a single unit on the South Acton Shuttle. *Ian Allan Library*

Below left: Interior of one of the clerestory-roofed 'G'-stock cars working the East London Line. *Author*

Right: Car 4148, a 'G'-stock vehicle dating from 1923, heading an East London Line train waiting to depart New Cross Gate for Whitechapel. *Author*

Below: A neat four-car rake of clerestory-roof 'K' stock dating from 1927 heads towards New Cross Gate on the East London Line. *Author*

Another anachronistic survival on the Underground was that of the steam locomotive. By the late 1950s those inherited by London Transport (it had bought no new ones) were venerable in the extreme. However, it was considered that their replacement by diesels would be uneconomic, given the relatively small amount of work they were called upon to perform by the Engineer's Department. Battery-electric locomotives were not sufficiently powerful, and therefore it was decided that GWR-built '57xx' 0-6-0 pannier tanks would make ideal replacements. To claim that they were a proven article would be something of an under-statement, for there were more than 800 of them, plus many more of a very similar design. Already they were no strangers to the Underground, a group having been fitted with condensing apparatus to work over the Circle Line to Smithfield meat depot. However, it was not these but a pair of an earlier variation with Dean-type cabs, Nos 7711 and 5752, which arrived in 1956/7, being renumbered L.90 and L.91. In all 13 entered London Transport service, although not all were at work at the same time. The final examples outlived steam on British Rail, not being withdrawn until 1971, and in the process created the rather extraordinary situation whereby the first and last ordinary steam trains on the Underground were worked by Great Western locomotives. Several of the panniers which served London Transport have been preserved, while special steam trains have been seen subsequently, notably during the phenomenally successful 'Steam on the Met' events staged in the 1990s.

Left: London Transport began the decade with an assortment of inherited steam locomotives. Pictured at Lillie Bridge depot in August 1956. No L31 was one of a pair of Hunslet 0-6-0Ts bought by the District Railway in 1930. *G. Clarke*

Below: Links between the Underground system and the GWR have persisted since the earliest times, none more so than in 1956, when Swindon-designed pannier tank No 7711 was transferred from British Railways to London Transport. This was the first of 13, some of which would serve on engineering duties until 1971, thereby outlasting BR steam by three years. It is seen in April 1957 at Neasden, where most were based. *A. A. G. Delicata*

· 11 ·

Coronation Year

THE year 1953 opened on a note of deep tragedy when at the end of January a combination of fierce storms and unusually high tides brought disaster at sea and the worst flooding of the 20th century in Britain. The Stranraer–Larne British Railways car ferry *Princess Victoria* foundered in the Irish Sea with great loss of life, fishing boats and their crews were lost, and down the East Coast flooding drowned more than 300 people, reaching right up the Thames Estuary. Canvey Island, just beyond the outer limits of London Transport territory, where many Londoners spent their holidays in caravans and chalets, suffered 59 deaths, and although no-one further upriver in Kent or Essex actually drowned there was extensive flooding at Abbey Wood, Dagenham and elsewhere. Bus services were disrupted, and right in the heart of London the Thames lapped the very parapet of the Embankment but, thankfully, did not overflow; had it done so, much of the Underground and Tube system would have been flooded.

With the onset of spring spirits lifted as the population looked forward to the great event of that summer, the Coronation. I was going to write that it would be impossible to conceive such enthusiasm for a royal event today, but when one considers the vast publicity surrounding every action of Princess Diana's, from her engagement to her death and beyond, perhaps not.

London Transport had, in a sense, had the opportunity of a dress rehearsal with the Festival of Britain two years earlier. It will be recalled that STLs, the newest of which was 12 years old, had been used on the special Festival services. Now, even though they were two years older and only a year away from the end of passenger service in the capital, the STLs were once again called upon to play their part in conveying the huge influx of visitors for the great event. More than 150 of the most recently overhauled examples — many of them Country Area vehicles, some with forward entrance — were chosen to supplement the Green Line fleet in transporting police, troops and schoolchildren, running excursions and augmenting ordinary services.

Left: STL1052, a lowbridge vehicle long associated with Godstone garage, moved westwards towards the end of its LT career and is seen here working from Guildford in February 1952. *Alan Cross*

Vast crowds came, not just to watch the actual procession itself, on a rather damp 2 June, but for weeks before and afterwards to view the decorations and take part in various festivities. As the summer moved on into the autumn, so the visitors gradually returned home, and the STLs, no longer needed, were delicensed, most of them never to run again in passenger service with London Transport. The class would linger on into 1954 but would not see another autumn. Even so, they outlasted — just — the SRT rebuilds. In 1949/50 production of bodies for new RTs was outpacing that of the chassis, so as a temporary measure these were fitted to 160 (of a planned 300) refurbished STL chassis. The resultant vehicles retained their old registrations, mostly in the final FJJ/FXT series, but were given low RT radiators and thus looked for all the world like standard RTs. Alas they were fearful impostors, and it quickly became obvious that the heavier body severely affected both acceleration and braking ability. Consequently the SRTs were found duties on routes with as few gradients as possible, and all were taken out of service in 1953/4; the chassis were then scrapped and the bodies transferred to new RT chassis in the 4397-4556 series.

Three classes which would be gone before the SRTs were the Bs, the Gs and the Ds. Just as RT1-151 were

Right: SRT34, the result of an unhappy combination of rebuilt STL chassis and standard RT body, stands at the Hampstead Heath terminus of route 24 in 1952; shortly afterwards the chassis would be scrapped and the body fitted to a new RT chassis. *F. G. Reynolds*

Below: One of the first batch of Bristols, B4, as delivered to Hanwell in wartime condition. *Omnibus Society*

known as 'prewar' RTs, even though all but the original had appeared after 1939, so the Bristols, Guys and Daimlers tend to be lumped together as 'wartime' buses, despite the fact that the last, a Daimler of the D182-281 series, did not take up work until November 1946.

The Bristols were the least numerous, just 29 being delivered, in two groups — K5Gs B1-9 in the spring of 1942, and K6As B10-29 at the end of 1945. The Guys were the most numerous, 435 of them being delivered between December 1942 and April 1946, whilst there were 281 Daimlers, delivered between May 1944 and November 1946. For the sake of completeness we ought to include STD101-11, which, although they had 'unfrozen' chassis, with most of the components dating from prewar days (or at least being of prewar quality), had wartime bodies and were put into service between December 1941 and August 1942. None of these types was popular with either crews or passengers, the STDs probably being the most disliked of all. It might be thought that these vehicles, well below the standard normally expected of London buses, would have been kept out of sight in the suburbs, but, although many did work such routes, a number also appeared regularly in the City and the West End. Oddest of all was the employment of Daimlers in Green Line livery on routes to/from Romford.

Above: B18, one of the postwar Bristols with the lower, more elegant radiator, at Golders Green.
F. G. Reynolds

Left: Northern Counties-bodied Guy G250, one of the better-looking wartime buses, stands outside Hornchurch garage alongside former Green Line T273, which appears to have been in a spot of bother.
D. A. Jones

My acquaintance with the 'wartime' types varied from intimate to non-existent. The Bristols, ensconced in far-away Hanwell, came into the latter category, as did most of the Guys, which inhabited huge swathes of that distant land, north and east of the Thames, known as Essex. I can recall only once travelling on a member of the G class, a Tottenham vehicle working the 76 — the first to be operated by the class — which I boarded at Victoria. There was only one other Central London route on which they worked regularly for any length of time, namely the 23 from Becontree Heath to Marylebone station.

STDs were a familiar sight, for they lived at the most central of all London garages — Gillingham Street, Victoria (GM) — and at the Crystal Palace terminus of the 137 came well within cycling distance from home. I even managed to take a photograph of one, withdrawn from service, as a trainer in Chelverton Road garage, Putney, which would have been quite interesting had not the camera shaken so badly that it was impossible to tell bus from garage.

Members of the D class passed the end of our road and my friend Hicks copped all 281 of them. But the

Right: STD88, in its final, all-red livery, still in excellent condition working the 113 from Hendon garage. *G. A. Rixon*

Below: Last days of the D class. Merton's D180 at the Clapham Common terminus of the 88, with an RTL, complete with full indicator display, behind. Beyond are another D and two STLs. *F. G. Reynolds*

Above: Although Morden was the heart of 'Daimler-land', other types did put in appearances on the station forecourt. STL2104 from Streatham (AK) garage calls in on its way to nearby Raynes Park. *Passport to Pimlico*, starring, amongst others, Stanley Holloway, was one of the classic Ealing comedies; no doubt 'Wisk' was a classic too. Posed modestly in the background is one of the somewhat less austere final series of Park Royal Daimlers based at Sutton garage. *Author's collection*

he had the advantage of living in Sutton, in the heart of Daimler-land, whilst Thornton Heath was served by just the one Daimler route (115), shared by Sutton and Croydon garages. The former used its Park Royal-bodied 'semi-utilities', with their unique livery of red and two cream stripes, so I got to ride these from time to time. They were better than my one experience of a Guy, which seemed to have very high windows and a rather sombre brown interior. Merton was home to the entire fleet of first-generation Ds, other than the Green Line examples, although they ended up there too, some still in green livery.

The G class began to be replaced even before the trams, sometimes with STLs but ultimately with members of the RT family, the last being taken out of service from Upton Park garage on 23 December 1952. The Bristols lasted a little longer, until April 1953. The wartime STDs had ceased passenger service in May 1951 but then did some work as trainers, and the last lingered on, out of use, until September 1955. Some 23 Daimlers were still operational at the end of 1953, but all had gone by the end of the first week of the New Year.

The worst feature of the wartime buses had been the bodywork, which used unseasoned wood. Chassis and engine were generally rather more satisfactory, and after service in London many moved on to the provinces and abroad, often rebodied. I renewed acquaintance with many of the Daimlers, fitted with handsome new bodies by the local firm of Harkness, in Belfast in 1961, while Edinburgh Corporation took a batch of Guys and transformed their appearance. The only 'utility' to survive into preservation with its original body is G351; a Park Royal-bodied vehicle originally (in February 1946) allocated to Upton Park, this was bought from Burton-on-Trent Corporation for preservation and underwent an extensive rehabilitation programme at Cobham. A great treasure, it is the only surviving example of a most interesting period in the history of the London bus.

Right: Dating from June 1943, G66, a Guy Arab with Park Royal body, ends its days with London Transport on learner duty. *Author's collection*

Below: The former London Transport B5, a Park Royal-bodied Bristol K5G dating from May 1942, finds a new lease of life with Hartlepool Corporation. *John Fozard*

· 12 ·

The Single-deck Story

Above: Green Line RF222 speeds past Croydon parish church on the cross-South London 725 route. *Author*

JUST as the RT family was ousting all other double-deckers, so the RF was doing much (but not quite so much) the same in the single-deck fleet. Chosen after considerable experimentation, the heavyweight AEC Regal IV chassis became the basis of the Private Hire and Green Line 'coaches' and Central and Country Area buses which constituted the RF class. Although there were minor variations, the bodywork of all versions was very similar, all 700 being bodied by Metro-Cammell.

The first 25 RFs were 27ft 6in-long, 35-seat 'coaches', painted in an attractive livery of dark green and pale grey with red lettering, which entered service with the Private Hire fleet in 1951, with LUC registrations. Next came the Green Line 'coaches', with LYF or MLL registrations. These, being 30ft long, seated 39 passengers and were decked out in standard Green Line livery; they also lacked the glass observation windows fitted to

the Private Hire vehicles. Delivered later than planned, the first, RF26, took up work on the 704 from Windsor to Tunbridge Wells in October 1951. Gradually they ousted all the prewar coaches — the Qs, TFs and, mainstay of the fleet since 1938, the 10T10s — the last, RF287, being licensed in November 1952. With clean, simple lines and a lack of ornamentation, they were not universally welcomed at first, but, like the RT, the design proved to be well thought-out and built to last.

The first red Central Area RFs, with MLL and MXX registrations, began work from Muswell Hill garage on route 210 on 11 September 1952. The Metropolitan Police, dear old-fashioned things that they were, refused to sanction passenger doors. Apparently they thought doors would slow down the entry and exit of

Above: RF19 was one of the original, 27ft 6in-long private-hire 1RF1/2s dating from 1951 and would later be converted to a Green Line coach. Behind is TF9, the only member of its 11-strong batch of 33-seat Park Royal-bodied private-hire coaches to survive the bombing of Bull Yard, Peckham, in October 1940; it had been built the previous year on the revolutionary Leyland Tiger FEC chassis, which had its engine mounted horizontally on the offside beneath the floor and pointed the way to postwar single-deck design, of which the RF was an early example. *Author's collection*

Below: Hoddesdon town square, with TF80 working Green Line route 715. TF14-88, placed in service between April and June 1939, were typical examples of the succession of revolutionary single-deckers introduced by London Transport in the 1930s. Leyland Tiger FECs, they had underfloor engines, anticipating postwar trends, but retained a half-cab layout. The introduction of the RF class saw their downgrading to buses in 1951/2; although employed here on a Green Line service, TF80 is by now in Country Area bus livery. *F. G. Reynolds*

Above: Predecessor of the TF was the AEC Q, with engine mounted on the offside behind the front axle. Unlike the TFs, none of the various Q designs perpetuated the half cab. They thus not only looked very modern but also had a greater seating capacity. The neatest variety of all was the 5Q5, the only one to take full advantage of the set-back front wheels by having the entrance at the very front of the bus, beside the driver. They could easily have operated as one-person vehicles, but this lay in the future, and all had been withdrawn by the end of 1954. Q163 appears to be highly desirable transport for a large number of Kingston's older residents. *Alan Cross*

Below: Representing an older but long-lived tradition is six-wheel LT1159, also seen in the single-deck stronghold of Kingston. The first single deck LTs — AEC Renowns classified 1LTL1 — entered service in January 1931. Altogether some 199 were built — there should have been 200, but the final example emerged as a double-deck coach. A number of these buses were rebuilt postwar, and the last was not withdrawn until January 1953, from Dalston garage. Two of these highly distinctive buses have survived, restoration of that in the care of London's Transport Museum having been completed. *Author's collection*

passengers; presumably they had no objection to their falling out. In most other respects the Central Area buses were very like the Green Line vehicles, but without the luggage racks and deep seat cushions. Delivery of red RFs was completed on 25 March 1953.

Green livery aside, the Country Area RF buses were identical to their red relations except for the installation of power-operated doors. Fittingly the first batch went to Reigate garage, in March and April 1953. All were in service by the end of the year, except for RFs 517, 647 and 700. These three were pioneers and indicators of the way the bus world was moving. The other 697 RFs all entered service with two-man crews, but falling traffic meant that this was a luxury which could not last, and the outstanding trio were fitted for one-man operation. Government regulations had for years meant that any bus with a capacity of more than 20 seats (latterly raised to 26) had to have both a driver and a conductor, but these restrictions could not be sustained, were relaxed and eventually abolished. The three one-man RFs worked first from Leatherhead garage on route 419, being moved in August to Hemel Hempstead for the 316. They represented the shape of things to come, and by the time the last RF was withdrawn from service the entire class had been one-person-operated for many years.

A rather surprising choice to replace the little Leyland Cub one-man buses was the GS. Looking as though designed by a committee, it had a modified Guy Vixen chassis, a bonnet by Briggs of Dagenham which (not surprisingly, with an address like that) had strong affinities with contemporary Fordson lorries, and an ECW body which looked as if it had set out expecting

Above: Passing a very shiny, very ugly Austin Cambridge, Central Area RF369 of Bromley garage heads through Beckenham towards Crystal Palace on route 227. Bedford Lemere's Bradford van has also managed to insinuate a bit of itself into the picture. *Author*

Below: Country Area RF563, on loan to the Central Area's Sidcup garage in 1957, on its way to Welling station on the 241. *Author*

to find itself sitting on a Bristol chassis, the proper repository for all ECW bodies, and then suddenly remembered it was going to serve London Transport and adapted itself accordingly. Yet it was generally agreed the result was an aesthetic success. The first GS went into service from Chelsham garage in October 1953 and worked regularly into Holland, which did not involve the driver's donning clogs and wearing a tulip behind his ear, Holland being a hamlet south of Oxted where the 464 and 465 routes terminated. By the end of the 1950s there was insufficient work for these anachronisms (as 20-seat, normal-control buses had by then become), and withdrawal began in 1959.

All prewar single-deckers had finished passenger service by 1954, although the handsome 10T10 Green Line coaches lingered as staff transports, the last of these (T716) not being sold until April 1957. By then the earliest postwar Ts, the Weymann-bodied 14T12s,

Above: TD18, one of 31 Weymann-bodied Leyland PS1 Tigers new in 1946/7 and based at Muswell Hill, heads for Golders Green on the 210. The batch would be displaced by new RFs in 1953. *Ian Allan Library*

Above right: Chelsham garage *c*1959. In the foreground is GS7, one of the little 26-seat modified Guy Vixens with a Perkins PG six-cylinder engine and ECW bodywork. Behind, the first of this final class of normal-control buses, GS1, lines up with a pair of RTs. *Author*

Left: T580, a 10T10 of 1938 demoted from Green Line duties with the advent of the RF class, serves out its time as a red-painted Central Area bus — albeit seen here outside Addlestone garage working a Country Area route. *F. G. Reynolds*

Right: Touring coach RFW7 leads an RT across Lambeth Bridge. *Pamlin Prints*

were also on their way out, none being in stock by New Year's Day 1960, whilst only nine of the final version of this diverse class, the 15T13s, lasted beyond that date. The TD class was another victim of the arrival of the RFs, as well as of falling demand and double-decking. The Weymann-bodied version had disappeared from passenger service by March 1958, and by the end of the 1950s heavy inroads had been made into the later, Mann Egerton buses.

One unusual type was the 15 strong RFW class of 1951. They had the same chassis as the RFs, but were 8ft wide and had proper coach seats for 39 passengers with glass cant panels. The bodies were designed and built by ECW but bore no resemblance to that firm's classic design on Bristol LS and MW chassis so familiar on long-distance coach services throughout the country. The RFWs were used on tours and excursions and were based at both Central and Country Area garages.

· 13 ·

Decline and Stumble

A recurring theme throughout the 1950s was the remorseless spread of private transport and the inroads the motor car was making into public transport. In 1951 the Government set up a working party to investigate London Transport. At the end of February 1953 it reported to John Boyd-Carpenter, Minister of Transport & Civil Aviation, finding that 'London has one of the best passenger transport systems in the world and it is served by a body of workers of all grades who have a fine tradition of loyalty and public service . . . the standard of service is high except for:

- acute overcrowding in peak hours,
- poor inter-change facilities between bus and rail, and
- some irregular and slow-running services which pass through congested streets.'

It went on to note that 'traffic congestion . . . is already becoming critical'. It advocated that 'working hours in Central London [should be] staggered . . . London Transport should experiment with special services, possibly at a fixed fare. Buses might be either standard double-deckers or special buses, possibly of the "standee" type.' It criticised terminals such as Victoria, where passengers had 'to stand in long and rather confused queues . . . [in] extreme discomfort, particularly during bad weather [which] must deter many passengers from using London Transport's services particularly if they can use private cars'.

LTE's relationship with the unions was not always happy; the Committee regretted 'that their invitation to the Transport and General Workers' Union to give evidence . . . was declined' and recorded that 'shortages of staff in certain grades are threatening to become serious . . . salaries attached to appointments in the higher levels have fallen below the levels in corresponding posts in industry. Similar considerations apply to other sections of the staff.'

Much of what it predicted did indeed come to pass, sooner or later, although, given its opening paragraph in praise of 'one of the best transport systems in the

Below: 'Feltham' 2157 does its best to avoid an unusual load, a Hillman Minx, a large Wolseley saloon and a cyclist at Kennington Oval whilst on its way to Tooting Broadway. *Author's collection*

world', it is a little odd that the Committee should have recommended either that LTE's status be changed to 'an entirely separate body responsible directly to the Minister', or that 'its functions be vested in the British Transport Commission'.

Two years later J. B. Burnell, Operating Manager, Central Road Services (of the LTE), wrote in *Passenger Transport* on 18 May 1955 about 'growing congestion in our towns, and we all know that the Minister of Transport is gravely concerned'. After noting at some length the dramatic increase in cars in the USA and the decline in the use of public transport, he observed that 'what has happened to them can happen to us. More and more cars are being used in England.' There had been a five-day bus strike in London in October of the previous year; this 'did not cause the hardship that previous strikes caused, however, because there was a much greater private car fleet . . . [and] congestion in the London streets was greater than in normal times. A private car journey from Mitcham . . . to the Oval . . . took 50 minutes against the normal 25 minutes.' Referring to Green Line services, which had worked throughout the strike, these 'normally maintain a high degree of regularity, but out of 38 coaches checked at Oxford Circus during the morning peak . . . none was early or on time, while nearly 50% were running ten minutes or more late'.

Mr Burnell noted, forcefully, that 'the strike did serve one purpose, it showed unmistakably that the bus is certainly not the "bête noire" of road congestion . . . indeed [it is] the most economical user of road space.' A police census showed that 'a bus passenger takes up 9.2 square feet while a car passenger takes up 46 square feet of road space'; in rush hours the disparity was some 300% greater. Whilst admitting that the job of car

manufacturers was 'to sell cars, and you cannot blame them for wishing to do this', he also noted that 'wages generally are good and often a whole family is working and earning . . . car manufacturers are setting out to capture the lower income groups . . . it follows that people in the bus world must attract them on to their side.'

An event which clearly took many people by surprise was a parade of vintage buses through the heart of London in the summer of 1954. *Passenger Transport* magazine reported that 'the pavements around Piccadilly Circus were packed solid with onlookers, and what a reception they gave them; the scene was reminiscent of great occasions of the past, such as Victory Night with cheering and waving on all sides . . . BBC Television and cinema newsreels also took part.' Clearly, whatever they felt about travelling on modern buses, the public loved old ones. The occasion was the 25th anniversary of the Omnibus Society, and a B type of 1910, a K of 1919, an S of 1920 and an NS of 1926, together with a replica Barton Daimler of 1908, all but the last from the London Transport collection, paraded from Earl's Court to Pall Mall. It was, perhaps, the first real occasion when the vintage-bus movement set out its stall as not just a hobby for boys who had never quite grown up but also a part of the Heritage scene, a celebration of Britain's industrial past. Mind you, if a writer in the 21st century dared to comment that the five-day journey from Twickenham to Land's End and back by local bus service by one of the special guests, Mrs Gertrude Leather, 'would not be unusual were it undertaken by the average male enthusiast, but it is an achievement for a housewife to do it off her own bat', he would be banned from approaching within 500m of a word-processor for the rest of his life!

· 14 ·

Deepening Doom and Gloom

THE year 1958 was notable — or maybe it should be notorious — for a strike which did more than anything else to drive Londoners from public to private transport, accelerating a trend which would not be reversed for another 40 years. That is not necessarily a condemnation of the bus drivers and conductors for going on strike, and the decline would certainly have continued, strike or not.

The editorial in the *Passenger Transport Year Book* for 1958, looking back at 1957, began thus: 'Each successive year appears gloomier for the road passenger transport industry . . . In fact, many will regard the year 1957 as one of the blackest in the history of road passenger transport in this country.' Commenting on a provincial bus strike, following which an increase of 11s (55p) a week was eventually agreed by both sides, it observed that 'further resistance to bus travel was expected as a result of the higher fares'. In London, wage increases or not, it was becoming harder and harder to recruit and hold bus and train men (and women), not only at London Transport but in the manufacturing industry, at AEC, Park Royal, Weymann and Duple, for example.

Statistics the year before the 1958 strike made unhappy reading. Mr B. H. Harbour, a member of the London Transport Executive, appearing before a transport tribunal in the summer of 1957 in support of an application for higher fares, reported that there had been 'a fall of 2,251 million passenger miles and 719 million passenger journeys on London Transport since 1948'. He went on: 'The motor car continues to be the biggest thorn in the side of the public transport operator . . . the worst feature is the creeping paralysis which it causes in our major cities. No undertaking has found the problem more acute than London Transport, and to alleviate the delays caused to buses in the centre of London through general congestion and street parking . . . some principal services subject to excessive delays have been split into sections — short and long in town and suburban.'

This splitting of long routes into much smaller sections was one solution to traffic delays which came to be applied more and more. In the mid-1950s Croydon

and Thornton Heath had six weekday routes — 12, 59A, 68, 109 (the busiest route in all London), 133, and 159 — linking them with the centre of London; nowadays there is none, nor has there been for many years. In 1950 there were also five Green Line routes connecting Croydon with Central London; these too have long gone.

The decline was not entirely due to road traffic congestion. The electrification of the railways certainly played its part, and although East Croydon had been well served by Southern Electric since the 1920s, frequency has increased dramatically; nowadays one turns up and feels most aggrieved if there isn't a train departing within a couple of minutes for the 20-minute journey to Victoria, London Bridge, Waterloo or Charing Cross. Elsewhere electrification on the intensive Great Eastern suburban service in and out of Liverpool Street and dieselisation at other London termini persuaded passengers to switch from buses and Green Line coaches.

Back to 1958, when negotiations over pay and conditions had been going on for months. An arbitration award in February did nothing to solve the dispute, and on Sunday 4 May the Transport & General Workers' Union brought its members out on strike. Not surprisingly the public was not amused. An even-handed editorial in the *Croydon Advertiser*, typical of informed opinion in the LTE area, noted that 'withdrawal of labour is perfectly legitimate' but also made the

Top right: A Metro-Cammell-bodied RTL on route 25 takes advantage of one of the first measures introduced in the 1950s to give buses priority over other vehicles as it turns out of Piccadilly opposite the Ritz and heads towards Bond Street and Oxford Street. *Ian Allan Library*

Right: During the disastrous strike of 1958 the People's League for the Defence of Freedom, a right-wing, anti-trade-union organisation, operated skeleton services using a variety of elderly vehicles. One such was this Leyland Cheetah, formerly of Lytham St Annes Corporation and seen here in service with its original owner. *Author's collection*

Above: RTWs 106 and 118 on Central London routes 15 and 8 negotiate roadworks in the Edgware Road. *Author*

indisputable point that 'the busmen, rightly or wrongly believing themselves to be the victims of unfair discrimination in the Government's economic policy . . . must cause inconvenience to someone — in this case the travelling public'. Even then — over 40 years ago — it noted that the majority of passengers were 'old people and the youngsters'.

The next issue, under the headline 'Strike: Little Inconvenience', stated that 'only people who are too reserved to ask for a lift have had any real difficulty in getting to and from work'. Tough luck on the meek, then. My three-mile daily journey from Thornton Heath Pond to the Art School at Park Hill, Croydon, remained as it had been since Easter, by BSA Bantam, and it was noticeable that so many people now had their own transport that there seemed no overwhelming desire to settle the strike, whatever the cost, as there would probably have been 10 years earlier. Busmen from Croydon garage got very cross with Croydon Trades Council when it spent nearly an hour discussing nuclear disarmament rather than the strike.

During the week ending 20 May all the busmen at garages serving the Croydon area voted to return to work, but as there was a narrow majority throughout London Transport to stay out, they did. The People's League for the Defence of Freedom, a right-wing political organisation, obtained temporary licences to operate seven routes in various parts of London. Based at Wandsworth, it operated a motley collection of vehicles, double- and single-deck. The strike dragged on into June and eventually came to an end after seven weeks, on 21 June.

At the beginning of July LTE admitted that, although it had no exact figures, 'considerably fewer' passengers were using its buses. Some former passengers were 'still travelling by main line or Underground'. (Tube and Underground trains had not been affected by the strike.) 'Many other [former passengers] are still going by car: during the strike arrangements were made between one neighbour and another, and reports indicate that in some cases arrangements are continuing . . . Forty per cent of London Transport passenger journeys are for distances of less than one mile . . . many people who decided to walk short distances during the strike are continuing to do so.' The strike was little short of disastrous, and by the end of 1958 there were 546 fewer buses scheduled for service.

· 15 ·

Too Many Buses
— and One New One

THE RT family wiped out all the prewar buses. The last STLs ended passenger service, from a number of Country Area garages, on 1 September 1954. They survived a little longer as trainers and staff buses, but even these duties came to an end in June 1955. Some saw further service elsewhere; I sat on the upper deck of one which served as a press grandstand at Crystal Palace in 1955; this was while I was carrying out the onerous duties of trainee newspaper reporter, observing local hero John Surtees (the only man to be both 500cc motor-cycle and Formula 1 motor-racing world champion) wipe out the opposition. Later, in the service of Her Majesty, Corporal John and I motor-cycled over from RAF West Malling one summer evening in 1957 to Chislehurst to photograph a couple of

STLs which the construction firm of Rush & Tompkins used as staff buses. This was typical of the afterlife of the STLs — the first standard London buses to find widespread use after their days in the capital were over — and ultimately contributed to the preservation of several. The postwar STLs departed soon afterwards, in 1955, all finding further owners, as did the STDs (all-Leyland PD1s), a number ending their days in Yugoslavia. One postwar STL (2692), which took itself off in the opposite direction, to the home of Desperate Dan, Dennis the Menace and Lord Snooty and his Pals — Dundee — lasted long enough to be preserved, restored to original Country Area condition.

Next it was the turn of the original RTs. In their last years they had spent some of their time, usually the period just before overhaul, as trainers. Passenger service came to an end in May 1955, other than for seven which were repainted green and sent to work on the 327 over a bridge at Broxbourne which would not take the slightly heavier postwar RT. Meanwhile the rest became full-time trainers or staff buses. The bridge at Broxbourne (which sounds like the title of a Harrison Birtwistle opera!) was strengthened in the summer of 1957, and the green 'prewar' RTs joined their remaining RT compatriots as trainers. This kept them busy for many years, the last not being sold until 1964. The prototype Green Line double-deck coach, RTC1, rebuilt in 1949 from RT97 (which, following war damage, had already been used to experiment with pay-as-you enter operation), saw out its time as a Country Area bus and was sold in 1955. The last survivor in the LTE fleet was, extraordinarily, RT1. This requires some qualification, for only half the bus was actually the prototype, the chassis being that of (one-time Cravens-bodied) RT1420; the two were united in 1954, when the body of RT1420 was damaged beyond repair. Together they formed mobile training vehicle 1019J and as such served for a remarkable 22 years. Now, following all manner of vicissitudes (including exile across the Atlantic), it is safely preserved.

The last RTs and RTLs had been delivered in 1954, but an over-optimistic estimation of needs meant that a number went into store. I was most excited to come

Above: STL1351 in service with Rush & Tompkins at Chislehurst in the summer of 1957. *Author*

Above: Pictured in 1951, three withdrawn STLs — 352, 1753 and 838 all in sombre all-over red — and former Green Line 10T10 T470 await disposal and eventual scrapping. *Author's collection*

Below: STL1836, with an earlier body than the roofbox one with which it was built, found further employment in East Anglia with Canhams. Alongside is an ECW-bodied Bristol K of Eastern Counties. *John Fozard*

Left: Relegated to driver-training duties, 'prewar' RT92 emerges from Chiswick Works after a lunchtime break in September 1959. *Author*

Below: RTC1, which ended its days as a Country Area bus, seen shortly before sale for further service on Merseyside. It could certainly have taken its own advice and sailed away from there to Ireland but so far as is known never did.
Author's collection

Right: Two of the final, 1954 delivery of OLD-registered buses on Waterloo Bridge. RTL1483 overtakes RT4468. *Author*

Below: One of the final batch of Country Area RTs not put into service until June 1959, East Grinstead-allocated RT4776, at West Croydon in October 1961. The crew are having a chat prior to setting off on the long journey on route 409 to Forest Row on the edge of the Ashdown Forest, setting for the legendary 'Winnie the Pooh' stories. At this time Mrs Milne, Christopher Robin's mother, was still living in one of the forest villages. No doubt Christopher himself would have travelled on the STs which worked the 409 in the 1930s. *Author*

Above: Four RTs lined up in front of Catford garage, November 1955. On the left (and shortly to be withdrawn and sold) is Cravens-bodied RT1518. *Author*

across a group of RTLs, with OLD registrations, hidden away in Reigate garage in the summer of 1955, prudently jacked up on blocks without tyres; keeping company with them were several CRs. LTE was in a quandary. It couldn't keep these brand-new vehicles stored indefinitely, yet there were no time-expired buses they could replace. It was decided that the 120 non-standard Cravens-bodied RTs would have to go. Non-standard they may have been, but they were still in superb condition, and (apart from RT1420, which tried to get under a low bridge at Norbiton and damaged its body beyond repair) all found new owners, who couldn't believe their luck at getting such an excellent deal. The last departed London in May 1957.

But worse, in terms of disposing of prize assets, was to follow. Even at the beginning of 1958 — before the disastrous strike — there were 121 new RTs and RTLs gathering dust. It was time to sell standard RTs and RTLs . . . and replace them with identical, newer versions. The inexplicable decision was made to dispose initially of those with the lowest numbers, *i.e.* in the RT152 and 402 series. Whoever came up with this bright idea hadn't realised that it was thus perfectly possible, because of body changes at overhaul, for vehicles with four- or five-year-old bodies to depart the fleet. This did indeed happen, as the oldest HLW- and HLX-registered RTs had been overhauled at the same time as the newest NXP- and OLD-registered buses. Later this nonsense ended, and buses were sold according to body age. It would take 21 years to

withdraw the standard RT from passenger service in London — surely some sort of record.

Before the last RTs and RTLs took up work, four prototypes of their successor, the Routemaster, were in service. Still with us in considerable numbers — in London and elsewhere — at the beginning of the 21st century, this remarkable bus does not therefore require description in great detail. Designed with enormous care, it was considered by many already out of date when the first production examples entered service in the summer of 1959, the first production rear-engined Leyland Atlanteans having started work in the provinces the previous year. Amongst these latter was a fleet bought by Maidstone & District to replace Hastings' trolleybuses; the Routemaster was designed with a similar purpose in mind for London.

It will be recalled that the decision to replace South London's trams with motor buses had put a question mark over the future of the world's largest trolleybus fleet, and on 3/4 March 1959 the beginning of the end arrived with the closure of Bexleyheath and Carshalton depots and the replacement of the 696, 698 and 654 routes. Because there were not yet sufficient Route-masters ready and there was a surplus of RTs, overhauled examples of the latter took over. As with the tram-replacement programme the opportunity was taken to

Above: Looking rather like two friendly dogs — and both destined to be discarded by their owner long before they were worn out — are Weymann-bodied T766 and Cravens RT1420 at Uxbridge. *Vanguard*

Below: Cravens RT1421 after being sold to Dundee Corporation heads past the Clydesdale Bank and a respectable Scottish matron in the city centre. Unusually Dundee made use of the route-number box. *John Fozard*

Above: The first standard RTs were sold in 1958 RT270 is seen in later life, beside the River Suir at Waterford, in the Irish Republic, while working for Kenneally Bus Service. *S. W. Lander*

Right: Someone in London Transport assumed that RT406 was a very early postwar RT and thus sold it to Bradford Corporation. Well, the chassis may have been, but the body was a lot more modern. Lucky old Bradford! *John Fozard*

Above and left: The shape of things to come: RM1, the first Routemaster prototype, on display at Chiswick in virtually original condition. The rear view demonstrates its ST/STL ancestry even more clearly than does the front. The minimal destination display, a weight-saving measure, would soon be replaced by London Transport's generously sized standard version. *London Transport / Ian Allan Library*

Above right: 3 March 1959, the last day of the 654 route and the beginning of the end for the London trolleybus. 'B1' No 91 of Carshalton depot speeds through a wet West Croydon on its way to Crystal Palace past a Commer van and a 'Jelly Mould' Austin A30. In the background, at the end of its long journey on the 630 from Harlesden, stands Hammersmith's No 1708, a member of the 'P1' class, the final prewar design, which entered service well into the war, in 1941. *Author*

Right: RT193 of Carshalton garage on trolleybus-replacement route 154 at Reeves Corner, Croydon (where trams now run), on 5 March 1959 — two days after the end of the 654 trolleybuses. *Author*

co-ordinate former trolley routes with motor-bus ones. Naturally enough, in the 40-odd years since trolleybuses disappeared from the streets of London there have been numerous route changes, such that it is difficult to trace the replacement services, although some of the numbers introduced then are still with us.

Five weeks after Stage 1, Stage 2 in April 1959 saw the removal of the 555, 581 and 677 from Clapton and Lea Bridge depots. Bexleyheath and Carshalton operated mostly the oldest vehicles in the fleet, and almost all were withdrawn and scrapped. The Bexleyheath ones met their end at Penhall Road, Charlton, the last resting-place of the trams, but all the others were broken up behind Colindale depot. Because the Clapton and Lea Bridge fleets were composed of relatively modern classes, their vehicles moved on — a pattern which was to be repeated throughout the replacement process — their places being taken by RTLs.

Next, on 18 August, came the turn of four routes, 661, 663, 691 and 693, worked by Bow and Ilford depots. Ilford was the home of the unique group of trolleybuses intended for service in South Africa but

Above: A forlorn group of trolleybuses in the Charlton scrapyard, 20 April 1959. From right to left are 'C2s' 190 and 188, 'D2B' 405B (rebuilt by East Lancs following war damage) and 'C2s' 191 and 189. *Author*

Left: Stripped of any reusable materials, the lower-deck remains of three 'L3' trolleybuses await their end in the scrapyard behind Colindale depot. *Author's collection*

Above: RM32, one of the earliest production Routemasters, seen in November 1959 at the Bloomsbury terminus of route 5, which had just replaced trolleybus route 665. *Ian Allan Library*

diverted during the war to London. There was a suggestion that they might yet reach their intended home, but although initially held back from scrapping, all eventually met their end at Colindale. RTLs replaced them and the Bow vehicles. The Bow trolleys, 'N1' BRCW-bodied AECs of 1939/40, moved westwards.

Stage 4 at last marked the entry into service (in its intended role as a trolleybus-replacement vehicle) of the Routemaster. The first production examples had worked on various Central London routes earlier in 1959 and were now gathered together at Poplar and West Ham depots ready to replace the trolleys used on the 567, 569 and 665 routes. Some 73 were needed, and out they went onto the streets of East London on 11 November, brightening up the late-autumn gloom, although, truth to tell, few of the trolleybuses they replaced wore the air of outdated veterans; right up to the end, they remained smooth-running, comfortable, environmentally friendly vehicles, overtaken by changing economic conditions and fashion rather than old age.

A curious statistic — aren't they all? — is that, despite withdrawals, the trolleybus-replacement programme meant that there were 122 more RTs and 237 more RTLs scheduled for service at the end of 1959 than there had been at the end of 1958. The next decade would see the end of the RTLs and the RTWs, 728 of

the former and over 250 of the latter going to Sri Lanka (or Ceylon, as it then was — and not half so good at cricket as it subsequently became), but the RT and RF classes, although slowly diminishing in number, would last much longer, outliving many of their successors. The Routemaster would do even better. There has never been a city bus anywhere to compare with the longevity of the RT and the Routemaster — a tribute to both the design and the maintenance standards of these remarkable vehicles. None of the trains running on the Tube or sub-surface lines in the 1950s still operates with Transport for London in the 21st century, although the Metropolitan 'A' stock is a late-1950s design, whilst over in the time warp which is the Isle of Wight some of the 1938 Tube trains still serve the public, trundling up and down between Shanklin and far out into the Solent to the end of Ryde Pier, where they keep company with supertankers and great liners such as the *Queen Mary 2*, something no-one who journeyed daily on them beneath the streets of London in the 1950s could surely, in their wildest dreams, have imagined.

Bibliography

Fares Please by O. J. Morris, Ian Allan (1953)
Overground by O. J. Morris, Ian Allan (1951)
Bare Empty Sheds by G. Harry Guilmartin
  (Tramway & Light Railway Society, 1986)
LCC Electric Tramways by Robert J. Harley
  (Capital Transport, 2002)
Green Line by Laurie Akehurst and David Stewart
  (Capital Transport, 2005)
Labour Relations in London Transport by H. A. Clegg
  (Augustus M. Kelley, 1950)
The Last Years of the General by Ken Glazier
  (Capital Transport, 1995)
A Lifetime of Bus Work by Robert Scanlan
  (Transport Publishing Co, 1979)
London Bus File, Double-deckers 1933-39 by Ken Glazier
  (Capital Transport, 2001)
London Bus File, Single-deckers 1933-39
  by Ken Glazier (Capital Transport, 2002)
London Buses Before the War by Ken Glazier
  (Capital Transport, 1996)
London Transport Tramways Handbook
  by D. W. Willoughby and E. R. Oakley
  (published by the authors, 1972)
The London Trolleybus, Volume 1 by Ken Blacker
  (Capital Publishing, 2002)
London's Underground, ninth edition, by John Glover
  (Ian Allan Publishing, 1999)
London's Underground Suburbs by Dennis Edwards
  and Ron Pigram (Baton Transport, 1986)
The Metropolitan Electric Tramways, Volume 2
  by C. S. Smeeton (Light Rail Transit Association,
  1986)
The STLs by Ken Blacker (Capital Transport, 1984)
Steam to Silver by J. Graeme Bruce (Capital Transport,
  1983)
abc London Transport Buses (various editions),
  Ian Allan Publishing
London Bus File 1955-62 by Ken Glazier,
  Capital Transport (1999)
London Transport Bus Garages by John Aldridge,
  Ian Allan Publishing (2001)
Routes to Recovery by Ken Glazier, Capital Transport
  (2000)
An Illustrated History of London Buses by Kevin Lane,
  Ian Allan Publishing (1997)

London Transport Service Vehicles by Julian Bowden-
  Green, LOTS (1978)
London Transport Service Vehicles by Kim Rennie
  and Bill Aldridge, Capital Transport (2003)
Electric to Diesel 1935-1962 by David Stewart,
  LOTS (1977)
London Tramway Twilight by Robert J. Harley,
  Capital Transport (2000)
London's Utility Buses by Ken Blacker, Capital Transport
  (1997)
The Circle Line by Desmond F. Croome,
  Capital Transport (2003)
RF by Ken Glazier, Capital Transport (1991)
RT by Ken Blacker, Capital Transport (1979)
Routemaster — Volume 1 by Ken Blacker,
  Capital Transport (1991)

Cobham Bus Museum Magazine (various editions),
  ed Bill Cottrell
London Bus Magazine (various editions), LOTS

The Croydon Advertiser
The Croydon Times
Middlesex Chronicle
Unpublished private diaries
Various local timetables, maps and guides
Guide to the 1951 Festival of Britain, South Bank site

Various issues of Passenger Transport
Various documents in the London Transport
  Museum